Women in Educational Management

A EUROPEAN PERSPECTIVE

edited by
Maggie Wilson

P·C·P

Paul Chapman
Publishing Ltd

Paul Chapman Publishing Ltd
144 Liverpool Road
London
N1 1LA

British Library Cataloguing in Publication Data

Women in educational management : a European perspective
1. Women school administrators – Europe 2. Women in education
– Europe 3. School administrators – Europe
I. Wilson, Maggie
371.2' 0082

ISBN 1853963216

Typeset by Anneset
Printed and bound in Great Britain

A B C D E F G H   9 8 7

Contents

Biographical Details

Giovanna Campani is Professor of Comparative Education at the University of Florence, where she was formerly a Senior Lecturer in the Department of Educational Science. She has participated in international research projects on women's education in Europe and in Italy and on immigrant women. Her recent publications have particularly concerned the areas of women's education from an international perspective in relation to wider socio-economic forces and new developments in the demand for the labour of immigrant women.

Marie-Françoise Fave-Bonnet is a Maître de Conférences (Senior Lecturer) in Educational Sciences at the Centre de Recherches Education et Formation at the Université Paris X at Nanterre. Her field of research was concerned with primary teachers. Her main research interests now concern French universities. She has written several articles about academics and, in particular, academic women in France.

Hannelore Faulstich-Wieland is Professor of Educational Science at the University of Hamburg and was formerly Professor of Women's Research at the University of Muenster. A qualified teacher, she has also worked at the Universities of Berlin, Goettingen, Dortmund, Hannover, and Frankfurt am Main. She has been a visiting scholar at the University of Siegen and the University of California at Berkeley.

Georgia Kontogiannopoulou-Polydorides is Professor of Sociology of Education and Social Policy at the University of Atnens. She has previously served for ten years as a professor at the University of Patras. She has coordinated numerous educational research projects and has published extensively in English and Greek. She is Coordinator for the Greek Centre of IEA Research. Her current research interests focus on education, social context, culture and attainment.

Kathleen Lynch is a founder member of the Equality Studies Centre at University College Dublin, where she is a Senior Lecturer in Education. She has written extensively on a wide range of equality issues both in sociology and in education. Her works include *The Hidden Curriculum* (1989) and *Irish Society: Sociological Perspectives* (with P. Clancy, S. Drudy and L. O'Dowd 1995). She has also been involved in a range of policy analyses and debates, including the Report of the Constitution Review Group on Ireland (1996).

Jorunn Oftedal is Deputy Head of the Gand Vidergaende Skole in Norway. She is a member of the Sandnes City Council and an elected member of the Board of Teachers' Associations. She has been Head of In-Service Education at Stavanger College of Education and a consultant at the National Education Office of Rogaland County.

Anna Picciolini works as a freelance researcher in the field of social policy analysis and intervention, as a journalist and as the coordinator of a social action group concerned with HIV/Aids education. She has formerly worked as a teacher and consultant on social problems to an Italian party political group. Her publications have particularly centred on policy towards and the needs of immigrant families in Italy.

Annelies Ruijs has worked as an educational researcher at the Institute of Applied Social Science at the Catholic University of Nijmegen. During this period she made several studies of women in educational management in primary, secondary and vocational education. She produced the final report of the 1990 conference on women in educational management in Vienna and was involved in the organisation of the 1995 conference on the same theme in Amsterdam. She is now a student counsellor at Nijmegen and continues her interest in the subject of women and education as a member of the board of the Foundation for Women in Educational Management (VrIOM).

Montserrat Santos is a state professor of secondary school education. She has been a secondary school headteacher, director of a teacher training centre and of a Spanish resource centre in Houston, USA. She is currently Deputy Director of the Liceo Español in Paris and International Secretary of the European Forum of Educational Administrators (EFEA). Her research has specialised in the role of the headteacher and she is the author of a number of books and articles on this topic. Recently she has focused on the subject of women and educational management and she has published a number of journal articles in this area.

Eva Széchy is Professor of Education at the Eötvös Loránd University in Budapest, where she has been teaching since 1966 after a career at the Ministry of Culture and Education. She has been a scientific advisor in the Pedagogical Research Centre on Higher Education and Head of the Hungarian Information Centre of the UNESCO/European Centre for Higher Education.

She has written and lectured extensively in Hungarian, English, German, Polish and Russian in the areas of educational theory, pedagogy in higher education and comparative education.

Ard Vermeulen is a senior educational researcher at the SCO-Kohnstamm Institute (Centre for Educational Research of the Faculty of Educational Sciences) at the University of Amsterdam. Her main field of research is school organisation and educational innovation, specialising in the topic of women and educational management. Her particular focus has been recruitment and selection procedures, barriers to promotion and strategies to overcome such barriers. She was involved in the organisation of the 1995 conference on women in educational management held in Amsterdam and is currently directing a research project on the mobility of women in the management of vocational training and adult education institutions.

Maggie Wilson is a Principal Lecturer in the School of Education at Oxford Brookes University, with a remit for developing international award-bearing work in the field of educational studies. She has worked as a secondary school teacher and has played an active role in development education. She has a particular research interest in gender issues in education and in comparative education. Among her publications are *Girls and Young Women in Education: a European Perspective* (1991) and *Gender Issues in International Education: Policy and Practice* (forthcoming).

Evie Zambeta teaches Educational Politics and Comparative Education at the University of Athens. She is the author of *Education Politics in Greek Primary Education 1974–1979* and has published articles on accountability in education and education as social policy. Her current research interests include analysis of European perspectives on citizenship education and on pre-school education policies.

Foreword

Few professions have readily welcomed women. Only in the relatively liberal era of the late twentieth century has women's membership of many professions become accepted and normal. But education is of all the learned professions the one which has been most open to women. It could indeed be argued that the early bond between mother and child constitutes a first and important stage of education, even if such education is informal and hard to define. Certainly women's role as mothers has often been cited to justify their entry to the teaching profession. Even so, for a goodly time after the development of the profession, women's teaching activity was limited paradoxically in many countries by the handicap of the marriage bar: their levels of activity were also limited until, after considerable resistance, they gained access to the higher education which would qualify them for teaching learners above the primary level - and for entry to other professions.

Curiously, now that women can freely enter all levels of teaching in most countries, some critics express dismay at this development, foretelling very bad effects of what is termed the feminisation of the profession. They see not professional equality but a takeover bid.

To what extent are such fears justified? Do we indeed have a situation in which women threaten to dominate the teaching profession, determining policy and occupying the key positions?

To find answers to these questions we need to look at the teaching profession in the context of women's general position in the labour market of different countries. We have to consider to what extent women in European countries are free to enter the employment of their choice: is there pressure on them still to devote themselves rather to the traditional role of mother and housewife? And, since no one would deny the importance of that traditional role, we have to see whether societies have enabled women to succeed in reconciling the demands of child-bearing and child-rearing with the also important demands of work outside the home.

Setting the question in this context, as the writers of the following chapters do, we discover that European societies still differ in the extent to which women's full-time, or even part-time, participation in paid employment is accepted, even if the trend is to ever greater participation. There is much variation in the social circumstances women encounter in the countries surveyed here: there is divergence in the provision of child-care and the organisation of school and daily life to facilitate, or make complicated, women's dual role. These chapters remind us also of the very different political climates in which European women have lived during this century - under dictatorships, the rigidity of the Soviet regime or the more tranquil democracies of The Netherlands or Norway.

An unexpected result of these surveys of reform and change in education is the realisation that well-intentioned changes can have most undesirable effects: merging schools to make more efficient units, making them coeducational to enhance equality opportunities can mean that many women are deprived of the chance to become heads of schools or colleges. The new political freedom of the former centrally planned economies, exemplified by Hungary, can lead to a reduction in child-care facilities and more difficult conditions for women in employment and coping with domestic chores - and a smaller representation of women at the higher levels of decision-making, in governments.

Yet when reading these accounts of management in education it must come as no surprise to find consistent evidence of the great similarities in women's career prospects and their place in decision-making in education throughout Europe. This book amply demonstrates that the pyramid and the glass ceiling are found everywhere, not only in the management of education but in other occupations. There simply are fewer women than men in top positions: and despite equal pay legislation, women, on average, receive less pay than men. It appears there is an oddly balanced feminisation of the profession.

Nevertheless, one of the great merits of the studies presented here is that they also show how affirmative action is going on in different countries, in different ways. The situation of women in educational management is in fact being improved, whether by planning in a former Polytechnic in England, by effective target-setting by the Netherlands' Ministry of Education and Science Memorandum on 'Equal Opportunities in Education 1993–96' and the Dutch 1997 Law on proportional representation of women in management positions in education, by the award of prizes and financial inducements, or by the Rogaland County Project in Norway. Equality in management remains elusive but there is this reassuring evidence of progress, in some cases, of considerable progress.

A further outstanding merit of these chapters is that readers are offered not a narrow discussion of one specific problem but an extensive view of European cultures in their diversity and unity. The situation of women in education reveals a great deal about the structure of the labour market and the economic progress of the countries in question. We receive succinct and useful information as to how schools and technical and higher education are organised in different parts of Europe. In fact, we have a remarkable contribution to the discipline of Comparative Education, illuminating our understanding of education in general.

This study of women in educational management shows not only what remains to be done but how admirably women's talents are already being employed to the benefit of all.

Margaret B. Sutherland
Professor (Em.) of Education
University of Leeds

Acknowledgements

I wish to record my thanks for the encouragement and support given by friends and colleagues during the course of this project, and to Oxford Brookes University for providing financial assistance for editing and translation.

In particular, I would like to thank my husband Bob for his invaluable help, my young daughter, Laura, for her patience throughout and my son, Alan, for not arriving too early.

1

Introduction

Maggie Wilson

Within Europe since the 1960s there has been rapid and often remarkable progress in the educational opportunities which girls and young women enjoy. Throughout the 1970s, spurred on by high profile international pressure and by the growing confidence of the women's movement, national governments attempted to create the conditions which would remove barriers to sex equality and give individuals equal access to education, training and employment. Legislation was couched within the framework of a liberal-democratic concern with creating a 'level playing field' to enable girls and women to compete on equal terms in the educational and employment arenas.

Such policies had an undoubted effect in quantitative terms. By the 1990s a near equalisation in the upper levels of secondary education and in higher education had been achieved in most European countries, with girls often outnumbering boys in academic secondary education (Wilson, 1991). By 1991–92 there were 102 females to every 100 males in upper secondary education in the European Union and 95 females to every 100 males in higher education (Eurostat, 1995a). However, differences among countries are also significant. While there were 151 females in higher education for every 100 males in Portugal, and over 110 in Denmark, France, Finland, Norway and Sweden, there were 71 in Germany and 83 in the Netherlands (Eurostat, 1995b). Nonetheless, in all European Union countries female students have taken the lion's share of the marked growth in enrolment in higher education to a greatly increased average of 39 per cent of 19- to 21-year-olds in 1991–92 (Eurostat, 1995a).

Within higher education, broad differences remain in the type of courses which students pursue, again with interesting country-by-country variations. Although, overall, female students tend to shun technologically orientated disciplines, the proportion represented in engineering, architecture and transport studies ranged from 31 per cent in Portugal, 22 per cent in Belgium and Greece to 10 per cent in Germany and the Netherlands respectively in 1991–92, with a European Union average of 16 per cent. In the broad area of the natural sciences, mathematics and computer science, while the EU average was 35 per cent female students, the proportion varied from 66 per cent in Portugal and 55 per cent in Ireland to 26 per cent in Germany and

23 per cent in the Netherlands (Eurostat, 1995b). Such discrepancies among countries serve to undermine any easy stereotypes concerning the relative 'liberation' of the North European Protestant woman in comparison with her Southern or Catholic counterparts and are also evident in data on women in the labour force and in teaching. However, the broad pattern remains of a significant differentiation of subject choice by gender at this level and at the level of upper secondary education, with profound consequences for the future employment of females, the next generation of professionals, managers, politicians and teachers.

In most widely accessible European data, there is a notable absence of information on the educational outcomes of a far wider group of school-leavers, the 77 per cent of 16–18-year-olds in the European Union who are in education and training. Of this group some 40 per cent will go on to form the backbone of the workforce at lower levels of employment. There is some evidence that even more marked disparities in subject choice exist in the field of vocational training, which merits wider research and policy attention (Bock and van Doorne-Huiskes, 1995).

WOMEN IN EMPLOYMENT

Partly fuelled by the increasing availability of a skilled and educated workforce and partly as a result of changes in the structure of the labour market, women's participation in employment has also changed dramatically since the 1970s. Women increased their share of the labour force from roundly 35 per cent of jobs in the EU in 1975 to 41 per cent in 1991. This period saw the emergence of the married working woman in particular and the increasing tendency to return to work or continue in the family business after the birth of children, albeit with variable patterns among countries (Plantenga, 1995). In 1992 the rate of 'economic activity' of women (i.e. employed or self-employed) ranged from over 63 per cent in Denmark to 34 per cent in Spain with an EU average of 44.6 per cent (*Social Trends*, 1995).

Corresponding with this growth in women's employment has been a sharp increase in part-time work and in 'atypical' employment (fixed-term, home-based, etc.) in the 1980s, which has afforded women flexibility in employment terms, but at a cost in terms of perpetuating a relatively weak market position. In 1991 82 per cent of all part-timers in the EU were women, and some 28 per cent of women worked part-time, as compared with 4 per cent of men (Plantenga, 1995). Once again there are substantial variations by country, with the highest rates recorded in Denmark, Germany, the Netherlands and the UK and the lowest rates in Greece, Spain, Italy and Portugal, ranging from around 60 per cent in the Netherlands to 7 per cent in Greece.

The image of the 'monstrous regiment of women' taking over the professions is to some extent supported by statistical evidence. Just over 40 per cent of professionals in the EU are women, with the highest rates, at over 50 per cent, in Ireland and Belgium and the lowest at under 35 per cent in

Luxembourg, France and Germany in 1992. Within the professions, the proportion of women in teaching, at an EU average of 60 per cent, is in sharp contrast to the proportion in occupations linked to physics, mathematics and science at around 13 per cent (Eurostat, 1995b). This relatively positive picture should also be placed against the backcloth of the overall situation of women in the workforce, with their higher rate of unemployment, lower pro rata rate of pay and higher representation amongst the low-paid in comparison with men.

Although this book is concerned with the relative prospects of promotion in a professional field and the obstacles to progress in this area, one of the key themes covered in each chapter concerns the overall work situation of women. Whether it is easy even to leave the front doorstep to go out to work, let alone succeed in a competitive field varies considerably among countries. A 1993 Eurobarometer survey posed the question as to whether marriage and children were perceived as obstacles to working life. Overall, over 20 per cent of respondents felt that marriage would present difficulties for women. Fifty four per cent opined that children would present an obstacle for the working woman and 8 per cent for the working man. The impact of having children was mentioned most frequently by respondents in Germany, Luxembourg, the Netherlands and the UK and least frequently by respondents in Portugal and Greece (Eurostat, 1995b). These differences may reflect the availability of family care networks as much as the presence or absence of progressive employment policies and state support. However, the overall message of the survey underscores the notion that men can expect to lead relatively carefree working lives, where children and domestic matters do not intrude.

Country-by-country variations in the provision of family leave and benefits can be marked, with comparatively generous provision in Scandinavia, Germany and the Netherlands. The issue of preschool childcare has been charted in surveys of provision across Europe, which revealed for example that 2 per cent of 3-year-olds in Ireland, the Netherlands, Luxembourg and the UK received publicly funded daycare in the late 1980s in contrast with 48 per cent in Denmark (Pot, 1995). Although these issues are crucial in enabling women to retain their position in the labour market, the years of compulsory school attendance can also be problematic. The length of the school day varies from 4 to 5 hours in Greece and Germany to 8 hours in France and the age of compulsory schooling from 5 years in the UK to 7 in Denmark. The greater the lack of congruence between school hours and working hours, clearly the greater the problems which will exist for working mothers, particularly where there is a strong cultural association between providing a cooked midday meal and being a good parent. Care provision outside of school hours is usually locally provided and very difficult to monitor. With the exception of Denmark and Sweden, provision is not widespread. In many countries, the private sector or informal arrangements are expected to fill the gap. Emergency leave for the care of sick children is likewise by no means universal and many women still have to take holiday time or 'disguised' time off for this purpose.

The decreasing cost and increasing availability of many technological aids to housework, such as microwaves, has resulted in a slight decrease of domestic work for women. Men also slightly increased their average share of domestic work in the 1980s across Europe. However, attitudes towards the domestic division of labour are changing very slowly, especially where children are present. One survey, based in seven European countries, showed that a mother of a child aged between 0 and 5 years spends an average of 19 hours a week more on household and family tasks than a childless woman, with little variation among countries. Children over the age of 5 almost cease to have any effect on the time men spend on domestic and family tasks (van der Lippe and Roelofs, 1995).

Family-friendly employment policies such as flexitime, job-sharing and the possibility of reducing working hours can clearly have an effect and have been recommended by the OECD (1991) and the European Network on Childcare (1993), which have called for a greater balance between employment and family roles in order to promote a better utilisation of human capital, enhance gender equality and improve the quality of life. Data from European sources on the average hours worked per week show some variations among EU countries, with the highest average for a full-time male employee in the United Kingdom. What such data do not reveal are variations in the culture of working practices in different European countries and the pressure on senior personnel to work long hours. Is the manager who finishes work by 6.00 p.m. considered to be efficient or possibly not pulling his or her weight? Although problematic to research, such issues may have a profound effect on patterns of family life and women's career decisions.

Finally, the presence or absence of women in political life has a significant bearing on state policy and also the public image of women as potential decision-makers. Bolstered by the inclusion of Finland and Sweden in the 1995 European Parliament, women have increased their representation here to 27.6 per cent of MEPs. Within national parliaments, the average female representation for the then 12 member states of the EU in 1994 was 13.6 per cent, with Greece, France, Portugal and the UK well below average. In contrast, the proportion of women MPs in Denmark and the Netherlands was around 30 per cent and in Norway, Finland and Sweden around 40 per cent (Eurostat, 1995b).

WOMEN AND TEACHING

Women teachers in Europe represent both a typical and an atypical group of employees. Teaching represents one of the most highly feminised of all professions and in many countries has been one of the few traditional avenues for female advancement. Yet here, two things are very clear. Firstly, the higher the educational level and age of student, the less women are to be found. Secondly, the higher the job level, the less women are represented, thus replicating the uneven patterns of participation seen in the wider workforce.

Thus in 1991–92, women represented 80 per cent of primary school teachers, around 50 per cent of secondary school teachers and 20–30 per cent of teachers in higher education in the European Union (Eurostat, 1995a). With variations in the traditional organisation and status of teaching among countries, average figures again mask differences, which will be explored in greater depth in the context of specific countries featured in this book. Female representation among primary school teachers ranged in 1991–92, for example, from 90 per cent in Italy to 50 per cent in Greece and among secondary school teachers from over 60 per cent in Ireland and Portugal to 40 per cent or less in Germany and the Netherlands. A higher percentage of women in secondary education is generally to be found in Scandinavia and Eastern Europe for differing reasons (Laemers and Riujs, 1996).

Within school systems, the pyramidal structure of the job hierarchy has been charted across Western as well as non-Western countries, irrespective of organisational structures, hiring practices, educational opportunities and roles and seniority systems (Schmuck, 1986; Davies, 1990; Shakeshaft, 1993). Where women have succeeded in gaining ground in terms of senior educational positions, this has often been as a result of the withdrawal of men into other occupations. Detailed comparisons of cross-cultural data are often hampered by differences in job titles, roles and the prestige of institutions. Even within the United States, administrative titles are not comparable across school districts (Shakeshaft, 1993). A systematic overview of the issue at an international level has not been provided by any international body. Data from national sources are scattered and vary in their degree of precision. Nonetheless, high profile attempts to chart the changing fortunes of women in educational management were presented to conferences held in Vienna in 1990 and Amsterdam in 1995. The first conference supported the rather pessimistic findings of earlier research concerning the under-representation of women in school leaderships and drew attention to the fact that women were more likely to gain headships in urban areas and in single-sex secondary schools (Riujs, 1993). By 1995, the situation for women had improved marginally in the counties represented, with the exception of Greece, with most countries reporting a 2–6 per cent rise in the proportion of female headteachers, albeit from different bases, giving rise to cautious optimism (Laemers and Riujs, 1996). Nonetheless, in six out of the sixteen countries which presented data, the percentage of female secondary headteachers was less than half of that of female teachers. Counter trends to the improved position of women in school management were also in evidence, delegates citing school mergers and the closure of single-sex schools as particularly disadvantageous to women.

At the level of higher education, problems of cross-cultural comparability are compounded by the greater variety of roles, institutions, conditions of work and career routes at this level (Sutherland, 1990). The relative importance of teaching, administration and research to career prospects varies among institutions and countries. Competition for senior posts is sharper in some disciplines and can be greatly increased as a result of funding cutbacks (Stiver Lie, Malik and Harris, 1994). The sector is often more varied than the school sector, with differences in prestige among types of institution. Nonetheless, yet again, a clear pyramidal structure of employment is all too apparent.

The increased proportion of women students stands in contrast to the proportion of women members of academic staff and still more to those represented at senior levels. Little information is available on the representation of women in the administrative structures or at the pinnacles of power, such as at the level of university rector or vice-chancellor. At the level of professor, women are generally minimally represented. In most European countries, the proportion of women professors is less than 10 per cent, and in several, such as Germany, the Netherlands, Austria, Greece and the UK, around or below 5 per cent. Positive exceptions are exemplified by Poland at 16 per cent, Turkey at 20 percent, and Spain at 38 per cent (Henniger, 1995; Laemers and Riujs, 1996).

The Amsterdam conference discerned a positive upward trend between 1990 and 1995 of a 2–3 per cent increase in the proportion of women professors in the limited number of countries for which data was available. In some countries, this doubled the percentage of female professors. An exception to this trend was again Greece, where the percentage of female professors dropped from 8 to 6 per cent for reasons which will be explored in the relevant chapter of this book.

AN OVERVIEW OF THE BOOK

Despite the problems of statistical and cross-cultural comparison outlined above, recent work in the field of comparative education has sought to discern broad trends and patterns across countries with broadly similar educational structures. The aim of this book is to contribute to this development, by giving an overview of the situation of women in educational management in Europe in the mid-1990s and detailed portraits of a selection of European countries. While not statistically representative of the great variety of population sizes, socio-economic or political compositions of European countries today, this selection is intended to give insight into similarities and differences across the spectrum.

Each chapter presents a broad picture of the structure of the education system concerned, the overall context of women at work in general and the position of women in the teaching force. The status of the teaching profession, promotional procedures and opportunities are outlined, along with governmental and political pressures for change, if these exist. The research base concerning cultural and organisational barriers to change is summarised, where available. It should, however, be noted that this varies enormously among countries and contrasts with the plenitude of research in the United States, where, as Shakeshaft describes, 'literally hundreds of studies indicate that negative attitudes towards women by those who hire constitute the major barrier to female advancement in school administration' (Shakeshaft, 1993, p. 49). Still less is available in most European research on the allied and very pertinent question as to whether women educational managers make a difference once in office.

The relative weight and salience of issues will clearly vary from country to country. In the cases of the Netherlands and the United Kingdom, for example, recent educational reforms and changes in the demands of promoted posts are particularly highlighted. In Ireland, the effects of the move from single-sex schools, often headed by religious personnel, to co-educational schools, is demonstrated. In the case of Hungary, the transition from a state socialist to a market economy has had such a profound effect on the working lives of women that this tends to overshadow equality issues, according to the evidence presented. In Germany the hierarchical structure of the education system is often inimical to the interests of women teachers and lecturers, while in Norway governmental commitment to sex equality has had substantial consequences. In France and Greece, apparently open systems for promoted posts at school level within highly centralised education systems mask processes of discrimination. The Greek chapter also raises the issue of the interrelationship between socio-economic and regional background and promotional success. In Spain the traditional family role of the woman runs counter to an open and democratic system of making school headship appointments, while the Italian chapter emphasises the congruence between the perceived caring role of female teachers, and their lack of promotion prospects.

At the level of higher education, the special pressures on women academics are highlighted, and the differences in selection procedures between countries emerge.

Where possible, successful strategies for change are exemplified in the form of positive case studies. These are summarised in a brief overview, which seeks to extrapolate from the experiences of the countries concerned, rather than attempting to provide a universal blueprint for the future.

REFERENCES

Bock, B. and van Doorne-Huiskes, A. (1995). The Careers of Men and Women: A Life-Course Perspective, in A. van Doorne-Huiskes, J. van Hoof and E. Roelofs (eds.) *Women and the European Labour Markets*, London, Paul Chapman Publishing.

Davies, L. (1990) *Equity or Efficiency? School Management in an International Context*, Lewes, Falmer.

European Network on Childcare (1993) *Employment, Equality and Caring for Children*, Annual Report 1992, Brussels, European Commission.

Eurostat (1995a) *Europe in Figures*, Luxembourg, Office for the Official Publications of the EU.

Eurostat (1995b) *Women and Men in the European Union; a Statistical Portrait*,

Luxembourg, Office for Official Publications of the European Communities.

Henniger, A. (1995) Women Academics at European Universities – Similarities and Differences, in C. Färber and A. Henniger (eds.) *Equal Opportunities for Women at European Universities*, Freie Universitat Berlin.

Laemers, M. and Riujs, A. (1996) A Statistical Portrait, *Context*, no 12. pp. 7–15.

van der Lippe, T. and Roelofs, E. (1995) Sharing Domestic Work, in A. van Doorne-Huiskes, J. van Hoof and E. Roelofs, op.cit.

OECD (1991) *Shaping Structural Change – the Role of Women*, Geneva.

Plantenga, J. (1995) Labour Market Participation of Women in the European Union, in A. van Doorne-Huiskes, J. van Hoof and E. Roelofs, op.cit.

Pot, L. (1995) Policies for Children and Parents in Four European Countries, in A. Van Doorne-Huiskes, J. van Hoof and E. Roelofs, op.cit.

Riujs, A. (1993) Women Managers in Education; a Worldwide Progress Report, in *Coombe Lodge Reports*, Vol. 23, nos. 7–8, pp. 519–676.

Schmuck, P. (1986) School Management and Administration; an Analysis by Gender, in E. Hoyle and A. McMahon (eds.) *The World Yearbook of Education: The Management of Schools*, London, Kogan Page.

Shakeshaft, C. (1993) Women in Educational Management in the United States, in J. Ouston (ed.) *Women in Educational Management*, Harlow, Longman.

Social Trends (1995) London, HMSO.

Stiver Lie, S., Malik, L. and Harris, D. (1994) The Gender Gap in Higher Education: a Conceptual Framework, in S. Stiver Lie, L. Malik and D. Harris (eds.) *The World Yearbook on Education: the Gender Gap in Higher Education*, London, Kogan Page.

Sutherland, M. (1990) Women Teaching in European Universities: Interviews and Information, in E. Byrne (ed.) *Gender in Education*, London, Multilingual Matters.

Wilson, M. (1991) *Girls and Young Women in Education: a European Perspective*, Oxford, Pergamon Press.

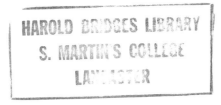

2

England and Wales

Maggie Wilson

Teaching as an occupation has traditionally attracted a high number of women in England and Wales. Its association with the 'natural' caring abilities of women and congruence with school hours made it a respectable career aspiration for an educated girl. Somewhat cloistered teacher training colleges, often in rural areas, provided a post-school education deemed appropriate for this group and until the 1970s teaching was one of the few career paths open to young women on a wide scale.

Since then, the improved educational attainment of girls and changes in the workplace have opened up wider opportunities. Nonetheless teaching is also becoming an increasingly female domain. As an occupation it exhibits the patterns of the wider labour market: a very mixed picture of success stories for the minority and constraints on women's participation for the majority.

WOMEN AT WORK

The last 25 years have seen a sharply increasing level of economic activity among women in the UK overall. In 1993 52 per cent of all women and over 70 per cent of 25–54-year-old women were in employment or self-employment. Women comprised 44 per cent of the civilian labour force, the second biggest proportion in the European Community after Denmark, contributing an increasing share of income to their households. For demographic and job-related reasons, this trend is predicted to continue into the next century, when, it is estimated, women will comprise 48 per cent of all employees by 2006 (*Social Trends*, 1995).

Despite these trends, there has been a fairly constant gap between male and female levels of pay since 1971 on average, although the gap between full-time employees has decreased. What complicates the picture is the increasing number of low paid, part-time women workers, who earn about 60 per cent of the male hourly average rate and 75 per cent of the female full-time hourly rate (*Social Trends*, 1995). Table 2.1 shows current employment patterns of male and female workers. Five times as many women work part-time as men and about 45 per cent of all women employees work part-time, a pattern strongly related to the age of their youngest dependent child. Recent rulings at European and national levels have considerably extended the employment rights of part-time employees with respect to redundancy, dismissal, pensions and maternity leave provision. However, the image and to some extent the reality of the part-time worker still tends to be one of low skills, low pay and lack of job security. High status part-time jobs are the exception, rather than the rule. Nevertheless, in 1992, 25 per cent of all professionals, 17 per cent of all managers and administrators and one-third of female teachers worked part-time (EOC, 1993).

Table 2.1   Full and part-time employment by gender (UK, thousands)[1,2]

Year	Males		Females	
	Full-time	Part-time	Full-time	Part-time
1984	13,240	570	5,422	4,343
1989	14,071	734	6,336	4,907
1994	12,875	998	6,131	5,257

Notes
1. Full/part-time is based on respondents' self-assessment. Excludes those who did not state whether they were full- or part-time.
2. At spring each year, includes employees, self-employed, those on government training schemes and unpaid family workers.

Source: Social Trends 1995, London, HMSO.

Women have started to make inroads into formerly male preserves, albeit at a slower rate than often popularly portrayed. A third of managerial and administrative posts are occupied by women and about a half of all business studies students are now female (DFE, 1994). The proportion of women in general management has risen from about 5 per cent in 1971 to 13 per cent in 1993 (EOC, 1993), but fewer than 10 per cent of non-executive directors, 6 per cent of executive directors and 1 per cent of main executive directors are women. In the political arena, 13 per cent of British MEPs and 7 per cent of members of the House of Lords were women (Macrae, 1996). The general election of 1997 raised the proportion of women in Parliament from 9 to 18 per cent.

A national campaign, Opportunity 2000, was launched in 1991 to improve equal opportunities in the workplace. Supported by leading companies, financial institutions, trade unions, the government and organisations such as the BBC, it is based on the 'business case' for equal opportunities policies. This argues that a neglect of such issues results in the financial costs of staff recruitment and retention problems, low morale, loss of staff time and potential customers (Hammond and Holton, 1991; Davidson and Burke, 1994). Some 'family-friendly' policies are now more in evidence in the workplace, although only a minority of employees benefit from such facilities as flexible working hours at present, as illustrated in Table 2.2. The

Table 2.2 Employees with flexible working patterns; by gender, Spring 1995 (%)

	Male	Female	Total
Full-time			
Flexible working hours	9.5	14.7	11.3
Annualized working hours	5.6	6.8	6.0
Four and a half day week	3.3	3.2	3.3
Term-time working	1.1	4.5	2.3
Nine day fortnight	0.5	0.2	0.4
Job sharing	-	-	0.1
All full-time employees[1] (=100%) (thousands)	10,872	5,953	16,734
Part-time			
Flexible working hours	6.9	8.8	8.5
Annualized working hours	3.9	5.5	5.2
Four and a half day week	-	-	-
Term-time working	4.6	10.4	9.5
Nine day fortnight	-	-	-
Job sharing	1.8	2.4	2.3
All part-time employees (=100%) (thousands)	817	4,634	5,451

Note

1. Includes employees who did not work flexible working hours or did not state them.
Source: Social Trends 1996, London, HMSO.

commercial sector has responded to changes in patterns of work; for example supermarkets are now open for longer hours. However, state provision of preschool childcare in the UK lags substantially behind European provision (Moss, 1992). Despite an increasing trend for women to take a short career break before resuming work – half are back at work after nine months – employer-provided workplace nurseries are still rare. Most parents rely on a patchwork of voluntary and private provision, supported by family and friends, as shown in Table 2.3. The majority of private or state nursery

Table 2.3 Use of day care services by preschool children: by age and type of provision, 1990 (England, %)[1]

	Age of child					All preschool children
	0	1	2	3	4	
Domestic premises[2]						
Father	19	18	24	24	24	21
Grandparent	22	24	25	22	18	23
Non-domestic premises						
Parent and toddler group	12	36	31	13	7	21
Day nursery	2	6	8	13	9	8
Playgroup	-	1	18	50	42	21
Nursery class or school	-	-	4	30	54	15

Notes

1. Children may receive day care from more than one source. Children attending school full time are not included.
2. Others providing regular day care in the mother's absence included friends, neighbours, childminders, nannies, au pairs, brothers, sisters and other relatives.

Source: Social Trends 1995, London, HMSO.

education is also part-time, often at times at variance with conventional working patterns. The school day ends at 3.00–3.30 pm. Although there are an increasing number of after-school and holiday playschemes, some government subsidised and often operating privately on school premises, demand still far exceeds supply (Maxwell, 1995). Delaying childbirth until well after the age of 30 is an increasing trend among professional women, who may thus also accrue responsibilities towards elderly parents at the same time as those towards school-aged children.

Research on women in management shows a largely consistent experience. Although women enjoy the challenge and 'buzz' of managerial positions, they often feel isolated, lacking suitable role models or support systems, experience direct or indirect discrimination and feel themselves to be over-visible, set up as test cases. Workplace expectations of mobility, for example job transfers or short-term placements, often conflict with family concerns; work can intrude on the home but not vice versa. Where women managers have partners at home, they still bear the brunt of housework. Single women managers lack the practical support from which many married men benefit at home and often feel labelled as oddities at work. Long working weeks of over 50 hours are virtually the norm, partly as a result of work overload, but also arguably a reflection of a work culture in which hours spent are deemed to represent commitment rather than time management skills. Faced with such demands, a higher than average proportion of women managers have joined a growing trend not to have children and there is increasing evidence of stress-related illness among UK women managers (Davidson and Cooper, 1992).

The pressures on women employees are, of course, not restricted to women in management. In a recent survey, two-thirds of respondents were reported to work routinely over their contractual hours, with 'pressure of workload' and 'workplace culture' cited as the main reasons for this. Two-thirds of those surveyed said that they did not spend enough time with their children and 71 per cent were unhappy with their hours and stress levels at work (Parents at Work, 1995).

THE EDUCATION SYSTEM OF ENGLAND AND WALES

Unlike other European states, education in England and Wales has not been nationally administered. The State has supervised and funded its administration through Local Education Authorities, which has created considerable diversity in the sector. The 1988 Education Reform Act altered this balance in favour of the State, while at the same time creating further diversity at school level, with the stated intention of giving more choice to parents. Education is compulsory between the ages of 5 and 16.[1] The great majority of children attend state schools – only 6.6 per cent of children attended private schools in 1994 – and official statistics on the teaching force concern state schools. About a third of schools in the state sector are 'voluntary', usually Church of England or Catholic, with slightly different arrangements for finance and governance than the mainstream sector. The education system comprises:

- nursery education for 3–4-year-olds, provided at the discretion of the Local Education Authority (LEA) in separate schools or in nursery classes within primary schools,
- primary education, usually for 5–11-year-olds and virtually always co-educational. In some LEAs middle schools provide a bridge between primary and secondary education, with respective ages of transfer at 8, 9 or 10 and 12, 13 or 14 years,
- secondary education, mostly provided in comprehensive schools and mostly co-educational; a category of selective 'grant-maintained' schools, funded directly by the State, has now been introduced at this level,
- post-compulsory further education, offered in colleges of further education (CFEs), tertiary colleges and sixth form colleges,
- higher education, offered in universities and colleges of higher education (CHEs).

The size of schools varies considerably and the salary levels of headteachers and deputy heads are partly dependent on the size of the school. Closures and mergers of smaller schools and single-sex schools have resulted in the loss of 2,800 primary and 775 maintained secondary schools between 1980 and 1992 (Mackinnon, Statham and Hales, 1995). There is some evidence that this has resulted in a disproportionate loss of headships occupied by women teachers and contrasts with the optimism of the 1960s and 1970s, when newly created promotional posts were relatively abundant (de Lyon and Migniuolo, 1989).

Along with the shift of control away from the LEAs, the 1988 Education Reform Act also introduced local management of schools. Maintained state schools now control 80 per cent of their own budgets and school governors have overall responsibility for budgetary management, staff numbers and appointments. In practice, much of this fiscal responsibility is devolved to the headteacher, particularly in primary schools, or to a team of senior staff in secondary schools. The role of the headteacher has thus changed considerably, from that of the 'extended professional' to one more akin to a company director.

With decreasing financial weight and legal powers, the LEAs now exercise far less influence on recruitment and selection procedures at school level. The school appointments system in England and Wales is a market-driven rather than a civil-service system. Candidates are 'free' to sell their labour anywhere or to apply to any school directly. Posts are advertised internally (for minor positions of responsibility) or externally. After several recent changes to the salary structure, salary points under senior management level are mainly awarded for qualifications, experience, responsibilities and to retain staff in shortage subject areas. Although there has been a move to more standard job descriptions, there is no standardised system of interviewing. The nature of the interview process and composition of the interview panel can vary considerably, even within the same LEA. Candidates for headships are usually interviewed by a panel of governors and the final decision rests with the full governing body. This comprises local government appointees, elected teachers and parents, co-optees from industry and commerce and church representatives in the case of voluntary schools. The Chief Education Officer of an LEA has a legal duty to advise on appointments and LEAs may offer guidance and training in equal opportunity matters, but formal equal opportunities policies will clearly have less of an effect than in the past. Current figures of the gender composition of governing bodies are not readily available. In 1992, three-quarters of governors in England were men (Ouston, 1993).

At the level of post-compulsory education, recent legislative changes have also had a profound effect. In 1993 colleges of further education became uncoupled from LEA control and 'incorporated' under a central funding council. At university level, a binary system of higher education existed from the mid 1960s to early 1990s, with a large part of the sector, the polytechnics and colleges of higher education, under LEA control. After a similar process of 'incorporation' and other legal changes, the polytechnics and many of the CHEs have now become 'new universities'. Government statistics have followed the old binary division of the sector, which complicates statistical comparisons.

Since incorporation there has been a similar trend towards devolution of budgetary management to cost centres, usually service or academic departments. The role of the head of department has changed correspondingly, demanding greater skills in the deployment of resources within systems of corporate planning. Within universities, professorships may be awarded as personal 'chairs', usually for 'excellence' in research, or may be synonymous with head of department posts. Under incorporation the institution's governors also have an enhanced role in selection procedures. Governing bodies comprise limited student and teacher representation, appointees from industry and the community, with an average female representation of currently just under 20 per cent (NATFHE, 1995a). The great majority of colleges and universities have equal opportunities policies, often inherited from the LEA and reworked in a new context, which can be more directly influential in the appointments process.

As in schools, there are no standardised selection and interview procedures across the country, although these usually exist for individual institutions. Many promotional posts are only advertised internally at 'middle management' level. In CFEs promotions are largely task-related. In universities there is still a mixture of criteria. In most new universities excellence in teaching, research and administration is a prerequisite, with some movement towards task-related definition. In the old universities, research tends to take pride of place, particularly since new funding arrangements have increased competition for research grants. This contrasts with systems of formal testing or accretion of years of experience (the 'old buffer' system!) more common in other European universities (Sutherland, 1990).

The education system has often been described as a flattened hierarchical pyramid, offering limited opportunities for individual advancement. In secondary schools a typical career route would follow either a pastoral or an academic line, through such middle-management posts as head of department, year or faculty. The old division of labour at deputy head level between the 'curriculum' deputy head (usually male) and the pastoral deputy head (usually female) now seems to be less rigid as other responsibilities, such as in-service education or resource management, are devolved to this level (McBurney and Hough, 1989; Wallace and Hall, 1993). However, only 10 per cent of primary and 5 per cent of all secondary teachers will become deputy heads, while 12 per cent of primary and 2 per cent of secondary teachers will reach the level of headteacher. How teachers, both male and female, respond to blocked opportunities has been well explored in British research, which has used a life history approach (see, for example, Sikes, Measor and Woods, 1985). At the level of higher education, opportunities for career advancement are also limited. About 20-30 per cent of university lecturers will become senior lecturers in the old universities or principal lecturers in the new universities, and only 12 per cent will become professors.

A full description of the impact of recent educational changes on the lives of 'ordinary' teachers or those in promoted posts is outside the scope of this chapter. Nevertheless, such changes form an important backcloth to the issue of equal opportunities in education, as the perceived quality of the job has a strong bearing on application and retention rates. Surveys of headteacher satisfaction at school level reveal complex and ambivalent attitudes. At all levels stress and overwork are strong factors. Primary headteachers derive considerable job satisfaction from their relationships with children, teachers and parents and are most concerned about work overload, the amount of paperwork now required and the relatively low status of the profession (Hill, 1994a). Secondary headteachers derive satisfaction from their leadership role and powers to innovate, but express negative feelings towards the time-consuming nature of new financial management requirements, increased paperwork and the shift in their activities away from pupils and colleagues. In general, they have welcomed their greater influence over staffing and budgetary decisions, but the cost is high in terms of immersion in committee work, public relations and micropolitics, especially at a time of staff cutbacks (Mercer, 1993; Evetts, 1994). Expressed stress levels tend to be higher among primary heads, especially those in small schools, and among female headteachers at secondary level (Cooper and Kelly, 1993; Hill, 1994a).

However, male headteachers are reported to suffer more mental ill-health, to exercise poorer coping strategies (exercise, relaxation, outside interests) and to resort to palliative strategies (alcohol, tranquillisers) to a greater extent. Analyses of salary levels show the greatest divergence between salaries of headteachers and other equivalent jobs to exist for heads of small primaries, at 9.2 per cent below average (NAHT, 1995). Compared with other industrial or commercial posts, headteachers enjoy fewer 'perks', such as company cars or private health insurance. In the 1994 survey of primary headteachers' views cited above, under a third would encourage their sons or daughters to enter the teaching profession, (Hill, 1994a). Quantitative analysis of headteacher 'turnover' rates shows that 30 per cent of vacancies at headteacher level are due to early retirement and 7 per cent to stress or ill-health. A significant decline in the number of applications per head or deputy head post has also been charted (Howson, 1995).

More limited evidence is available at the level of further and higher education and is largely derived from trade union sources. In further education recent changes in contracts for lecturers have resulted in a greater number of casual staff and increased workloads for core staff. In higher education a near doubling of the age-participation rate of 19–20-year-olds between 1981 and 1994, accompanied by a substantial increase in the number of mature students, but not by a corresponding increase in the resource base, has created strains in the system, particularly in the new universities and CHEs. In a 1994 survey, 75 per cent of further and higher education lecturers reported 'unacceptable' stress levels and 20 per cent were planning to take early retirement in the next few years. Relatively long hours of work were routine; heads of department in universities worked an estimated average of 55 hours per week (Earley, 1994).

It could be argued that some of the changes experienced by teachers and lecturers in promoted posts have overtaken incumbents. In time, a new breed of educational managers, steeped in the new work culture and more attuned to the demands of corporate planning, will replace those who have adapted uneasily to new exigencies. The implications of such changes for women teachers and lecturers will be explored later in this chapter. The next section provides a snapshot of the situation of women teachers in the educational system at present.

WOMEN IN TEACHING – THE FIGURES

School teaching has long been something of a stronghold of women's employment and there is some evidence that the feminisation of the profession is increasing (DFE, 1992). In 1994, 18 per cent of full-time primary teachers and 50 per cent of secondary teachers were male. Slightly more than twice as many education students are now female as male (DFEE, 1996). In common with the overall situation of working women, a high proportion of women teachers are employed part time, where it is rare to be considered for promotion. Eighty one per cent of part-timers in nursery and primary education and 50 per cent in secondary education are female (DFEE, 1996). In addition a far higher proportion of women teachers are on fixed-term contracts, particularly among those who work part time, as Table 2.4 shows. Since the introduction of local management of schools, the number of part-timers employed has increased by over a quarter (NASUWT, 1995). As the overall number of supply teachers has been reduced, it is interesting to note that gender differences here are not as great overall.

Table 2.4 Qualified secondary school teachers by type of appointment and status, 1992 (in thousands)

Type of Appointment	Males		Females	
	F/time	P/time	F/time	P/time
Permanent	85.8	2.0	76.1	7.7
Fixed Term	1.5	4.0	2.9	13.8
Supply	0.2	1.8	0.4	1.5
TOTAL	87.5	7.8	79.4	23.0

Source: Secondary Schools Staffing Survey, 1992, London, DFE.

The distribution of male to female teachers across job grades is given in Table 2.5. The disparity between the sexes in obtaining primary school headships is particularly marked and gives credence to the popular perception that a talented male teacher can experience a meteoric rise in this sector. It should also be noted that these figures do not include part-time staff and thus give a skewed picture. Pay levels of teachers reflect this hierarchial distribution; full-time women secondary teachers earned 86 per cent of the male rate and primary teachers 91 per cent in 1992–3 (DFEE, 1996). Changes since 1985 have not been substantial, as Table 2.6 illustrates. There are marked regional

Table 2.5 Percentage of men and women at each grade in maintained primary and secondary schools in England and Wales, 1992[1]

Grade	Nursery and Primary		Secondary	
	Men	Women	Men	Women
Head Teacher	32.1	7.3	3.8	1.1
Deputy Head	18.4	8.6	6.4	3.4
Allowance E	0.1	0.0	6.6	2.3
Allowance D	0.5	0.2	19.1	8.6
Allowance C	1.8	1.5	11.2	9.6
Allowance B	14.0	14.0	21.2	23.3
Allowance A	10.1	18.8	9.7	15.7
Main scale (no allowance)	23.0	49.5	21.8	35.5
Any other scale	0.1	0.1	0.3	0.3
Total number of teachers	33,535	145,377	100,883	97,157
Total percentage of teachers	18.74	81.26	50.92	49.08

Note
1. Full-time teachers only.
Source: Statistics of Education: Teachers in Service, 1992, London, DFE.

Table 2.6   Percentage of men and women teachers at each grade in maintained primary and secondary schools in England, 1985

Grade	Nursery and Primary		Secondary	
	Men	Women	Men	Women
Head Teacher	32	7	3	1
Deputy Head	20	8	4	2
Senior teacher	0	0	6	3
Scale 4	0	0	18	6
Scale 3	12	8	27	19
Scale 2	27	42	23	29
Scale 1	9	35	19	40
Total percentage of teachers	22	78	45	55

Source: de Lyon, H. and Migniuolo, F. (1989) (eds) *Women Teachers – Issues and Experiences*, Milton Keynes, Open University Press.

and national variations in these patterns. The proportion of headteachers who are women shows marked regional variations, being far higher in metropolitan areas than in the rural counties and in the south-east and midlands, than the north (O'Connor, 1994). In Wales only 8 per cent of secondary and 43 per cent of primary schools were headed by women (Lloyd Ball, 1996).[2]

Data on women personnel in other influential positions are less forthcoming. However, the number of women Chief Education Officers rose from 1 out of 108 in 1970 to 16 in the late 1980s (Heron, 1991). The position of black women in education is not addressed in official statistics.

The further education sector in England and Wales is generally under-researched, and official data on the distribution of staff are not readily available. Formerly bastions of male technical expertise, the majority of full- and part-time students are now female, although this distribution varies enormously between subject areas. A survey of 38 CFEs conducted in 1991 by the Inspectorate found that although the average proportion of male staff in colleges was 65 per cent, the actual percentage varied from 43 to 90 per cent among colleges. Somewhat dated figures on staffing patterns at all levels are provided in Table 2.7, in the absence of more recent data. In 1996, 14 per cent of college principals were women, which represents a real increase since the 1980s.[3] Regional differences are again in evidence, with better opportunities for women in the metropolitan areas, in particular the former Inner London Education Authority (Wild, 1994). The use of hourly paid staff in this sector, excluded from many employment rights, is growing, but data on its extent or gender composition is not available.

In higher education, national statistics on staffing patterns in the new universities and CHEs have only been available since 1991. Combined figures are now available for both old and new universities. However, the discrepancy betweeen the two sectors is striking, as Tables 2.8 and 2.9 show. The proportion of women members of academic staff has increased since 1980–81, when 15.5 per cent of lecturers overall, 6.4 per cent of readers and senior lecturers and 2.6 per cent of professors in the old universities were women (Sutherland,

Table 2.7 Proportion of women in maintained, assisted and grant-aided establishments of further education[1]

Grade	1984	1988
Principal	5.6	5.5
Vice Principal	9.3	10.9
Head of Department	10.8	12.6
Principal Lecturer	8.5	13.4
Senior Lecturer	15.9	19.3
Lecturer Grade II	27.5	36.4
Lecturer Grade I	36.9	36.4
Mean for all Grades	24.4	29.1

Note
1. By 1988 lecturer grades one and two had merged, so 36.4% is for the new grade.

Source: R. Wild (1994) Barriers to Women's Promotion in Further Education, *Journal of Further and Higher Education*, Vol. 18, no. 3.

Table 2.8 Full time academic staff at old universities by grade and sex, 1993–94[1,2]

Grade	Men %	(n)	Women %	(n)
Professors	94.5	(5484)	5.5	(319)
Readers/Senior Lecturers	88.0	(9264)	12.0	(1259)
Lecturers	72.9	(23195)	27.1	(8620)
Others	57.2	(3304)	42.8	(2468)
Total	76.5	(41247)	23.5	(12666)

Notes
1. Great Britain only.
2. Includes staff not wholly university financed.

Source:*University Statistics 1993–94. Volume 1 – Students and Staff* (1994), Cheltenham, Universities Statistical Record.

Table 2.9 Full-time academic staff at new universities and colleges by grade, 1992

Grade	Males	Females
Head of Department	85	15
Principal Lecturer	82	18
Senior Lecturer	73	27
Lecturer	54	46
Researcher A	72	26
Researcher B	59	41
Other	54	46

Source: *Gender Audit for the New Universities and Colleges* (1994), London, NATFHE.

1985). In 1994–5, 27.6 per cent of all university academic staff and 8.2 per cent of professors were women (HESA, 1996). In both the old and new universities, there is often a striking discrepancy between the proportion of female students in any area of study and the proportion of female lecturers, partly as a result of the rapid growth in female enrolments in the last decade. Table 2.10 shows the variance of female employment among departments, which can also offer very uneven chances of promotion, especially in the

Table 2.10   Full-time academic staff by departmental group, 1994–5

Departmental Group	Males %	Females %
Engineering and Technology	91.0	9.0
Agriculture, Forestry and Veterinary Science	73.3	26.7
Biology, Mathematics and Physics	81.0	19.0
Architecture and Planning	83.4	16.6
Administrative, Business and Social Studies	70.5	29.5
Other Arts	74.0	26.0
Education	59.0	41.0
Language Based Studies	61.0	39.0
All Academic Staff	72.4	27.6

Source: Compiled from Resources of Higher Education Institutions 1994–5 (1996), Cheltenham, Higher Education Statistics Agency.

Sciences and Engineering. The subject mix offered by institutions also influences the proportion of women employed overall, which ranges from 17 to 36 per cent. According to recent research, the proportion of females who are professors ranges from none at all to 32.6 per cent (Griffiths, 1996).

As with data on schools, official figures often only provide a partial picture. Part-time staff, who now constitute 19 per cent of lecturers in the new universities, are not included. In the old universities, the proportion of part-time staff on fractional contracts has risen at twice the rate of full-time staff to about 8 per cent of all staff (AUT, 1995). Figures for hourly paid staff are not available for the old universities. This group, however, makes up about half the part-timers in the new universities (NAFTHE, 1993). Expedient and flexible, hourly paid staff receive virtually no staff development opportunities and have no job security. Part-time staff on fractional contracts have more mixed experiences. About a half of those in the new universities are on permanent contracts, although very few achieve promotion. Over a half of all part-timers are women.

Women are also disproportionately represented among lower grade research staff (categorised as 'others' in Table 2.8), who likewise are generally on short-term contracts, receive lower rates of pay and have limited staff development opportunities (NAFTHE, 1995b). Although there is some evidence of more even promotion prospects at the top level of the senior lecturer grade, there is also evidence of a disproportionate number of women being appointed at the bottom level or below in the new universities (NATFHE, 1994). This continuing, and possibly increasingly unfavourable, situation for women has been described as amounting to an 'academic proletariat' in universities (Acker, 1993).

Data on the distribution of academic-related staff are now more readily available than in the past. In the 1980s, women tended to be represented in the top grades only among library staff (Jackson, 1990). In the 1990s a growing number of appointments in other areas of administration, such as in finance or marketing, has resulted in some change. An estimated 12 per cent of top administrative jobs are now occupied by women, and the number of women vice-chancellors has risen to 6 out of a total of 104 (Williams, 1995).

Criticisms of this kind of data, fairly well documented in the research literature and now becoming more widely available in some sectors as monitoring procedures are improved, stem from the argument that such data represent a static view of the system and do not serve as good predictors of future change. In higher education, for example, there is a bottleneck of lecturers in promoted posts, now in their late 40s to mid-50s. Once they retire, rapid change may occur in access to such posts by women at the top of the lecturer (old universities) or senior lecturer (new universities) scales. However, within this category, a smaller group will form a 'pool of promotability', possessing appropriate qualifications and experience, than appears in organisational diagrams. At school level, one researcher has attempted to discern promotion factors, using regression analysis (Grant, 1987). While such work clarifies the weighting of variables at the point of application and promotion, it fails to raise broader questions about the situation of women in teaching, for example justifications of the negative evaluation of career breaks for raising children among selection panels. It is to this broader explanation of the 'glass ceiling' for women teachers and lecturers that we now turn.

WOMEN IN SCHOOLS

Reviewing the relevant field, Valerie Hall makes the charge that 'compared to the United States, research on women in educational management in Britain is still in its infancy' (Hall, 1993, p. 23). Gender, she argues, is treated as a separate and marginal issue in the literature on school leadership. Research on women in educational management is characterised by armchair theorising, anecdotal testimony and lack of empirical roots.

Compared with many European countries, however, it could be asserted that the UK is fairly well served in the provision of official statistics and can draw on a relatively rich research base at school level. Research at the level of higher education and particularly further education, is less plentiful and Hall's comments on the scope of research are well targeted. Research is mostly concerned with blockages to women's promotion and to a more limited extent with the experience of being in promoted posts. Much of the evidence is based on self-report, by questionnaire or by interview. In some accounts the basis of sampling is not clear and interviews are limited to 'success stories', uncorroborated by faculties or colleagues. Statistical data and interview material is often presented without reference to changes in the education system and opportunities available. There has been little research on the views and actions of the mostly male power-holders. Nonetheless, Hall's current research on the observed differences in women headteachers' management styles, Evetts' (1994) research on the life-stories of headteachers and the research by Farish *et al.* (1995) on the process of selection interviews begins to redress this imbalance.

An often cited study in this field, published in 1985, still provides one model of good research practice. Based on detailed research on secondary schools in one LEA, Hilda Davidson tackled the 'unfriendly myths' levelled at women teachers. These included the assertions that:

• women teachers do not want responsibility or promotion,
• women teachers are not promoted because they are less well qualified than their male colleagues,
• women teachers have fewer years of experience,
• women teachers leave to have babies,
• women teachers are absent more often than men.

In 1983, Davidson put these myths to empirical test in one LEA. She found that men were promoted more quickly, but did not have more years of teaching experience on average. More male teachers in her sample were graduates, and men were more successful in gaining secondments to improve qualifications. Only 3 per cent of teachers had taken maternity leave in the year of study, compared with 1.5 per cent who had taken long-term leave for other reasons. Rates of absence for all reasons were similar for both sexes and low overall. Today, such 'myths' still abound in staff rooms and senior common-rooms. When women try to challenge them rationally, they can be subjected to ridicule (Burgess, 1989; Cunnison, 1989).

Subsequent research at school level partially upholds Davidson's findings. Men and women do not express dramatically different career aspirations (Grant, 1987; Hill, 1994b). There is some evidence that women make fewer applications for promoted posts, particularly externally (Ozga, 1993). Research draws our attention, however, to the role of 'patronage', 'gatekeepers' and 'mentors' in this process. Here there is some evidence that women are encouraged to apply for posts less often by advisors and inspectors (Jayne, 1989). Women also tend to target their applications more selectively, so that when they do apply for headships, they are often more successful (Grant, 1989a; Ouston, 1993). They may also adopt something of a cost–benefits approach in deciding whether the price to pay for promotion is too high (Hall, 1993).

There are consistent accounts of women teachers' lack of career plans, which can often give the appearance of 'drifting' in conventional career terms. However, this surface judgement obscures the way in which many women construct a 'rather messy mosaic of life and work events, rather than following a clearly, well-staged, well-signposted career map' (Grant, 1989b, p. 119). Ambitiousness may fluctuate in response to events external to teaching. The decision to have children may well be interpreted as a signal of changed commitments, but may simply represent a different phase in the life cycle of teachers (Riddell, 1989; Evetts, 1994). Willingness to move geographically in order to secure promotion is likewise often seen as a mark of commitment. Research into the views of both male and female teachers shows that this is generally an unpopular option (Grant, 1987). The majority of headteachers are in fact appointed within their 'home' or neighbouring LEA and job-related moves are not the norm.

With a declining number of headships available, the average age of attaining a first headship has risen for both men and women. At primary school level, this is now 35–39 years for men and 40–49 years for women (Hill, 1994b). This discrepancy between the sexes can be explained to some extent by career breaks. More male secondary teachers, for example, have over 16 years' total teaching experience (DFE, 1992). However, it should be noted that only a small minority of women teachers have taken career breaks of over one year's duration (NASUWT, 1995). Indeed, in common with other women professionals, there is a growing trend to delay childbearing and to take statutory maternity leave only or to remain childless. This is reflected in the more even figures on teaching experience of under 15 years. A career break for family reasons is not always seen as disadvantageous at primary school level (Hart, 1989). Much depends on the way the break in service is managed to enable women to retain their foothold in teaching. On return to work, a lack of flexible working arrangements, pre-school and after-school childcare and the domestic support systems more commonly enjoyed by male teachers on the way up, may pose greater problems.

Although a slightly higher proportion of male secondary teachers are trained graduates, data are too limited and contradictory to explain discrepancies at promoted levels (Grant, 1987; Hill, 1994b). More significant is the research evidence on the progress of teachers in school hierarchies. Women are more likely to be given cross-curricular posts of responsibilities, which are more complex and less readily understood than their male counterparts', or posts which involve pastoral concerns to a greater degree (Weightman, 1989). They are less likely to be awarded incentive allowances and are often given lower allowances than men for similar responsibilities (McMullen, 1993). They are less likely to be given substantial staff release for in-service training. The introduction of staff appraisal in schools is proving to be something of a double-edged sword. While it could offer women greater access to staff development opportunities linked to career planning, this is often not the case. There is some evidence that male appraisers can be overprotective of women appraisees and that appraisal reinforces gender-stereotyped views of attributes and behaviour (Freeman, 1992; Hall, 1993). Interviews with senior women teachers attribute encouragement to both male and female mentors, but this is clearly not uniform. At the interview stage, there is evidence of the continuing practice of asking women applicants questions about their home lives and family plans and the continuing perception of them as a 'bad risk', especially by governors (Grant, 1987;

Evetts, 1994). Black women candidates, in particular, find that their experience is not recognised and that judgements about personal style influence outcomes (Walker, 1993). In one small-scale study, candidates feared the judgements of women governors most, as they felt that they were making invidious comparisons with their own lives (Burgess, 1989).

If women do succeed in jumping these hurdles, the experience of headship can be equally problematic and this in turn will influence women lower down the hierarchy. Like their counterparts in industry, senior women teachers are made visible by their relative scarcity, lack mentors of the same sex and often feel isolated and constantly 'on trial'. This sense of visibility is clearly heightened in the case of the few senior black teachers (Al-Khalifa, 1989; Walker, 1993). Work overload and long hours are the norm (Ouston, 1993; Ozga, 1993). Interviews with women in the most senior positions, such as Chief Education Officers, suggest that 70 to 80 hour working weeks are not uncommon (Heron, 1991). Visibility becomes even more acute at this level. Pauline Perry, describing her days as Chief Inspector, remembers having 'the wrong pitch of voice in discussions' and being 'the only patch of colour at a table surrounded by dark suits' (Ozga, 1993, p. 89).

Some senior women minimise references to domestic concerns (Al-Khalifa, 1989). Others downplay the exigencies of the juggling act, as exemplified in a letter from a Chief Education Officer who stated that, 'It is not only perfectly feasible to combine a CEO's job with having young children, 80 hour week, weekend work and all, but there are positive professional advantages in being a parent' (TES, 1991, p. 19). Caring responsibilities are not always tied to parenthood. Grant noted the concerns of women deputy heads with substantial responsibilities towards elderly parents as well (Grant, 1989b).

Interviews with senior women teachers often reveal a high level of self-critical reflectiveness. Unwilling to be cast either as 'one of the boys' or in a stereotypically feminine role, it may take a while to evolve a confident personal style in office, drawing on a repertoire of available management styles. In common with women managers in other spheres, women headteachers claim to spend a higher proportion of their time 'on the ground'; to exercise co-operative planning at meetings and to adopt more informal communication styles (Adler, Laney and Packer, 1993). They are said to listen more than men; to sympathise; to be prepared to apologise and to be able to resolve conflicts with skill; to be 'enablers' and 'empowerers' (Al-Khalifa, 1989; Hall, 1994). However, research into the attitudes of men and women headteachers often show that both sexes favour an open, democratic style of management, at least in theory (Jones, 1990; Evetts, 1994). Whether this commitment is translated into practice remains open, without substantial further research.

Whatever the case, the demand for greater corporate planning in schools inevitably impacts on management style. Based on systematic planning, goal-setting and the harnessing of resources – physical and human – to achieve such goals, the qualities required of educational leaders are changing. 'Individuals seeking or achieving promotion in the new organisations, both public and private, are required constantly to demonstrate their competence and effectiveness and to achieve high levels of measurable performance' (Evetts, 1994, p. 120). Financial and directional skills are at the forefront, although the ability to motivate remains a strong imperative. For some, this new managerialist approach is the very antithesis of women's preferred management style: instrumental; task-orientated; detached; technicist; almost synonymous with masculinity. Others simply observe that these demands cut across the management styles most preferred by women and so could act as a disincentive to more 'people-oriented' teachers applying for promotion. Whether teachers of either sex will be able to harness external demands to more emancipatory management practice in the future remains an open question.

WOMEN IN FURTHER AND HIGHER EDUCATION

The experience of women in post-compulsory education has much in common with the situation in schools. Similar issues of juggling home and work demands in often unsympathetic environments arise. Women lecturers have often been channelled into counselling or administrative duties, where they cannot demonstrate other competencies (Howe, 1986; Jackson, 1990). With far fewer institutions in existence, the issue of whether to move for job reasons comes more to the fore (Sutherland, 1985). Appraisal schemes are not always linked with staff development opportunities and can dwell on women's perceived defects rather than strengths (Bagilhole, 1993). With far fewer women in the sector, let alone in promoted posts, the issues of visibility and isolation can be even more acute. Senior women in the sector represent even more of a pioneering cohort, anticipating the advance of the 'monstrous regiment'.

In each sector, particular concerns are influenced by the prevailing work culture and practices. In further education, an absence of female role-models for women lecturers is particularly marked, especially as promotions tend to favour expertise in such subject areas as engineering and technology (Howe, 1986; Wild, 1994). Although over 90 per cent of colleges have equal opportunities policies, systematic monitoring of outcomes has been far less prevalent (HMI, 1991). In 1989, only 15 per cent of a sample of 200 colleges monitored equal opportunities, 13.5 per cent offered training in equal opportunities and 3.5 per cent had designated equal opportunities teams (Warwick and Williamson, 1989). Where Equal Opportunities Officers were in post, they were often allocated only 1 to 4 hours per week in which to carry out their duties. Women participants at a follow-up seminar reported fatigue in the face of 'inhospitable psychological climates' (p. 34).

Networks, such as the Network of Women Managers in Further and Compulsory Education, are increasingly providing lateral support to women in the sector, but the uncoupling of the CFEs from local authority control may well result in even less vigorous support for equal opportunities policies.

A discrepancy between the existence of equal opportunities policies and the practice of equal opportunities is also marked in higher education. In 1994, 93 per cent of UK universities (old and new) had equal opportunities policies and 72 per cent guidelines on fair recruitment and selection. However, only 42 per cent provided training in equal opportunities for staff involved in recruitment, and only 21 per cent made training compulsory (Wright, 1994). Without careful implementation, such policies can remain a form of 'equispeak', addressing only surface issues (McCann, Jones and Martin, 1991). In the new universities, the legacy of LEA equal opportunities policies, combined with stronger recruitment training policies, may offer some explanation of the relatively favourable situation for women, compared with the old university sector. Yet even here, policies are often concerned with the 'rules of the game', rather than outcomes. In 1994, 75 per cent of all universities had monitoring systems in place, yet gaps in data produced, for example concerning short-term contracts, can be eloquent.

As noted earlier, the work culture of British universities is changing rapidly. The self-image of the sector was based on the notion of collegiality, but even in the past an emphasis on individual excellence, often forged in the cut and thrust of abrasive academic debate, ran counter to this (McAulay, 1987). Women were assigned roles as one of the 'chaps', as inferior or invisible in many university departments, which at the same time relied on women lecturers to bear the brunt of lower-level committee work and lower-status teaching. Excluded from networks and informal sponsorship, women often do not achieve 'take-off' in research terms, where access to research budgets and assistance can bring cumulative advantages.

A 1989 analysis of publications rates by type of institution and by gender showed that women were more numerous among the non-producers and fewer among the high producers of research, but lacked any exploration of the reasons behind this pattern (Halsey, 1990). Clearly, the effects of career breaks and the presence of young children will have an impact, especially in areas of rapidly changing knowledge. Yet this is not a sufficient explanation. In a recent case study, only 56 per cent of a sample of women lecturers were married and 30 per cent had children; 75 per cent felt that they had been discriminated against directly or indirectly (Bagilhole, 1993). Most women lecturers take a short maternity leave break but often experience poorly managed career break schemes, which place a burden on their colleagues, and face inflexible working arrangements on their return (The Hansard Society, 1990). In the new universities, teaching commitments are far greater and both men and women lecturers have to carry out research in their 'spare time', unless research grants are available for staff replacement.

For lecturers with family responsibilities, annualised hours offer greater flexibility within timetabled commitments than for teachers in schools. However, research seminars are often held in the early evenings. A double standard has also been noted, whereby absence from the work place is permitted for conference attendance but not for child-related reasons. One response is a rigid segregation of the home and work spheres, where children are simply not mentioned in the professional context.

There has been little research into the career motivation of women academics in the UK. In 1985, Margaret Sutherland noted the familiar phenomenon of 'drifting', with unclear career plans, which still seems to prevail where there is a climate of indifference towards women's futures and in departments where women are very much in the minority (see also Jackson, 1990). Once women lecturers constitute a 'critical mass' of over 15–20 per cent of a department, they may be perceived as more of a threat, especially if they try to rock existing practices (West and Lyon, 1995). In this context, it would not be surprising if the often heard cry that women do not apply for promotion was partially true. However, monitoring of this issue is yet in its infancy and statistics are only available on an institutional basis. As noted before, promotions criteria vary to some extent between the old and new universities, with more emphasis on entrepreneurialism and professional or industrial experience in the latter. However, in both, unwritten rules and expectations may undermine stated criteria in selection interviews (Farish *et al.*, 1995).

Since the female professor or head of university department is such a rare animal, there has been very little research into their goals, management styles or experiences. In many institutions the number of female professors can be counted on one hand, which has obvious implications for their visibility (Acker, 1993). In such a minority situation, they tread a thin line between assertiveness and abrasiveness and may be overloaded as mentors to women lecturers in their departments. Single women can be seen as particularly threatening by male colleagues, who fear what they perceive as over-commitment to the role. In common with headteachers, the nature of the job demands greater managerial skills, particularly over declining financial resources. The extent to which this will affect women's promotional chances and management style at this level again remains an open question.

PRESSURES FOR CHANGE

Unlike several of our European neighbours, such as the Netherlands or Scandinavia, government policy towards equal opportunities for women has been marked by its absence. There have been no targets, no quotas; it has not been considered a particular issue. In contrast, many LEAs have had a long track-record in promoting equal opportunities and, although their power is diminishing, they can still be a source of information and influence on schools, for example in monitoring application rates and outcomes and publicising these. In the wider arena of employment, the influence of the Opportunity 2000 Group in pressing the 'business case' for equal opportunities has already been noted, as has the concern with the equal treatment of employees at EU level. From 1991 onwards the Committee of Vice-Chancellors and Principals of Universities has outlined a model of good practice for the higher education sector and has monitored its implementation. The Labour government elected in 1997 has promised greater attention to equal opportunities, and has added this to the portfolio of the (female) social services minister. It is not clear yet to what extent raised expectations of change will be met.

Pressure from below is gathering pace. National networks, such as the Women in Higher Education Network or Through the Glass Ceiling, act as general information exchanges and support groups. LEA-based fora for senior women teachers or university-based groupings can offer more specific and immediate forms of support and act as local catalysts for change. In 1990 the Hansard Commission provided a useful summary of strategies for change, included here as Table 2.11. In practice, such strategies for change can be undermined by financial pressures, which push equal opportunities way down the agenda; by systematic muddle and the exploitation of ambiguities; by inertia or negative reactions. Change can be limited to high-profile, low-cost measures, which lack commitment. Nonetheless, positive models are now more readily available, and it is to one such that we briefly turn.

Like many former polytechnics, Oxford Brookes University left LEA control in 1989 with an equal opportunities policy in place, concerning employment matters. This ensured that the institution complied at minimum with the employment law on such issues as sex and race discrimination, and maternity leave, and provided policy guidance in the areas of job-sharing, career breaks and sexual harassment. However, during the early 1990s, there was substantial criticism by interested parties, such as the women's staff forum and trade unions, that the translation of such policy into practice was insufficient. The Polytechnic had also recruited a higher proportion of female students than the national average (52 per cent in 1989–90) and an awareness of their needs, for example in relation to childcare, led to measures which were of potential benefit to both staff and students. The attainment of university status in 1992 provided a backcloth to a wide-ranging examination of current practices under the umbrella of the Agenda for Brookes Initiative. As a result of an external consultancy report on equal opportunities, which called for a new and vigorous approach, the Equal Opportunities Action Group was established with a fairly generous budget. The remit of the group included the further promotion of fair treatment of staff and students with disabilities and from ethnic minority groups, as well as gender issues. Its terms of reference were to advise the Vice-Chancellor on all aspects of equal opportunities, to monitor existing patterns, to identify discrimination and to

Table 2.11   Strategies for change

BARRIERS	STRATEGIES
Organizational Barriers	
Unfair selection or promotion procedures	Equal opportunities policy
	Equal opportunities training
	Dual interviewing
	Precise job specifications
	Objective assessment criteria
	External advertising
	Equal opportunity audits
	Monitoring
	Targets
Inflexible working arrangements	Senior level part-time/jobsharing
	Flexi-time
	Working at home
	Annual hours
	Other flexible arrangements
Mobility	Requirement dropped or modified
	Dual career job search
Age Limits	Requirement dropped
Traditional Roles	
Work and family life	Career break schemes
	Workplace nurseries
	Childcare vouchers
	Parental leave
	Enhanced maternity leave
	Other childcare help
Attitudinal Barriers	
Lack of confidence	Equal opportunity advertising
	Headhunting
	Internal promotion policies
	Women-only training courses
Prejudice	Boardroom commitment to change
	Equal opps training for managers
	Awareness training for all staff

Source: Hansard Society (1990) *The Report of the Hansard Society Commission on Women at the Top*, London, The Hansard Society for Parliamentary Government.

recommend appropriate targets and action. Meanwhile, the Personnel Department had begun to monitor staffing patterns and had appointed a designated Equal Opportunities Officer. The former Chair of the Equal Opportunities Commission was appointed as a governor and a high-profile woman barrister as Chancellor. The proportion of women governors rose from 23 per cent in 1990, already above the national average, to 31 per cent in 1996.

A public demonstration of support for equal opportunities was provided by the presence of governors at a mandatory awareness training programme for managers of academic and service departments and academic course leaders. In addition, the Vice-Chancellor has been described by the group as 'a powerful advocate in all decision-making fora' (EOAG, 1995, p. 3). Although there are no recipes for success in this field, a combination of demonstrated commitment from the top and a groundswell of support from below is often considered conducive to success. Wider mobilisation of support was attempted through visits by EOAG members to department meetings and accessible dissemination of information about activities, research projects and policy recommendations in the University's staff bulletin. This did not always have the desired effect. There was some initial criticism that the Group was an expensive talking shop and was in danger of spreading itself too thinly across too many issues and of championing a cause which was not the most pressing at a time of budgetary constraint. There was a suggestion that some of the early initiators of policy measures also felt robbed of their achievements or that efforts were being duplicated. In fact, measures initiated by the EOAG together with other parties such as Student Services, the Personnel Department and trade unions have contributed to an overall improved climate of equal opportunities. These include the establishment of a childminder network and half-term playscheme, an improved maternity support scheme and permitted absence for parents to care for sick children (also as a result of a change in the law).

In 1995–6 a half-time Head of Equal Opportunities was appointed from among the academic staff on a temporary basis with continued funding for the Group. Among the Group's staff-related objectives was attendance at advancement panels for teaching staff with a view to ensuring and reporting on good practice. In comparison with average figures for the new universities, Brookes presents a relatively favourable profile, as illustrated in Table 2.12. The University also came second in a 1996 league table of the percentage of female professors appointed, with 26.1 per cent compared with 5.7 per cent at the University of Oxford (Griffiths, 1996). As is the case in many universities, the recency of statistical monitoring does not facilitate the identification of long-term trends, nor is it yet possible to establish to what extent this is directly attributable to an equal opportunities policy. Analysis of promotions from senior to principal lecturer level in 1993–4 did, however, show that although a slightly lower proportion of women applied than were represented at this level, a higher proportion were both shortlisted and

Table 2.12   Academic staff at Oxford Brookes University by grade, 1996[1]

Grade	Male %	Female %
Researcher A	57	43
Researcher B	48	52
Lecturer	34	66
Senior Lecturer	62	38
Principal Lecturer	76	24
Management[2]	75	25

Notes
1. Compiled from personnel records at Oxford Brookes University.
2. Management includes service departments as well as academic departments.

appointed. However, the proportion of women appointed on a temporary basis was significantly higher than the male rate. Lower down the academic hierarchy, the University has just begun to monitor the proportion of male to female teaching staff on temporary contracts. In 1995–6 approximately 20 per cent of staff were on part-time fractional contracts and 18 per cent were on fixed-term contracts. Of these two groups 56 per cent were female. Hourly paid staff comprised a much bigger group in terms of individuals employed: again 58 per cent of this group were female. Compared with the overall representation of women in the teaching force, it is evident that women are disproportionately represented among staff on such contracts. Without long-term data it is not yet possible to establish trends or to assess whether the success stories at the top are being off-set by an increasing reliance on the 'academic proletariat' at the bottom.

After discussion at a joint staff committee, it was decided that the establishment of any quantitative targets in relation to staffing patterns would not be helpful. However, the issue of equal opportunities is now firmly embedded in planning procedures and in the University's own five-year strategic plan. Academic departments have been required to include a statement on equal opportunities in their own strategic plans, the scope of which is determined at this level. The structure of accountability is somewhat blurred at this point and the consequences of non-compliance or a tokenistic approach are not clear. With a greater emphasis on the devolved powers of heads of department, there is a danger that central University policy and advisory guidelines could be ignored or flouted. Nonetheless, the Central Management Team of the University has expressed commitment to reviewing the strategic planning process in relation to equal opportunities outcomes.

At department level, commitment to equal opportunities varies considerably. In a 'gender-friendly' context, staff development and appraisal should result in specific careers guidance which takes into account personal circumstances and goals. The proportion of women lecturers who are in receipt of University research funds should be raised through targeted guidance and support. Policy on the management of career break schemes in action is currently being reviewed by the EOAG. The Group has also raised concern about the position of part-time staff and of research staff, arguing that particular attention should be given to career routes for staff in these categories. The experience of women in senior positions should also inform practice and the demands of such posts be reviewed. In this case study policy initiatives have given a clear lead in a direction which goes beyond limited quantitative outcomes. The work of the Group has progressed from the stage of problem definition, through a period of coalition building to a point where the University has been mobilised to incorporate the goal of equal opportunities (Price and Priest, 1996). The challenge is now to ensure that a pervasive and deep-rooted ethos of equal opportunities will deliver the promise of change.

CONCLUSION

Throughout this chapter it has been evident that structural changes in the education system and financial constraints on the sector have to some extent resulted in the relegation of equal opportunities issues. Schools, colleges and universities exhibit patterns similar to the wider workplace. In an overall climate of rationalisation and limited resources, the education system has to find ways of delivering the service more economically and this is often at the expense of its most vulnerable employees, in this case, women.

Nonetheless a strong case can be made for the retention and development of equal opportunities policies in order to maximise human resources – as well as to work towards social justice. Although there is evidence of women gaining ground in the middle ranks of the system, changes at the top remain limited so far. If equal opportunities policies do result in more equitable representation of women in educational management, will those newly appointed recognise their responsibilities as path-finders?

NOTES

1. Separate and more centralised systems exist in Scotland and Northern Ireland, under the respective auspices of the Scottish and Northern Ireland Offices. It has been beyond the scope of this chapter to cover these countries as well. Statistics are published separately for schools but statistics on higher education are aggregated for the UK. For an account of women in educational management in Scotland, see, for example, Marsh, L. (1988) Survey Feedback and Policy Formulation: Equal Opportunities and Promotion in Strathclyde, *Scottish Educational Review*, Vol. 21, no. 1, pp. 26–35; Darling, J. (1992) The Best Man for the Job: Women Teachers' Promotion and the Strathclyde Research, *Scottish Educational Review*, Vol. 24, no. 1, pp. 45–46. For Northern Ireland, see Chapter 7. For an account of Wales, see Lloyd Ball, below.
2. In Scotland, there are 48 female headteachers, representing 5 per cent of Scottish heads, and 15 per cent of deputy heads are female (*Context*, 1996, no. 12).
3. Author's own calculations from FEFC sources.

REFERENCES

Acker, S. (1993) Contradictions in Terms; Women Academics in British Universities, in Arnot, M. and Weiler, K. (eds.) *Feminism and Social Justice in Education*, Lewes, Falmer.

Adler, S., Laney, J. and Packer, M. (1993) *Managing Women*, Buckingham, Open University.

Al-Khalifa, E. (1989) Management by Halves: Women Teachers and School

Management, in de Lyon, H. and Widdowson Migniuolo, F. (eds.) *Women Teachers – Issues and Experiences*, Milton Keynes, Open University.

AUT (Association of University Teachers) (1995) *Part-time, not Part Person*, London.

Bagilhole, B. (1993) How to Keep a Good Woman Down: An Investigation of the Role of Institutional Factors of Discrimination against Women Academics, *British Journal of Sociology of Education*, Vol. 14, no. 3, pp. 261–74.

Burgess, R. (1989) Something You Learn to Live With? Gender and Inequality in a Comprehensive School, *Gender and Education*, Vol. 1, no. 2, pp. 155–64.

Cooper, C. L. and Kelly, M. (1993) Occupational Stress in Headteachers: A National UK Study, *British Journal of Educational Psychology*, Vol. 63, no. 2, pp. 130–43.

Cunnison, S. (1989) Gender Joking in the Staffroom, in Acker, S. (ed.) *Teachers, Gender and Careers*, Lewes, Falmer.

Davidson, H. (1985) Unfriendly Myths about Women Teachers. In Whyte, J., Deem, R., Kant, L. and Cruikshank, M. (eds.) *Girl Friendly Schooling*, London, Methuen.

Davidson, M. and Burke, R. J. (1994) *Women in Management: Current Research Issues*, London, Paul Chapman Publishing.

Davidson, M. and Cooper, C. (1992) *Shattering the Glass Ceiling: the Woman Manager*, London, Paul Chapman Publishing.

DES (Department of Education & Science) (1992) *Statistics of Education: Teachers in Service, England and Wales*, London, HMSO.

DFE (Department for Education) (1992) *Secondary Schools Staffing Survey*, London, HMSO.

DFE (Department for Education) (1994) *Education Statistics for the UK*, London, HMSO.

DFEE (Department for Education & Employment) (1996) *Education Statistics for the UK*, 1995, London, HMSO.

Earley, P. (1994) *Lecturers' Workload and Factors Affecting Stress Levels*, London, NATFHE/NFER.

EOAG (Equal Opportunities Action Group) (1995) *Report for 1993–5*, Oxford Brookes University.

EOC (Equal Opportunities Commision) (1993) *Women and Men in Britain*, Manchester.

Evetts, J. (1994) *Becoming a Headteacher*, London, Cassell.

Farish, M., McPake, J., Powney, J. and Weiner, G. (1995) *Equal Opportunities in Colleges and Universities*, Buckingham, Open University Press/Society for Research into Higher Education.

Freeman, A. (1992) School Teacher Appraisal and Gender Issues, *Educational Change and Development*, Vol. 12, no. 2, pp. 1–4.

Grant, R. (1987) A Career in Teaching – a Survey of Middle School Teachers' Perceptions with Particular Reference to the Careers of Women Teachers, *British Educational Research Journal*, Vol. 13, no. 3, pp. 227–39.

Grant, R. (1989a) Women Teachers' Career Pathways: Towards an Alternative Model of Career, in Acker, S. (ed.) *Teachers, Gender and Careers*, Lewes, Falmer.

Grant, R. (1989b) Heading for the Top: the Career Experiences of a Group of Women Deputies in one LEA, *Gender and Education*, Vol. 1, no. 2, pp. 113–25.

Griffiths, S. (1996) Chipping Away at the Glass Ceiling, *The Times Higher Educational Supplement*, 26 July, p. 16.

Hall, V. (1993) Women in Educational Management: a Review of Research in Britain, in Ouston, J. (ed.) *Women in Educational Management*, Harlow, Longman.

Hall, V. (1994) Making a Difference: Women Headteachers' Contributions to Schools as Learning Institutions, paper presented to the BEMAS Conference in Manchester.

Halsey, A. H. (1990) The Long, Open Road to Equality, *Times Higher Education Supplement*, no. 901, 9 February, p. 17.

Hammond, V. and Holton, V. (1991) *A Balanced Change: Achieving Cultural Change for Women, a Comparative Study*, Berkhamsted, Ashridge Management Research Group.

The Hansard Society (1990) *The Report of the Hansard Society Commission on Women at the Top*, London, The Hansard Society for Parliamentary Government.

Hart, L. (1989) Women in Primary Management, in Skelton, C. (ed.) *Whatever Happens to Little Women?*, Milton Keynes, Open University Press.

Heron, E. (1991) The Monstrous Regiment Advances, *Times Educational Supplement*, no. 3902, 12 April, p. 12.

HESA (Higher Education Statistics Agency, 1996) *Resources of Higher Education Institutions 1994–5*, Cheltenham.

Hill, T. (1994a) Primary Headteachers: Their Job Satisfaction and Future Career Aspirations, *Educational Research*, Vol. 36, no. 3, pp. 223–35.

Hill, T. (1994b) Primary Headteachers' Careers: A Study of Primary Heads with Particular Reference to Women's Career Trajectories, *British Educational Research Journal*, Vol. 2, no. 2, pp. 197–207.

HMI (1991) *Equal Opportunities in Further Education: a Survey of Good Practice in England and Wales*, London, HMSO.

Howe, T. (1986) The Organisation of Women in Further Education: Changing the Focus?, *Journal of Further and Higher Education*, Vol. 10, no. 2, pp. 3-13.

Howson, J. (1995) *An Assessment of the Labour Market for Senior Staff in Schools*, London, National Association of Headteachers.

Innes, S. (1994) *Making it Work, Women, Change and Challenge in the 1990s*, London, Chatto and Windus.

Jackson, D. (1990) Women Working in Higher Education: A Review of the Position of Women in Higher Education and Policy Developments, *Higher Education Quarterly*, Vol. 44, no. 4, pp. 297–324.

Jayne, E. (1989) Women as Leaders of Schools: the Role of Training, *Educational Management and Administration*, no. 17, pp. 109–14.

Jones, M. L. (1990) The Attitudes of Men and Women Primary School Teachers to Promotion, *Educational Management and Administration*, no. 18, pp. 11–16.

Lloyd Ball, H. (1996) Welsh Women and Educational Management, *Context*, no. 12, pp. 30–31.

de Lyon, H. and Migniuolo, F. (1989) (eds.) *Women Teachers, Issues and Experiences*, Milton Keynes, Open University Press.

Mackinnon, D., Statham, J. and Hales, M. (1995) *The System: Education in the UK, Facts and Figures*, London, Hodder and Stoughton.

MacRae, S. (1996) *Women at the Top: Progress After Five Years*, London, The Hansard Society for Parliamentary Government.

Maxwell, E. (1995) More than Somewhere to Go, *Times Educational Supplement*, no. 4118, 2 June, p. 6.

McAulay, J. (1987) Women Academics: A Case-Study in Inequality, in Spencer, A. and Podmore, D. (eds.) *In a Man's World*, London, Tavistock.

McBurney, E. and Hough, J. (1989) Role Perceptions of Female Deputy Heads, *Educational Management and Administration*, no. 17, pp. 115–18.

McCann, J., Jones, G. and Martin, I. (1991) Behind the Rhetoric: Women Academic Staff in Colleges of Higher Education in England, *Gender and Education*, Vol. 3, no. 1, pp. 15–28.

McMullen, H. (1993) Towards Women-Friendly Schools, in Ouston, J. (ed.) *Women in Educational Management*, Harlow, Longman.

Mercer, D. (1993) Job Satisfaction and the Headteacher: a Nominal Group Approach, *School Organisation*, Vol. 13, no. 2, pp. 153–64.

Moss, P. (1992) Perspectives from Europe, in Pugh, G. (ed.) *Contemporary Issues in the Early Years*, London, Paul Chapman Publishing.

NAHT (National Association of Headteachers) (1995) Unpublished evidence to the School Teachers Review Body.

NASUWT (National Association of Schoolmasters and Union of Women Teachers) (1995) *The Career Prospects of Men and Women in the Teaching Profession*, Birmingham.

NATFHE (National Association of Teachers in Further and Higher Education) (1993) *Losing Out: A Study of Part-time Lecturers in the New Universities*, London.

NATFHE (1994) *Gender Audit for the New Universities and Colleges*, London.

NATFHE (1995a) *Governance in Higher Education*, London.

NATFHE (1995b) *Research Staff in the New Universities and Colleges of Higher Education*, London.

O'Connor, M. (1994) Ambitious Women Should Head for the City, *Times Educational Supplement*, no. 4064, 20 May, p. 2.

Ouston, J. (ed.) (1993) *Women in Education Management*, Harlow, Longman.

Ozga, J. (1993) *Women in Educational Management*, Buckingham, Open University Press.

Parents at Work (1995) *Time Work and the Family: Research Report*, London.

Price, L. and Priest, J. (1996) Activists as Change Agents: Achievements and Limitations, in Walsh, V. and Morley, L. (eds.) *Breaking Boundaries: Women in Higher Education*, London, Taylor and Francis.

Riddell, S. (1989) 'It's Nothing to do with Me' – Teachers' Views and Gender Divisions in the Curriculum, in Acker, S. (ed.) *Teachers, Gender and Careers*, Lewes, Falmer.

Sikes, P., Measor, L. and Woods, P. (1985) *Teachers Careers, Crises and Continuities*, Lewes, Falmer.

Social Trends (1995), London, HMSO.

Social Trends (1996), London, HMSO.

Sutherland, M. (1985) *Women Who Teach in Universities*, Trentham, Trentham Books.

Sutherland, M. (1990) Women Teaching in European Universities: Interviews and Information, in Byrne, E. (ed.) *Gender in Education*, London, Multilingual Matters.

TES (Times Educational Supplement) (1991) no. 3904, Letters page, 26 April, p. 19.

Walker, C. (1993) Black Women in Educational Management, in Ozga, J. (ed.) *Women in Educational Management*, Buckingham, Open University.

Wallace, M. and Hall, V. (1993) *Senior Management Teams in Action*, London, Paul Chapman Publishing.

Warwick, J. and Williamson, A. (1989) *Equal Opportunities (Gender) Policy and Practices in Colleges of Further Education*, London, Further Education Unit Research Report no. 505.

Weightman, J. (1989) Women in Management, *Educational Management and Administration*, Vol. 17, no. 3, pp. 119–122.

West, J. and Lyon, K. (1995) The Trouble with Equal Opportunities: the Case of Women Academics, *Gender and Education*, Vol. 7, no. 1, pp. 51–68.

Wild, R. (1994) Barriers to Women's Promotion in Further Education, *Journal of Further and Higher Education*, Vol. 18, no. 3, pp. 83–96.

Williams, E. (1995) Lipstick and White Collars, *Times Higher Education Supplement*, no. 1186, 28 July, pp. 18–19.

Wright, A. (1994) A Sisterly Hand up the Ladder, *Times Higher Education Supplement*, no. 1129, 24 June, p. 13.

3

France

Marie-Françoise Fave-Bonnet

The experience of French women in educational management is very similar to that of French women in other fields: the possibilities are considerable, but there are difficulties in 'making the move' needed to secure responsible jobs.

FRENCH WOMEN AT WORK

The percentage of women in work has risen steadily since the end of the 1960s, despite the economic crisis and unemployment. Women currently account for 44 per cent of the working population, and the proportion of women between 25 and 49 rose from 71 per cent in 1985 to 77 per cent in 1994. There are more than 11 million women in work in France (INSEE, 1994).

This growth is due mainly to the increase in paid work by women and to the growth in the tertiary sector (which employs more women) as opposed to the industrial sector (traditionally a more masculine preserve). There is also a significant demand for work by women: the economic factor plays an important part here, given that women's wages are no longer a secondary source of income, but a crucial part of the family budget and a safeguard against unemployment. For women, work is also a means of ensuring security in case of divorce.

Over and above the economic aspect, however, the need for independence and personal development undoubtedly also greatly influences the desire to work. A woman's identity is increasingly linked to her professional identity. A good indicator of this change is the rise in the numbers of women pursuing a career despite family commitments: amongst women between the ages of 25 and 54, the proportion in work is 77.6 per cent for women with 1 child, 71.4 per cent with 2 children, and 41.7 per cent with 3 children. Thus, only when there are 3 children does the rate of employment show a significant decline – although 1 woman in 3 between the ages of 30 and 34 holds a job as well as bringing up 3 children (Aubin and Gisserot, 1994).

Part-time employment has increased as work has become more flexible: 29 per cent of women in employment currently work part time, mainly in the tertiary sector. But for 36 per cent of women, part-time work is something imposed on them (INSEE, 1996). On the other hand, the French system of free state nursery schooling, in which children are cared for from the age of 2, facilitates women's working lives. In 1994, 35.3 per cent of children aged 2 and 99.3 per cent of children aged 3 were attending nursery school (INSEE, 1996). One should also remember the length of the school day (usually 8.30 to 16.30), which may run from 7.30 to 18.00 if the local authorities run creches before and after school, and the presence, in all schools, of canteens where children can have their lunch.

However, this increase in women's employment remains concentrated in essentially 'female' areas such as the tertiary sector. In addition, there has been only a slow rise in the percentage of women in positions of responsibility: in 1992, women accounted for 31 per cent of managers in the intellectual professions, as opposed to 24 per cent in 1982, but they accounted for only 22 per cent of managers in business. The securing of positions of responsibility by women must not be confused with their securing positions of power. Thus, in 1992, despite their presence in the executive ranks of government service, women occupied less than 6 per cent of posts 'awarded at the discretion of the government', including, most notably, heads of government departments (5.5 per cent women), préfets (2.6 per cent), and ambassadors (2 per cent) (Aubin and Gisserot, 1994).

Differences in salary between the sexes also persist: on average 27 per cent in the managerial category, despite the 1983 legislation on job equality. In public service, where the principle of equal pay for equal work is very strictly applied, job structures are such that the difference in men's and women's salaries is still 15 per cent.

The French example that most clearly reveals this exclusion of women from positions of power is that of politics. It should be remembered that in France, women have only had the vote since 1945, and that the percentage of women in parliament is the lowest of all the countries of Europe except Greece (5.5 per cent). In 1993, the proportion of women in the Assemblée Nationale was 6.1 per cent, and in the Sénat 4.8 per cent.

There is thus still a reluctance to entrust important positions to women. But there is undoubtably also hesitation, on the part of women, about envisaging career-development. This self-censorship continues to be strong in all sectors and, as we shall see, in careers in education.

Education is one of the areas of employment that are regarded as 'female'. It also 'attracts' women because of its conditions of work: secure civil-servant status, a work timetable that can be fitted in with family life, the opportunity of working part-time. In recent years, education has also been one of the sectors in which recruitment opportunities have been maintained. Between 1985 and 1993, the average annual growth of the educational workforce was greater than that for the working population as a whole: 1 per cent as compared with 0.5 per cent for all workers. Staff had to be recruited in order to meet the increase in numbers of pupils in secondary and then in higher education. This increase was due to the huge extension in the time spent in education: the proportion of a particular generation of children going on to take the *baccalauréat* – in other words, completing full secondary schooling – rose from 34 per cent in 1981 to 67 per cent in 1995. More staff also had to be recruited to replace the significant numbers of teachers who had been employed in the 1960s and 1970s and were now retiring at every level of the system (DEP, 1995a, note 95–23).

This recruitment did benefit women, but we shall see that the increase in numbers of women took place mostly at the lower grades, not in positions of responsibility.

THE FRENCH EDUCATION SYSTEM

In order to assess the position of women within the school and university system, we need briefly to recall the history of women's schooling in France (Lelièvre and Lelièvre, 1991). Girls were for a long time excluded from education because it was run by the Church until the eighteenth century. Whereas state-run primary and secondary schooling for boys was instituted as early as the start of the nineteenth century, it was not until the end of that century that any educational establishments for girls were set up. At the beginning of the twentieth century, women, even if educated, had to stay 'where they belonged', that is to say, at home. It was only after the Second World War, with the advent of the Fifth Republic, that mixed schools appeared and that girls' schooling increased. Whereas in 1900, there were only 624 female students for every 27,000 male students at university, by 1971 the numbers had been equalized (Baudelot and Establet, 1992), and in 1995, 55.3 per cent of university students were women.

Nowadays, the problem of girls' education is no longer one of numbers – given that they receive the same amount of schooling as boys – but one of integration into the workplace. As a rule, girls succeed better than boys at school, and they build up a significant fund of educational resources at the outset, but boys are better at making use of what they know in open competitions for professional advancement. Women are more ·affected by unemployment, and are hived off into branches of a very specifically female kind. This is because their input occurs in areas that are educationally and socially less prestigious. Hence, only 36 per cent of students in university science departments are women. Sociologists offer three possible explanations for this situation: 1) having internalized their subordinate position, girls exclude themselves from scientific and technical sectors and veer towards sectors which are 'objectively socially less advantageous'; 2) girls anticipate a future in which they will have to reconcile family life and working life; 3) they are less attracted by 'educational and social values that attribute a central role to mathematics, competition, and hierarchical management functions'

(Marry, 1995). Girls' schooling has thus not had any effect on stereotyping and differentiation in the workplace (Duru-Bellat, 1990). These differences will resurface when we consider managerial posts in schools and universities.

The French education system is a public service administered by the central ministry of education. Depending on the political tendencies of the government, higher education is either administered by a secretary of state attached to this ministry, or else it has its own separate ministry. In the latter case, higher education is combined with research. At the time of writing (July 1996), education in France is overseen by a ministry covering the whole of the education system: the Ministry for Schools, Higher Education, and Research.

In the analysis that follows here, we shall mainly consider state education. Most private educational establishments are, in any case, under contract to the French state, and it is the state which pays the teachers. Furthermore, the proportion of teachers working in the private sector is not very great in France: in 1994, it stood at 12 per cent of teachers in first-stage education (*maternelle* and elementary schools), and a fifth of teachers in second-stage education (*collèges* and *lycées*).

There are three main levels in the French educational system.

Primary education

The first stage, namely primary schools, comprises the non-compulsory *maternelle* (or nursery school), which takes children from the ages of 2 to 5, and compulsory elementary school, which takes children from the ages of 6 to 11. The teachers employed in these schools have always had a standard status and training, which means that they are free to ask for a transfer to another nursery or elementary school as they wish. Previously, training took place at an *école normale*, or teacher-training college, but since 1990 it has been provided in *Instituts Universitaires de Formation des Maîtres* (IUFMs – institutes of teacher training attached to universities). One of the purposes of setting up these institutes was to provide unified training centres for primary and secondary teachers. For admission to an IUFM, applicants must have a *licence* (involving 3 years of university study after the *baccalauréat*). In the first year, students are prepared for an examination in the various subjects to be taught at school, leading to the *Certificat d'Aptitude au Professorat des Ecoles* (CAPE). The second year is devoted to practical training, with a large number of sessions in the classroom. At the end of these 2 years, the students are awarded the status of *professeurs des écoles*.

The proportion of women employed at the first stage is high: 76 per cent (314,200 teachers in 1995), with an average age of 41. Teachers with non-permanent status represent less than 1 per cent of the total (DEP, 1996a, note 96–01).

Secondary education

The second stage, secondary education, takes place in two kinds of establishment: the *collège*, which takes pupils for 4 years, that is to say up to the age of 16, when compulsory schooling ends; and the *lycée*, either general or vocational, which, over a period of 3 years, prepares pupils either for the *baccalauréat* or for a vocational qualification.

The status of teachers in these establishments (in which 56 per cent of the staff are women) is determined by their training and by competitive entry, and results in differences whereby the hours of work or salary for one grade may be double those for another. At the top of the ladder are the *agrégés* (35,159 in number), who have undergone a rigorous examination, the *agrégation*, for which study always takes place in a university, after a *maîtrise* (or Master's degree) in a specific discipline (arts, maths, etc.) – in other words, 4 years after the *baccalauréat*. Fifty per cent of *agrégés* are women. The majority of teachers at the secondary stage are *professeurs certifiés*: they number 184,000, of whom 60 per cent are women. They are recruited via another examination, the *certificat d'aptitude à l'enseignement du second degré* (CAPES), study for which takes place in an IUFM, as for the elementary school teachers, but with courses at university. The same applies to teachers in vocational *lycées* (53,700), where the proportion of women is lower – only 45 per cent. These examinations take the form of written tests on various subjects, followed by an oral if they pass the written part.

Other teachers at the secondary stage, although many in number, have no training and have not entered any competitions. They are usually employed on the basis of a *licence*. This group includes: *chargés* and *adjoints d'enseignement* (non-certified teachers, 15,900 in number, of whom 61 per cent are women); *professeurs d'enseignement général des collèges* (PEGCs – former primary school teachers seconded to a *collège*) of whom there are still a great many – 48,200, including 59 per cent women. The final category, the *maîtres-auxiliaires* or auxiliary teachers, do not have permanent status and can be laid off from one year to the next. Despite plans gradually to do away with this grade and to institute internal examinations, this group is still relatively large in number: 31,780, of whom 57 per cent are women (DEP, 1996a, 1996b, notes 96–01, 96–02). As is clear from the above, the proportion of women is greatest in the lower grades.

Higher education

In France, higher education is more diversified than in any other European country, and its various branches are highly structured, each having fixed functions and specific organizational and educational features. These different post-*baccalauréat* courses of study can be divided into 2 broad sectors: one is 'open' to all those who have obtained their *baccalauréat* – this is the university sector; and the other is 'closed', with access by selection, on the basis of school records or competition. This 'closed' sector includes: the *Grandes Ecoles (Polytechnique, Ecole Nationale d'Administration, Ecoles Normales Supérieures*, etc.) and the establishments which prepare students for entry to them; the *Instituts Universitaires de Technologie* (IUTs, attached to universities); the *Sections de Techniciens Supérieurs* (STSs); and also private, paramedical, social, administration and business schools. Hence, when one talks of teachers in higher education, this does not include those – such as the staff of *Sections de Techniciens Supérieurs* or preparatory establishments – who form part of secondary education, nor those working in private institutions. In 1995, there were 69,438 teachers working in higher education, of whom 34.6 per cent were women.

There are 3 groups of teacher-researchers (*enseignants-chercheurs* – the official term) with permanent status: *professeurs*, who make up a quarter of higher education teaching staff (13 per cent women); the *maîtres de conférences* and *maîtres-assistants* (senior lecturers and lecturers), who make up the largest proportion, namely 40 per cent of the total (34.6 per cent women); and the *assistants* (assistant lecturers), who have enjoyed permanent status since 1983 but are no longer being recruited and now represent only 3 per cent of all staff (35 per cent women) (DEP, 1995b, note 95–40).

Recruitment is by competition, on the basis of research publications and interview. For positions as *professeurs*, candidates must have obtained their *habilitation* (accreditation to supervise research – the *thèse d'Etat* was abolished in 1985), and for posts as *maîtres de conférences*, they must hold a doctoral thesis. Candidates are assessed by 2 committees of specialists in the discipline concerned, one at local and one at national level. The sequence, weight, and composition of these 2 committees have fluctuated continually in line with the vagaries of politics.

In addition to *enseignants-chercheurs* with permanent status, higher education staff in 1995 comprised 11.4 per cent *moniteurs* and *attachés* (post-graduate teaching assistants), and 17 per cent secondary school teachers, *lecteurs* (university assistants), and *maîtres de langues* (language assistants) (DEP, 1995b, note 95–40). More than a quarter of permanently employed teachers at university thus do not have university status in the strict sense. To these must be added part-time and contract lecturers, records of whom are never kept and whose ranks are steadily growing with the increase in student numbers. These various categories are recruited locally, for a fixed period. A local survey has shown that the numbers of women employed in these precarious grades is huge – except in law and economics (Fave-Bonnet, 1996). We shall return to the hierarchy in university disciplines when we take a closer look at the position of women in university 'government'.

The correlation between hierarchy and numbers of women employed is striking. The higher up one goes in the hierarchy, the more women tend to disappear: they account for 76 per cent of staff in primary schools, 56 per cent in secondary schools, and 34 per cent in higher education. In addition, as we have just seen, there is another kind of hierarchy within the secondary and higher education systems, in which women are massively over-represented in the lower grades. It is crucial to have a grasp of these features if one wants to understand the position of women in educational management.

WOMEN IN EDUCATIONAL MANAGEMENT

The overview of the school and university system presented highlights the distinctive features of each level. A similar situation exists in management. At the first stage, each school is run by a *directeur or directrice* (headteacher), who has no prerogatives over recruitment, promotion, or teaching methods, because he or she is a teacher like others, but simply performs various administrative and organizational tasks. Headteachers are recruited by the *inspection d'académie* (school inspectorate) of the particular *département* (local authority), from amongst a list of suitable candidates. The list is open to teachers with at least 3 years' service, on the recommendation of a joint committee comprising: the relevant national and a regional school inspector; representatives of school headteachers; and trade unionists. Some *départements* are currently experiencing a staffing crisis, following an increase in responsibilities over the last few years. Since 1989, schools have had more autonomy than before, but it means more responsibilities for the headteacher without more powers. What is more, many of the teachers concerned have not been relieved of their class responsibilities, and so have to complete these management tasks in addition to their teaching activities. Lastly, the remuneration received for undertaking headship responsibilities is considered by some to be derisory in relation to the duties involved; managment bonuses do not increase the salary of a teacher by more than about 10 per cent.

Each school also has to have a headteacher, even if there is only one class and one teacher in the school, and so there is an increasing number of cases in which classroom teachers are acting as headteachers without having actively wanted to do so. The situation is so confused that in its most recent statistics, the Ministry of Education, which is usually meticulous in its records of numbers of staff, no longer makes a distinction between the two job grades. The last available figures (1993) indicated that 64 per cent of headteachers were women, whereas women made up 79 per cent of the total numbers of primary school teachers (DEP, 1994a, note 94–10).

The real position of power in primary education is therefore that of the *Inspecteur de l'Education Nationale* or national inspector, who monitors and inspects teachers, takes part in their recruitment and further training, and acts as advisor to the *inspecteur d'académie* (regional inspector). Recruitment to the inspectorate is by open competition for each subject specialism (on the basis of career records and an interview), and to take part a candidate must hold a *licence* and have 5 years' service in the national educational system. Only 29 per cent of inspectors in first-stage education are women, even though women's success-rate in the competition for recruitment is much the same. The heavier workload and longer hours involved result in fewer women applying for such posts.

At the second stage of education, women represent only 30 per cent of headteachers (*principal or proviseur*) of *collèges* and *lycées*, directorial staff, whereas they make up 56 per cent of teaching staff in secondary education as a whole. Although heads of secondary schools do no teaching – unlike their colleagues in the primary sector – their workload is extremely heavy, sometimes more than 40 hours per week, and, in some schools, difficult. They do not have much power – on the one hand because the schools are managed by *conseils d'administration* (governing bodies) on which teachers, parents, and pupils are represented, and, on the other hand, because they have no influence on the careers of teachers in their schools. Most of the posts in the school system can be obtained by competition, and then by transfer, at the request of the person concerned. Headteachers have no say in the choice of candidate. In a 1994 survey, three-quarters of secondary headteachers expressed regret at not being able either to appoint technical, supervisory, and administrative staff directly, or have some say in their appointment. Half of them believed they should be involved in the appointment of permanent teachers. Similarly, half of them regretted only being able to grade teachers on administrative performance and not on teaching (DEP, 1994b, note 94–43).

One can therefore understand why women seldom apply for these posts. Whereas they make up 56 per cent of the teaching staff in these schools, they represent only 39 per cent of candidates for these jobs. And yet they have a higher success-rate than men: in 1994, they accounted for 54 per cent of the top quarter of successful candidates (DEP, 1996c, note 96–04). The fact that competition is nationally based is also undoubtedly a deterrent for women: for the first-rank competition for *professeurs agrégés* and for the second-rank competition for *professeurs certifiés*, candidates have to be over 30 years of age and have been teaching for 5 years. But most importantly, the ranking of successful candidates in the open competition determines their allocation to the vacant posts on offer, and the prospect of changing schools, or indeed areas, in order to secure these jobs is a more problematic one for women. Where there are two or three vacant posts, candidates may have some choice in where they are allocated, according to the results they have obtained. This is however seldom the case.[1]

The same kinds of problems occur in the case of regional school inspectors – the *inspecteurs d'académie* – who have the same tasks as national inspectors but work with secondary school teachers and heads. Here, women number only 23 per cent. It should be noted that to be a candidate for such a post, one has to have completed 5 years' service and be either an *enseignant-chercheur*, a *professeur agrégé*, a headteacher, or a national inspector – grades in which, in any case, women are poorly represented.

At the very top of the educational hierarchy, the proportion of women is even smaller: 17 per cent in the case of *secrétaires généraux* or *recteurs* (directors of education, appointed to a region by the national ministry of education); 16 per cent in the case of *inspecteurs généraux* (chief inspectors of schools, whose task is to assess the overall educational system and to provide advice to the minister of education); and 16 per cent in the case of ministry heads (DEP, 1996a, note 96–01). The proportion of women exactly duplicates the hierarchy, in reverse, as Table 3.1 illustrates.

Table 3.1 Percentage of women teachers and managers in primary and secondary schools in France in 1993 (%)

	Teachers	Headteachers	Inspectors
Primary	76	64	29
Secondary	56	30	23

Source: DEP, 1994a.

Case Study: Women in University Management

University education does not have the same kind of organization as primary and secondary education: there are no inspectors, only elective posts. In addition, various committees are in charge of the running of universities, in line with legal stipulation about academic autonomy. One might therefore ask whether women find it easier to find their niche in an elective, as opposed to a competitive, system.

Although the internal organization of each university is very different, one can nevertheless distinguish 4 broad areas of responsibility: management of the *Unités de Formation et de Recherche* (teaching and research centres or faculties); the management of laboratories; participation in various university committees; and university headship.

In contrast to the situation at the primary and secondary levels, there are no statistics on the position of women in the running of universities. However, we have conducted a number of surveys (by questionnaire, interview, and analysis of relevant papers) which show up the low percentage of women in key university posts and the reasons for this dearth (Fave-Bonnet, 1992, 1993, 1995, 1996; Fave-Bonnet, Gendreau-Massalou, 1993).

(a) A university is made up of various *Unités de Formation et de Recherche* (UFRs), comprising a number of courses and research laboratories. This system replaced (in 1968) the former single-subject faculties. The dean of a UFR thus has to answer to the faculty committee – made up of representatives of teachers, administrative staff, and students – for the smooth running of a disparate, and sometimes factious, entity comprising teaching departments for various disciplines and several research laboratories. Running a UFR is therefore not an easy task. It is also a demanding one, given that it is combined with the usual teaching and research commitments of a university lecturer. One can understand why women are reluctant to stand in UFR committee elections. In our interviews, some women said they did not dare put themselves forward for these kinds of tasks for fear of feeling 'out of place' or coming across as 'too ambitious'. In the survey conducted by questionnaire in 1991 (1,048 questionnaires), 12.5 per cent of those who had been deans of UFRs or faculties were women (11 women as compared to 77 men). But the proportion of women who had been departmental heads – a lower-grade position, but one that can also be demanding – was about 22 per cent (34 women as compared to 123 men). Sometimes there is a shortage of candidates, and some only agree to stand 'under friendly pressure from colleagues' (Fave-Bonnet, 1993). In 1995, in a large university city (with 3 universities), there were 5 women heads of UFRs, IUPs (*Instituts Universitaires Professionnalisés*), or IUTs (*Instituts Universitaires de Technologie*), out of a total of 57, in other words, 8.7 per cent were women.

(b) Management of a laboratory is a very well-regarded work in an institution such as a university, where research holds pride of place. It is almost always entrusted to a professor, which reduces the chances of women gaining access to such posts, since they are in a minority in this grade. In addition, women have to have proved their skills as researchers in order for colleagues to promote them to this position. In our survey by questionnaire (1991), about 14 per cent of those who had been heads of laboratories were women (19 women compared with 118 men). In the large university city, the figures are lower because they are a 'snapshot' of women's situation at a given moment: there were 35 women heads of laboratories and research centres out of a total of 456 – in other words, an average of 7 per cent were women (Fave-Bonnet, 1996).

(c) Participation in one or other university committee is determined by an electoral procedure that is very strictly regulated, in order to ensure that the different components (teachers, administrative staff, students, outside parties) are represented. It seems that a more formally organized system favours women: about 22 per cent of those who had been members of a university committee were women (82 women as compared with 298 men). It should be noted that the 3 university committees do not all have the same power: the *conseil des études* deals only with educational matters; the *conseil scientifique* manages research; whereas the *conseil d'administration* rules on proposals made by the first two. Places on this last committee are therefore much more coveted.

(d) Headship represents the pinnacle of power in a university. The *président* is elected jointly by the 3 university committees, on which, as we have seen, women are poorly represented. In 1985 there were 3 women *présidents* of universities in France (Laufer and Delavault, 1988), and in 1996 there were 5 (out of a total of 87) – in other words, 5 per cent. It should, however, be noted that in the survey by questionnaire, women accounted for 9 per cent of deputy heads of universities (3 women as compared with 28 men).

One should not conclude from these figures that women do not take on any responsibilities: what we are talking about here is the 'glass ceiling' – in other words, positions of power rather than of responsibility. In the survey by questionnaire, for example, 30 per cent of those who said they had undertaken additional responsibilities were women (79 out of 182). The responsibilities which respondents listed often included demanding commitments such as the running of study and career centres, a particular course, a lecture-series, etc. (Fave-Bonnet, 1992).

In fact, because all the positions of power are determined by election, professorships in the 'dominant' disciplines are favoured – which partly explains why there are so few women in such positions. The subject hierarchy is a function of the history of university education. As far back as 1789, Kant drew a distinction between the '3 higher faculties' (theology, law, and medicine) and the rest. If one looks at the proportion of professors who are women (13 per cent in all), the same hierarchy emerges – in science (8.8 per cent), medicine (9.3 per cent), and law (13.2 per cent), as compared with the arts and social sciences (25 per cent). In 15 years, the proportion of women in professorships has increased by only a little more than 1 per cent in the sciences, 4 per cent in medicine, 6 per cent in law, and 9 per cent in arts. In the multidisciplinary universities, it is the scientists, lawyers, and doctors who most often occupy positions of power.

When asked about this, women university teachers do not say they have been victims of discrimination. On the contrary, they usually express great satisfaction at being involved in a profession that allows them to manage their own input and time. It should be remembered that, of all the various activities undertaken by university staff, only the annual teaching commitment is stipulated in detail: 192 hours of teaching, which may be arranged in course in large lectures (more than 100 students) in seminar groups (with 30 to 40 students) or laboratory-based practicals (with 15 to 20 students).

This great degree of freedom enjoyed by university teachers leads to even greater career differences for women than for men. These differences stem from the personal and professional scope which the job of university teacher allows. The nature of this scope is ill-defined, because some careers have not been 'thought out', and, in any case, such scope is hedged about with all sorts of constraints.

These career differences stem basically from the different inputs. These may be internal (research, teaching, administrative/collective responsibilities) or external (private life, family life, other professional activities, social activities). For women, the range of these inputs is broader, and this leads to very different career profiles and explains the lack of attraction women feel for university management.

The particular subject-area of the *enseignants-chercheurs* leads to differences in input as regards research and attitudes to other activities: in physics, for example, research takes precedence over all other activities; in law, economics, and medicine, the option of simultaneously engaging in outside activities deters individuals from assuming administrative responsibilities.

Rank and age lead to differences in position: a young woman lecturer is well advised to prepare her *habilitation* in order to gain a professorship, rather than investing her energies in administrative tasks that will be of no benefit to her career. Conversely, at the end of a person's working life, these kinds of activities can round off a successful research career.

Family commitments and the position of the spouse also influence the degree of importance attached to professional activity, particularly as regards income. Several of the women interviewed (single, divorced, those with husbands on low incomes, etc.) reported serious financial difficulties that prevent them from getting help with housework and child care. In addition, women are in a minority in those subject areas, like medicine and law, where extra income is available (Berthelot, 1992). Finally, where women do devote themselves to administrative tasks, these do not, as we have seen, bring much, or any, remuneration – in contrast to the running of UFRs, or to headships of universities, which entitle their holders to annual allowances (in 1995 these were, for example, 53,000 frs. for a university head and 33,000 frs. for the director of a UFR).

Lastly, as elsewhere, there are significant psychological and cultural deterrents. The special form of 'renunciation' in which women engage in regard to knowledge and power is undoubtedly reinforced in the male-dominated world of the university. Like all minority groups, women have to adapt to the values of the dominant group: the spirit of competition, the career-based outlook, and the sheer weight of the hierarchical system often prove very difficult for women to bear. In our survey cited earlier, 67 per cent of the women said that university life was still governed by an autocratic 'mandarinate' whereas the proportion of men who said this was smaller (58 per cent). Some women said they no longer felt like playing the game.

Table 3.2   The position of women in French universities

Position	%
Teachers:	
Senior Lecturers	35
Professors	13
Managers:	
Deans	9
Presidents	5

Source: DEP, 1995b, and Fave-Bonnet (1996).

In more general terms, considering the whole range from primary-school teacher to university professor, it is clear that the picture of a harmonious balance between family life and career which is supposed to be the privilege of the teaching profession is not borne out in reality: 'every step taken in one or other area of activity implies choices or sacrifices in the other', as is shown by Marlène Cacouault in regard to secondary-school teachers (Cacouault, 1995).[2] Whether or not a woman enters a career path as headteacher or inspector in primary or secondary education, and whether she takes on responsibilities in higher education, is determined to a great degree by her family situation. Those that do are single women, divorcees, and those whose husbands have a high salary and a secure job; or they are women whose children are grown up and who are setting out on a new career.

THE LACK OF NATIONAL POLICIES

The principle of representative democracy in France is based on representation of the individual, not of the group. For this reason, the *Conseil Constitutionnel* opposed the introduction of quotas by gender in the electoral law of 1982. In France, there are no quotas by gender in any area of political, trade union, economic, or social life. Even though the introduction of quotas into electoral rolls periodically comes up for discussion, nothing has changed. The only exception was Michel Rocard's socialist roll in the 1984 European elections, which contained equal numbers of male and female candidates.

However, there are some women in the professions who are exceptions to the rule. But is it not the case that they get noticed precisely because they are rare? The first example concerns an elected post: for the first time since its foundation by Colbert in 1666, the *Académie des Sciences* has a woman president (for 1995 and 1996); she is Marianne Grunberg-Manago, a long-established authority in biological research. But out of a total of 136 members, only 4 are women.

The second example concerns appointments: at the time of the first Chirac government, in May 1995, the number of women in the government was unprecedentedly high – of 41 ministers or secretaries of state, 12 were women; after the first reshuffle in November 1995, there were only 4 out of a total of 32 members.

As in the political sphere, women's scope in the school and university system is extremely restricted, whatever the mode of access to positions of responsibility – be it by appointment or by election. Opinions concerning quotas are very divided, even among feminists. In relation to the education system, some consider that quotas on membership of recruitment committees are a neccessity for realising equality of opportunity, particularly as at all levels (primary, secondary and university) such committees comprise a majority of men. Others maintain, on the contrary, that the recruitment process should be competency-based rather than based on sex-related criteria. Recent examples from political life, where women have been nominated *de jure* rather than on the basis of their competence in a particular sphere, have done a great disservice to the idea that women are altogether fit for high responsibilities.

Nonetheless it is only access to management posts that will do away with prejudices. Women in France should have the confidence to compete for positions of responsibility and to demonstrate their skills in them. That is the way to ensure any change in the French situation.

NOTES

1. The ratio of male to female headteachers does not exhibit particular regional differences, as is the case in some European countries, as the system of recruitment is a national one.
2. There has been virtually no qualitative research in France into the experience of women teachers and headteachers, other than the work of Marléne Cacouault on secondary school headteachers.

REFERENCES

Aubin, C. and Gisserot, H. (1994) *Les Femmes en France: 1985–1995*, report for the United Nations, La Documentation Française, Paris.

Baudelot, C. and Establet, R. (1992) *Allez les filles!*, Seuil, Paris.

Berthelot, J.-M. (1992) *Les enseignants-chercheurs de l'enseignement supérieur: revenus professionnels et conditions d'activités*, Documents du CERC (Centre d'Etudes des Revenus et des Coûts), 105, La Documentation Française, Paris.

Cacouault, M. (1995) Images, carrières et modes de vie des enseignantes des années soixante à la décennie quatre-vingt-dix, *Recherche et Formation*, no. 20, INRP, Paris, pp. 17–31.

DEP (Direction de l'Evaluation et de la Prospective), *Notes d'information*, Ministère de l'Education Nationale, Paris:

DEP (1994a) 94–10 Les Personnels du Ministère de l'Education Nationale au 1er Janvier 1993.

DEP (1994b) 94–43 Les Chefs d'Etablissements du Second Degré et la gestion des ressources humaines

DEP (1995a) 95–23 Les personnels de l'Education en 1993.

DEP (1995b) 95–40 Les personnels de l'Enseignement Supérieur en 1994–1995.

DEP (1996a) 96–01 Les personnels de l'Education Nationale et de l'Enseignement Supérieur au 1er Janvier 1995.

DEP (1996b) 96–02 Les enseignants des établissements publics du second degré en 1994–1995

DEP (1996c) 96–04 Les concours de recrutement des personnels de direction, d'inspection et des conseillers d'administration scolaire et universitaire.

Duru-Bellat, M. (1990) *L'Ecole des filles: quelle formation pour quels rôles sociaux*, L'Harmattan, Paris.

Fave-Bonnet, M.-F. (1992), L'opinion des enseignants-chercheurs sur leur profession, *Savoir, Education, Formation*, no. 2, April–June, Sirey, Paris, pp. 161–170.

Fave-Bonnet M.-F. (1993) *Les enseignants-chercheurs physiciens*, Paris, INRP/SFP.

Fave-Bonnet, M.-F. (1995) Les femmes universitaires en France: une féminisation, mais différenciée, contribution to the international colloquium, in *Les femmes et l'Université dans les pays de la Méditerranée*, Toulouse, forthcoming.

Fave-Bonnet, M.-F. (1996) Les femmes universitaires en France: une féminisation et des carrières différenciées, in *Egalité, Equité, Discrimination: Hommes et Femmes sur le Marché du Travail, les Cahiers du Mage (Marché du Travail et Genre)* 1/96, IRESCO-CNRS (Institut de Recherches sur les Sociétés Contemporaines-Centre National de la Recherche Scientifique), pp. 83–91.

Fave-Bonnet, M.-F. and Gendreau-Massalou, M. (1993) The role of women in the administration of higher education in France, in *Women in Higher Education Management*, UNESCO-Commonwealth Secretariat, Paris, pp. 69–80.

INSEE (Institut National de la Statistique et des Etudes Economiques) (1994) *Employment Survey*, INSEE, Paris.

INSEE (Institut National de la Statistique et des Etudes Economiques) (1996), *Social Statistics*, INSEE, Paris.

Laufer, J. and Delavault, H. (1988) *Responsabilité des femmes dans la conduite de leur carrière et enseignement supérieur*, UNESCO Round Table/Fédération Internationale des Femmes Diplômées d'Universités, UNESCO, Paris.

Lelièvre F. and Lelièvre C. (1991) *Histoire de la scolarisation des filles*, Nathan, Paris.

Marry, C. (1995) *La place des femmes: les enjeux de l'identité et de l'égalité au regard des sciences sociales*, La Découverte, Paris.

4

The Federal Republic of Germany

Hannelore Faulstich-Wieland

THE STRUCTURE OF THE EDUCATION SYSTEM

The German education system is organized federally: each of the federal *Länder*, now numbering 16, has its own cultural administration and its own school system. However, as a result of the activities of the *Ständige Konferenz der Kultusminister der Länder* (KMK – Standing Conference of the Ministers of Education and Culture of the *Länder*) a number of agreements exist that are intended to ensure broad comparability and easy interchange within the school system. This means it is possible to present a picture of the basic structure of the educational system for the Federal Republic as a whole (see Figure 4.1).

Following voluntary attendance at kindergarten, compulsory schooling for all children begins at the age of 6. Because of the reform of the abortion law (sect. 218), sufficient places are in future to be made available for three- to six-year-olds. Currently there are virtually no childcare facilities for children under the age of 3. The kindergarten system for the children aged 3 to 6 often provides childcare only on a half-day basis, from 8 to 12 o'clock. Bigger cities like Berlin or Frankfurt/Main provide all-day childcare institutions and also after-school classes, but these are rare in the total German context.

Attendance at the *Grundschule* – the primary sector of the school system – lasts 4 school years. After that, children enter *Sekundarstufe I* (Secondary Level I). Within this there are 4 different types of school: the *Hauptschule*; the *Realschule*; the *Gymnasium*; and the *Gesamtschule*. In some *Länder*, entry into these schools is preceded by a two-year orientation period. The *Hauptschule* is more geared towards a future vocational education path leading to skilled manual work. The *Realschule* combines the possibility of continuing education at the upper level of the *Gymnasium* – which requires a reasonable grade-point-average and enrolment in French as a second foreign language – with an orientation towards vocational education leading to service industry or technical jobs. The *Gymnasium* is academic and scientifically oriented and ensures its successful students entry into institutions

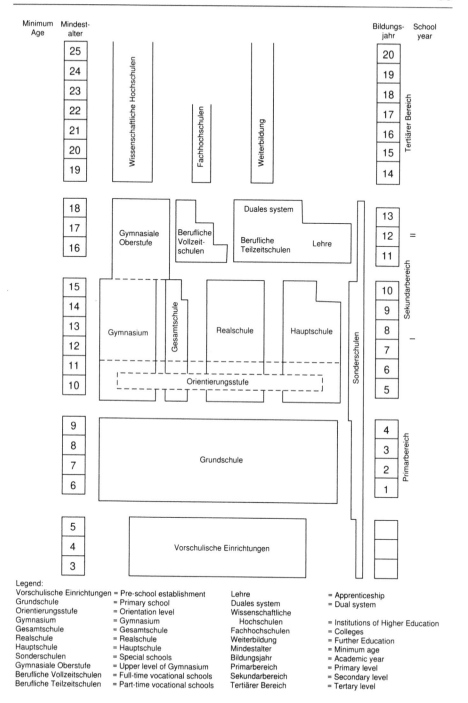

Figure 4.1 Structure of the educational system in the Federal Republic of Germany
Source: Arbeitsgruppe Bildungsbericht 1994, p. 19.

of higher education. The *Gesamtschule* is a comprehensive or integrated system of all three types of school. The comprehensive system comprises all the three types of secondary education. Students are allocated to one type but may take courses in another section. The integrated type of *Gesamtschule* offers mixed ability groups in the main with some streaming in subjects such as mathematics and foreign languages. The *Gesamtschule* issues leaving certificates which equal either *Hauptschule, Realschule* or entry-permission to the Secondary level(II) of the *Gymnasium* – depending on the performance of the students.

With the exception of Berlin and North Rhine-Westfalia, compulsory education ends after 9 years' full-time schooling.[1] Children attending a *Sonderschule* (special school) or a *Hauptschule* then leave, although a number of *Länder* offer the option of a tenth year at the *Hauptschule*. In the other types of schools, Secondary Level I continues until the end of the tenth school year. After that – depending, amongst other things, on performance – children move either into the upper level of the *Gymnasium*, where they can obtain their *Abitur* (leaving/university entrance certificate), or into part-time or full-time vocational schools. Regulation of vocational education is not a matter for the *Länder*; it is dealt with by the Ministry of Education, Science, Research and Technology.

The higher education sector comprises universities and *Fachhochschulen*. The entry requirement for the universities is the *Abitur*, and for the *Fachhochschulen* there is a special *Fachabitur*, which can be taken in vocational secondary education. Both institutions offer diploma or degree level work but university graduates usually obtain better paid jobs. Most subjects are offered in the *Fachhochschulen* as well as in the universities, but the orientation of the *Fachhochschulen* is in theory applied. Intending teachers must normally enrol on a four-year course at university, where they usually study two main subjects and some social sciences in order to teach in primary and secondary schools, and must pass a special state examination, although there are variations in the compulsory courses to be taken between *Länder*. Higher level qualifications are demanded for *Gymnasium* teachers. They may then get a job as a *Referendar* or probationer in a school. The probationary period lasts two years and combines teaching under supervision and study through seminars.

In the higher education sector, the prerequisite to become a university 'professor' (equivalent to senior lecturer in the British system) is a Doctorate, followed by the *Habilitation*, the publication of a second book-length thesis, which has to be approved by a University Commission. There then follows an oral presentation to the Faculty the aspiring professor wishes to join, who are empowered to decide whether to finally bestow *Habilitation*. In the *Fachhochschulen* the prerequisite is a Doctorate and five years work experience in a non-academic field. Below the rank of professor the great majority of staff are employed on a non-tenured basis as *Assistenten*, on short-term contracts of a maximum of six years. In any university over 80 per cent of staff are in this position. Once scholars are ready to apply for a professorship, the law stipulates that this must be at a different institution: recruitment must come from outside. This generates a high level of competition to 'stay in the game' until tenure is achieved (Kriszio, 1995).

This chapter is largely confined to the general school system. General schools are organized on the basis of year-groups. In each school there is at least one class per year-group, and schools usually have more than one year-group intake. In the *Grundschule* or primary school the teacher (generally female) does most of the teaching on an interdisciplinary basis. From the third school year, there is more differentiation by subject, and subject-teachers are also employed. From Secondary Level I, teaching is divided mainly on the basis of subjects, and those members of the teaching staff who spend 5 hours or more per week in 'their' class act as form teachers. The number of hours of compulsory attendance also increases from the first to the last class – though the basic organizational principle is half-day schooling. In primary schools, the children are only in school for 3 or 4 hours in the morning. In some *Länder* (particularly Hamburg, Lower Saxony, and North Rhine-Westfalia) efforts are increasingly being made to institute 'full half-day schooling', that is to say assured care of children between 8 o'clock and 12 (or 1) o'clock. From Secondary Level I, children generally have 6 hours of school per day, and in the higher classes this may in some cases rise to 7 or 8. But school organization is not geared to lunch-breaks and canteens, and the children are sent home between 1 and 3 o'clock. Full-day schools do exist, but they are the exception. In some *Länder* it is mainly the *Gesamtschulen* that are organized as full-day schools, although this is not always the case. Other types of schools are sometimes run on a full-day basis, and comprehensives sometimes on a half-day basis (especially in Hesse). In Berlin, a relatively high proportion (27.9 per cent) of children at the primary level and at Secondary Level I attend a full-day school; in Brandenburg the figure is 13.7 per cent, in North Rhine-Westfalia 11.1 per cent, in Hesse 8.3 per cent, with the other *Länder* lying well below the 3 per cent level (Böttcher, 1995, p. 54).

Teachers are mostly federal employees and are well paid relative to the average income. However, there are tremendous differences between the school types. Teachers in primary schools earn the least, teachers in *Gymnasien* are the best paid, receiving about 10 to 15 per cent more than teachers in *Grundschulen* or *Hauptschulen*. Additionally, teachers in primary schools have the most, and those in *Gymnasium* the least, class contact time, ranging from 24 to 28 hours per week in 45 minute blocks. There are form rooms for the teachers in each school, but usually they do not have a place to work – preparation of classes, correction of tests and so on has to be done at home. This creates an image of the teaching profession as if it were a half-day job, for which teachers would be very well paid. In terms of public opinion teachers have lost their former social status and are now criticized for being lazy and for failing educational standards.

There is no formal career structure for teachers. Most remain in the classroom, although a small percentage will become department heads, assistant teachers, headteachers or educational administrators. The process of becoming a headteacher is described later in the chapter.

WOMEN IN GERMAN SOCIETY

The fact that the school system in the Federal Republic is organized on a half-day basis is of particular relevance from a gender-related point of view: the system of schooling assumes that one of the parents – usually the mother – will be available when children come out of school, either as expected or unexpectedly (for example, when lessons are cancelled). In Germany, care and provision are regarded as tasks that naturally fall not to schools but to the family. This is important in understanding why the rate of employment amongst German women continues to be low compared to the rest of Europe. Despite this, in 1992 it stood at 59.5 per cent for 15- to 65-year-olds amongst the female population (Bellenberg and Klemm, 1995, p. 24). But regional variations are considerable, and between the old (formerly West Germany) and the new *Länder* (formerly East Germany) in particular there are major differences. In 1991 82.5 per cent of children under the age of 18 in the new *Länder* had working mothers or were living alone with a working father. In the old *Länder* this was the case for only 48.2 per cent of the children (ibid., p. 23). In the old *Länder* 40.2 per cent of the working mothers work less than 20 hours per week, 42.7 per cent between 21 and 39 hours, and only 17.1 per cent 40 hours or more. In the new *Länder*, on the other hand, the norm is for mothers to be employed full-time: 78.7 per cent were working 40 hours and more, and only 3 per cent were employed part time for up to 20 hours per week (ibid., p. 25). This reflects the development of women in German society on the whole: the overall increase in the employment rate was mainly due to the rise in the employment of married women (see Table 4.1),[2] but this was mostly due to an increase in part-time jobs.

After World War II and the establishment of the two German Republics there has been a very different development: in the former Federal Republic of Germany women mostly went back into the family after the men came home and re-entered civil employment. The ideal was for a woman to become a housewife and mother. In the former German Democratic Republic there was an entirely different situation. Because of the previously socialist ideology both sexes were supposed to participate in the workforce. The government provided childcare institutions to ensure the possibility for both parents to go out to work. Even after German unification, it is still the norm for women in the new *Länder* not to stay at home. Patterns are rapidly becoming westernized. Many more women than men are becoming unemployed, and childcare facilities are not being maintained. The unemployment rate in the old *Länder* was 9.2 per cent for both sexes in 1994: in the new *Länder* it was 10.9 per cent for men and 21.5 per cent for women (Hanesch, 1995, p. 263).

Table 4.1   Employment rate for women related to age

Age	Total		single	married	
	1990	1961	1990	1990	1961
15–20	37.3	73.7	37.2	39.4	62.8
20–25	75.7	75.9	79.1	63.7	52.5
25–30	71.6	52.8	84.3	62.3	40.4
30–35	66.9	44.1	90.1	60.0	36.0
35–40	68.0	45.1	92.7	63.1	37.2
40–45	69.4	45.2	91.9	65.5	37.7
45–50	66.7	41.5	90.0	62.3	34.6
50–55	57.8	38.1	85.2	53.3	31.2
55–60	43.8	33.2	74.1	39.2	26.5
60–65	12.5	21.4	21.3	11.0	17.8

Source: Bundesministerium für Frauen und Jugend (BMFJ) 1992, p. 45.

Women are mainly employed in jobs in the white-collar and office sectors and also in the healthcare system. They are mostly to be found in administrative but not in management posts. As a result of this the average income of women is still only about two-thirds of the average income of men (BMFJ 1992, pp. 50–1).

In the old *Länder* there is still a slight disagreement about the entitlement of women to work. In a recent poll 36 per cent of women and 35 per cent of men said that they thought women should remain housewives.[3] In the new *Länder* nobody fully agreed with this statement and only 8 per cent partly agreed (Statistisches Bundesamt 1995, p. 517). Nevertheless, these cultural perceptions of working women still function as a barrier for women, since they are expected to be responsible for household and childcare, regardless of their employment status. Restrictive shopping hours, to enable the family duties of the mainly female sales force – make it difficult for people to combine full-time jobs and family work. Shops open usually between 9 a.m. and 6 p.m., Monday to Friday – often with a lunch break from 1 to 3 p.m. – and 9 a.m. to 1 p.m. on Saturday.

Given these arrangements it is all the more understandable that the teaching profession offers for many women the best option for combining work and family commitments. Even so, many women have to opt for a reduced teaching commitment (i.e. part-time post). From 1960 to 1994 the distribution of female and male teachers has changed tremendously: in 1960 only 38.3 per cent of the full-time teachers were women. By 1994 this had risen to 59.2 per cent (BMBFT, 1995, pp. 104, 106).

THE ORGANIZATION OF EDUCATIONAL ADMINISTRATION

In order to be able to describe women's participation in educational management, it is first necessary to give a few details about administrative organization. In line with the federal structures for schools this is specific to the *Land* concerned, but here too there are comparable organizational forms. All *Länder* have a ministry responsible for schooling – and sometimes also for cultural matters in general, and for higher education. These ministries have responsibility for organization, standardization, and planning, within the framework of the state regulations of the educational system (*Schulgesetze*) in their *Land*. They discharge this duty mainly by providing staff, material resources, and finance, and also through legal and administrative regulations (Arbeitsgruppe Bildungsbericht, 1994, p. 98).

In most of the German *Länder* there are two further levels of educational authority: the education departments within the *Bezirksregierung* or *Regierungspräsidium* (district or regional governments) as an upper division of authority; and the education offices (*Schulämter* or *Schulaufsichtsämter*) at the local level (ibid., p. 99ff) as a lower division. For an individual school, the competent authority is the *Schulrat* or school inspector, who has charge over curricular, legal, and administrative matters (*Fach-*, *Rechts-*, *Dienstaufsicht*) – a triple distinction which in practice it is not always easy to make (Bildungskommission NRW, 1995).

Within the individual schools, there are various forms of headship, ranging from direction by a single person – the Rektor or the Rektorin (female head) in primary schools – through deputies, to more extensive school management teams in *Gymnasien* and *Gesamtschulen*, in which there are, in addition to an overall head, heads for each of the levels and/or subject areas. The competencies of school management also vary according to regional regulations; their nature depends on the responsibilities that have been accorded the various participation committees. Heads or members of their management teams are usually trained teachers and retain some teaching commitments whilst performing their headship duties. Headteachers are appointed by the state, often on the recommendation of regional authorities or in response to open advertisement. The local school has no role in the selection process. In turn, classroom teachers are appointed by the regional authorities and staff appointments are not part of a headteacher's brief. Headteachers are paid about 10 to 20 per cent more than classroom teachers and are on a higher civil service level.

Before we move on to the concrete issues related to the participation of women in educational management, the relevant data that are available will be presented. It should be said at the outset, however, that although systematic statistical data exist for schools, teaching staff, and pupils, there are none for school administration. Wolfgang Böttcher writes that: 'the relevant statistics do not cover size or output of the administrative apparatus: 16 ministries of education, as well as numerous bodies at the intermediate and lower levels of the education authority, evidently hold no interest in terms of educational statistics' (Böttcher, 1995, p. 40).[4] In addition, there are no official data on gender ratios in school management.[5] The only official list is one published by the Ministry of Education of Lower Saxony. It dates from October 1991, presents figures for the period up to the end of September 1990, and is entitled *Promotion for Whom? Career Advancement in Schools. What Part Do Women Have in it?* However, some as yet unpublished data from the Ministry of School and Adult Education of North Rhine-Westfalia for the period of 1992 to 1994, and data about the proportion of female to male heads in all 16 *Länder* from a research project by Mechthild von Lutzau (Lutzau and Metz-Göckel, 1996) are included in the following section, which outlines the situation of women in educational management.

WOMEN IN EDUCATIONAL MANAGEMENT

The data show a markedly uneven distribution of women and men at the various levels of the educational system and in its administration, as illustrated by Figures 4.2 and 4.3.

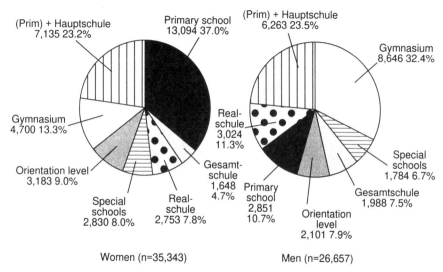

Figure 4.2   Distribution of male and female teaching staff in schools in Lower Saxony
Source: Own figures based on *Niedersächsische Kultusministerium* 1991, Table 1.

It emerges that overall there are more women than men employed as full-time teachers: in 1990 in Lower Saxony, for example, 57 per cent of all full-time teaching staff in general schools were female, and 43 per cent male. Female teachers were mainly to be found in primary schools (37 per cent); only 13 per cent were teaching in *Gymnasien*. Male teachers, on the other hand, were employed chiefly in *Gymnasien* (32 per cent); only 5 per cent were in primary schools. In North Rhine-Westfalia we find nearly the same figures: here too 57 per cent of all teachers are female and 43 per cent are male.[6] The distribution to the different types of school, however, show only slight differences – mostly due to the fact that there are no separate schools for the orientation level.

More than half the female teachers in Lower Saxony do not work full time;

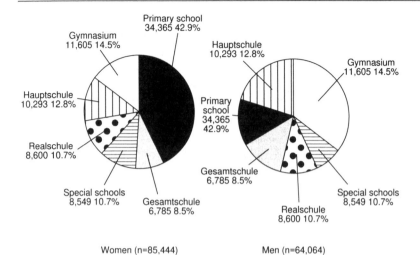

Women (n=85,444)   Men (n=64,064)

Figure 4.3   Distribution of male and female teaching staff in schools in North Rhine-Westfalia
Source: Own figures based on Statistischer Bericht zum Frauenförderkonzept der Landesregierung Nordrhein-Westfalen – Ressortbeitrag des Ministeriums für Schule und Weiterbildung (ehemals Kultusministerium), *Erhebungszeitraum* 1.1.92–31.12.94, hekt. Man. 1996, p. 5.

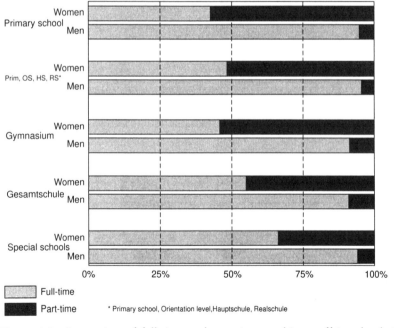

Figure 4.4   Proportion of full-time and part-time teaching staff in schools in Lower Saxony by gender
Source: Own figures based on *Niedersächsisches Kultusministerium* 1991, Table 1.

in the case of the men, however, only 6.8 per cent are employed part time (see Figure 4.4). In primary schools and *Gymnasien*, most women are not employed on a full-time basis. In *Gesamtschulen* and special schools there are comparatively more women working full time, possibly because many *Gesamtschulen* are full-day schools in this *Land* and because of the particular nature of work in special schools. However, there is no research or official explanation for these differences.

If one breaks down the figures to show how the sexes in the various school types are distributed amongst the teaching, administrative, and headship categories (see Figures 4.5 and 4.6), the gross disparity is particularly clear in the case of primary schools. In this area it is virtually the case that if a man is employed in a primary school, then it is as a headteacher, or at least a deputy head. This is more striking in the figures for Lower Saxony than in North Rhine-Westfalia, because of a slight change in time. The group with least share in headship responsibilities are women working in *Gymnasien*.

Even if one takes the relative proportions of women and men heads within individual school types as a basis for comparison (see Figures 4.7 and 4.8), it emerges that only in the primary school domain is the proportion of women in school management greater than one-third. In special schools, it is one-quarter. For Lower Saxony we know that this is a result of the fact that, of

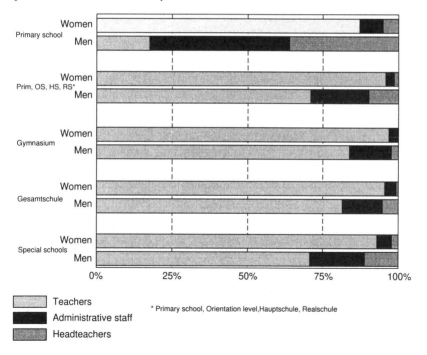

Figure 4.5 Proportion of teaching staff, administrative staff, and headteachers in schools in Lower Saxony by gender
Source: Own figures based on *Niedersächsisches Kultusministerium* 1991, Table1.

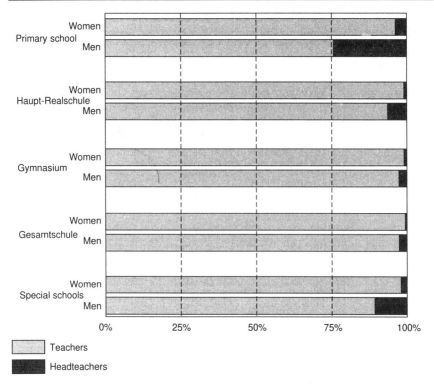

Figure 4.6 Proportions of teaching staff to headteachers in schools in North Rhine-Westfalia by gender
Source: Own figures based on Statistischer Bericht zum Frauenförderkonzept der Landesregierung Nordrhein-Westfalen – Ressortbeitrag des Ministeriums für Schule und Weiterbildung (ehemals Kultusministerium), *Erhebungszeitraum* 1.1.92–31.12.94, hekt. Man. 1996, p. 5, p. 13.

43 special schools for the mentally disabled, 17 are directed by women. The picture is confirmed in the case of the *Gymnasien*: these are firmly in the hands of men; female heads are the absolute exception. Again here, the data from North Rhine-Westfalia show a slightly better picture, but the differences are still huge. Overall, the proportion of women heads to men heads is 23.6 per cent to 76.4 per cent in Lower Saxony and 26.5 per cent to 73.5 per cent in North Rhine-Westfalia. These figures are well representative of the average position in the old *Länder* (see Figure 4.9), although there are tremendous differences between the *Länder* (see Figure 4.10). In the new *Länder* a virtually inverse situation exists: on average there are 58.5 per cent of female heads to only 41.5 per cent of male heads. This is probably due to the fact that there is a larger proportion of female teachers here, and the former DDR encouraged women to take advantage of management and career positions to a far greater extent.

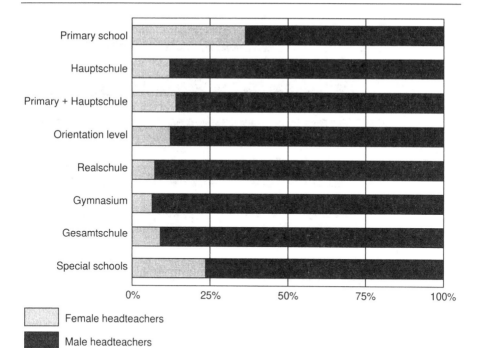

Figure 4.7 Proportion of women and men headteachers in various school types in Lower Saxony
Source: Own figures based on *Niedersächsisches Kultusministerium* 1991, Table 1.

In higher education, the percentage of women professors is still very low and does not correspond with the percentage of female students in any department. Before unification, women were equally underrepresented as professors in the former East and West Germanies at about 5 per cent. In East Germany, an additional position, equivalent to the rank of professor, called Dozenten, existed. In this group, the percentage of women was about 12 per cent, so that the proportion of women among higher education lecturers was on average 9 per cent. In addition most university staff gained tenure after completing their doctorates and about 40 per cent of this group were female (Kriszio, 1995).

In contrast, the system in West Germany, described earlier, where most posts under the rank of professor are on a short-term basis, has resulted in a less favourable situation for women. Although the proportion of lower-rank university assistants has increased from 17 per cent in 1982 to 22.5 per cent in 1991, the requirement to be mobile at an age when family demands are highest has a discriminatory effect, despite affirmative action programmes adopted by many universities.

Since unification, the system has been restructured along Western lines. This has resulted in a quantitative reduction of both male and female lecturers

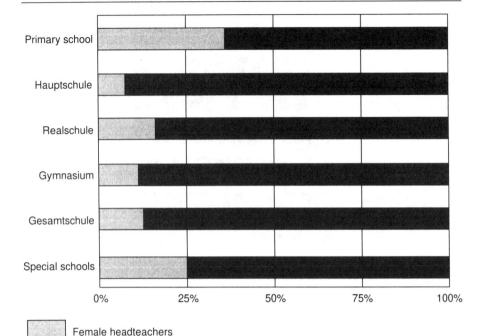

0%   25%   50%   75%   100%

Female headteachers

Male headteachers

Figure 4.8   Proportion of women and men headteachers in various school types in North Rhine-Westfalia

Source: Own figures based on Statistischer Bericht zum Frauenförderkonzept der Landesregierung Nordrhein-Westfalen – Ressortbeitrag des Ministeriums für Schule und Weiterbildung (ehemals Kultusministerium), *Erhebungszeitraum* 1.1.92–31.12.94, hekt. Man. 1996, p. 13.

and a loss of tenure for those under the rank of professor, apart from job losses for political and 'quality' reasons. Competition for new short-term contracts and for professorships has intensified, with fears that scholars from the fomer East will lose out to those from the former West Germany. Evidence of the effects of this on women's representation is mixed, varying between 16.8 per cent of professors in Berlin to 6.7 per cent in Sachsen-Anhalt (Kriszio, 1995). The prognosis for non-tenured female staff remains a concern.

Data on the position of women in educational administration at *Land* level – here using the Lower Saxony data again – reinforce the picture formed so far. Of senior teachers (*Studiendirektoren*) at *Gymnasien* employed as heads of subject areas, 6.7 per cent are women (*Niedersächsisches Kultusministerium* 1991, Table 2). Of departmental advisers (*Dezernenten*) in education offices, women account for 13.7 per cent in the case of curriculum-related posts and 31 per cent in the case of posts relating to educational psychology (i.e. 19.4 per cent overall). Only 4.1 per cent of the

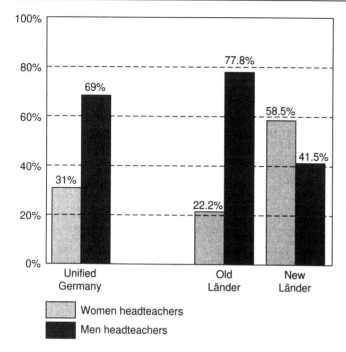

Figure 4.9 Proportion of women and men headteachers in the old and new Bundesländer
Source: Von Lutzau/Metz-Göckel, 1996, p. 225.

education offices are headed by a woman (ibid., Table 4). The situation in district governments is no better: of departmental heads, 11.4 per cent are women, and of departmental advisers, 17.7 per cent (ibid., Table 5).[7]

When it comes to the causes of the unequal distribution of the sexes in management positions, there are, according to the Ministry of Education in Lower Saxony, two views on the promotion of women:

- 'We would like to see women promoted, but they don't want to be';
- 'Women would like to be promoted, but they're not allowed to be'. (ibid., p.1)

At the conference on 'Women and School' held in Dortmund in 1988, Anne Ratzki, herself the head of a *Gesamtschule*, pointed out that to argue that there were no women willing to apply for jobs was a way of playing safe:

As a rule, an education authority picks its staff and heads by approaching people personally and encouraging them to apply. I know many qualified women, but none has ever been approached; on the contrary, when they were interested in a headship and approached the education authority, they were mostly given to understand that another applicant (a man, of course!) was already being considered. This kind of 'old-boy-network' crops up again and again.

(Ratzki, 1989, p. 136)

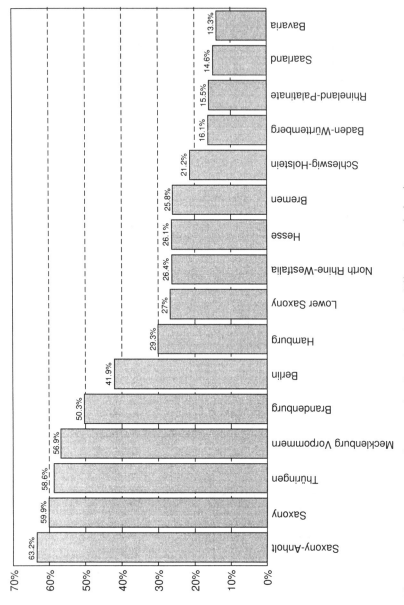

Figure 4.10 Proportion of women headteachers in the different Bundesländer
Source: Von Lutzau/Metz-Göckel, 1996, p. 224–5.

So what plausible explanations are there, in fact, and are there any indications of change during those 8 years since this statement was made?

BARRIERS TO PROMOTION OF WOMEN INTO MANAGEMENT

There are at least three different arguments which explain why women are underrepresented in management. One emphasizes the attitudes of women teachers in keeping them from accepting leadership positions for themselves. Another sees them primarily as victims of discrimination, and a third involves a shift in the conceptualization of leadership. The basis of these arguments will be examined in turn.

Women Teachers' Fear of Loneliness in the Management Role

Investigations by Heidemarie Krüger and Charlotte Röhner, and also by Karin Flaake, have clearly shown that women teachers do indeed have worries about assuming positions of leadership.[8] 'Women seem to forgo in advance – in their own desires and ideas – opportunities of putting their interests into practice in leadership positions' (Flaake, 1987, p. 5). This renunciation seems, on the one hand, to be motivated by social anxieties:

> What is important to woman teachers is to cultivate good contacts with their female and male colleagues. But they see these as under threat, because they believe that in senior positions in the educational hierarchy, regulations and instructions have to be imposed on the teaching staff. What they most fear is the social isolation that seems to be associated with management positions.   (Krüger, 1986, p. 90)

Another motive is fear of losing contact with teaching: woman teachers believe that they will have too much administrative work and will be able to do less teaching (ibid., p. 91). In so far as both these worries are concerned, woman teachers are not very different from men teachers: the latter cite similar fears (see Flaake, 1988, 1989a, 1989b, 1990; Haller and Wolf, 1993, 1995). In the case of the women, however, there is the additional factor of the family situation, in the sense of 'worry about availability in the dual working-world of career and family' (Krüger, 1986, p. 91). This is the crucial difference: the responsibility which women have for family relations not only burdens them with more work; it also means that, conversely, they have no backing – for example, from their partner – in professional conflicts. Thus women often slot into the prevailing gender arrangement and forgo any attempt to secure management positions. It is this behaviour that provides the justification for the previously quoted view that 'Women don't want to'.

Discrimination against Women

It may still be true of many woman teachers that they carry out their professional duties without any thought of career advancement – something, which, incidentally, should probably not be viewed as 'a bad thing'.[9] Even so, accounts by women who have gained some overview of women's approaches to job applications in the context of in-service training of woman teachers show that the claim that 'Women would like to be promoted but are not allowed to' is still justified. Here too, the gender-specific division of labour plays a central role: Anne Ratzki reports that the question of the care of the family was explicitly used as a criterion of assessment for management positions – in the case of women, but not of men (Ratzki, 1989). In addition, there is evidence of explicit discrimination in the form of documents going missing, untrue statements, negative assessments that are only vaguely substantiated (Lührig, 1990).[10] In most *Länder* affirmative action plans have been introduced to ensure equal opportunities for women. These guarantee that there are women responsible for equality questions and give them the possibility of gaining some control over the documents and selection processes.

For a long time – and even now, in certain *Länder* – the possibility of exercising a management function was linked to full-time employment. In Germany it was not so much a problem of a 'long hours culture' in heading a school (as it is in other areas of management and in other countries), but it was considered unthinkable that management functions might require less than a full-time job. This meant that to apply for a management position automatically became impossible for more than half of all women teachers. The fact that management positions are now open to part-time teachers as well may therefore be viewed as an achievement in terms of women's rights. It means that women who wish both to take on management positions and have enough time for their family commitments now have the chance of seeing how this works out (see Hahn and Weiß-Hennerici, 1995). We shall return to this point later on.

Do Women Have a Different Management Style?

In the early 1990s there has been a movement to argue that women would manage things much better than men and that therefore more women should be promoted. I regard approaches that justify increased participation by women in management by reference to sex differences, in line with this notion, as problematical. A serious attempt to do this was made, for example, in a paper by Elisabeth Jacobs and Hans H. Münch in 1992 in the journal *Schulmanagement*. Here it was stated, for example, that 'The "female" management style is based, amongst other things, on an intense perception of feelings ... The "male" management style, in line with the "Cartesian myth", only acknowledges a person's rational side' (Jacobs and Münch, 1992, p. 22). Even though the paper stresses that 'male' and 'female' behaviour is not tied to biological sex but is socially conditioned, and thus learnable, the representation it offers is none the less ultimately still ontological in character: no consideration is given to the role played, on the one hand, by feelings, and, on the other, by rationality in management behaviour; each is played off against the other. No account is taken either of the fact that modes of behaviour are simply not acquired in a 'gender-neutral' fashion, but within a gendered context, nor that the same behaviour can be perceived and judged in very different ways – depending, precisely, on whether it is a woman or a man who is exhibiting it.

In my opinion, a stand has to be taken against arguments that try to oppose discrimination against women by pointing to their 'special qualifications': women are not better people, and their right to share in management functions does not depend on their acting better or differently from men. That said, one has to admit that women do indeed often exhibit a different kind of behaviour from men, and they naturally bring this to the exercise of management functions. Investigations into the ways in which women and men teachers shape their professional roles reveal a number of gender-related differences. But these differences do not only have positive benefits; they also harbour problems and risks. Thus, women teachers' greater focus on people (see Wirries, 1991b; Terhart *et al.*, 1993; Terhart, 1995) also brings with it the risk of more rapid burn out. Hence Karin Flaake warns against a situation where

> if women assume management positions. . . people expect them – and perhaps they expect themselves – to change everything, in line with the fantasy . . . that everything good, but also everything bad, lies within their own power, within the power of women. Here too it is important, and also a relief, to recognize and accept the limits – one's own and those imposed by institutions – and to stick with the idea of the 'little bit different', the small changes that women can effect in schools if they bring their qualities out of the purely private sphere and make them public, propound them with confidence, and try to introduce them into management positions as well.   (Flaake, 1989b, p. 131)

This plea helps to get the management style debate out of the polarization of masculine and feminine qualities in an unhelpful and unsubstantiated way, and still empowers women to bring to bear what they have been taught during their female socialization without overestimating their possibilities of changing 'the whole school system'. There is a coincidence of women's interests with the proclaimed objectives of modern school management theories, for example in motivating 'human resources' to a maximum extent. This certainly is a reason to employ women – but not simply because of their gender (see von Lutzau and Metz-Göckel, 1996).

EXAMPLES OF WOMEN IN HEADSHIP POSITIONS

In the survey carried out by Heidemarie Krüger and Charlotte Röhner, women who have been willing to take on (and have been granted) headship functions describe their work as 'an extension of teaching tasks and responsibilities' (Krüger and Röhner, 1985, p. 39). They thus do not in any way confirm the reservations expressed by women teachers about the obligations and nature of this kind of post. Administrative work, they say, is undoubtedly necessary, but does not imply a huge degree of involvement, nor does it put a stop to opportunities for pedagogical creativity. However, the women heads did report various social conflicts arising from 'the dual function (of being on the one hand a colleague and on the other a person of official authority)' (ibid., p. 41). As far as the issue of compatibility between the public and the private spheres of their lives was concerned, one important factor was that the women had developed a view of themselves 'which tended away from the notion that they bore total responsibility for the family' (ibid.). This change in attitude is supported by a recent study by Mechthild von Lutzau, based on interviews with 30 women heads in all types of schools, all of whom received help and understanding from their partners. In general terms two aspects appear to be changing: women's interest in combining family and work and men's acceptance of promoting their partners through moral as well as practical support (von Lutzau and Metz-Göckel, 1996).

In what follows two very different examples will be offered of how women can participate in educational management, that is to say in the management and structuring of schooling.

Women Heads in *Gymnasien*: A Job-Sharing Example

In Hesse, an example already exists of how women can fulfil management functions despite a (continuing) reduction of working time. Roswitha Hahn and Mechthild Weiß-Hennerici began their new job as head of the Secondary level II in a *Gymnasium* in the school year 1994/5. Mechthild Weiß-Hennerici describes it as follows:

> Whereas I take care of the children in years 10/11 on four (out of six) teaching days[11] per week, my partner is responsible for years 12/13 for the same time-span but staggered with mine. This results among other things in our being particularly available to colleagues teaching in the year-groups involved. In addition, we are both available at any time to deal with questions relating to school regulations or administrative matters, and can provide authoritative and reliable information.
>
> (Hahn/Weiß-Hennerici, 1995, p. 200)

They have divided up their tasks on a division-of-labour basis (see Figure 4.11). Their experiences so far are summed up as follows:

> As well as the work involved in trying to combat staff scepticism about the innovative management-structures in the school, there is the job of asserting oneself within the 'all-male squad' in the management team. This requires a lot of time and, sometimes, nerves of steel! On the other hand, there is the opportunity of getting women's approaches adopted within the institution of 'school', working from a management position, and also the chance which the 'tandem-style appointment' brings of constant review by one's partner, of a kind of continuous supervision – all of which augurs some worthwhile successes in the near future.
>
> (ibid.)[12]

First Head's Tasks
Tutor training Yr 11

Advice sessions Yr 11
Survey of course needs Yr 11
Preparation and conduct of
course selection, reselection,
and deselection Yr 11
Preparation of exam papers

Printing of reports
Advice sessions for 10th
class (pupils and parents)
Reception into Yr 11
Pupils trips abroad

Both Heads' Tasks
Work-related meetings/full
staff-meetings
Heads' meetings
Exam committee (Abitur)
Arrangements with sports
department

Allocation of teaching commitments
and participation in timetable
planning
Work with school council
Partents' evenings

Computer work
Statistics

Designing forms

Second Head's Tasks
Tutor training Yr 12/13

Advice sessions Yr 12/13
Survey of course needs Yr 12/13
Preparation and conduct of course
selection, reselection, and deselection
Yr 12/13
Preparation of exam papers

Printing of reports
Career advice

Organization of Abitur
Review of individual pupils' plans for
the Abitur

Figure 4.11 Division in tasks in women heads' job-share
Source: Hahn/Weiß-Hennerici 1995, p. 201.

MOTIVATION AND FURTHER TRAINING OF WOMEN HEADS

For some years now, opportunities for further training have been made available to women teachers interested in headship positions (see Lührig, 1989a; Wirries, 1990, 1991a, 1991b; Collignon, 1991; Rotering-Steinberg and Wilhelm, 1993), and also for new women heads. The degree of interest in such opportunities can be inferred from various surveys: The Working Party on Women's Issues of the *Deutsche Philologen-Verband* (German Association of Philologists) conducted a survey amongst women *Gymnasium* teachers, asking, amongst other things, about shortcomings in, and suggestions concerning, promotion.

> The following topics are raised, particularly by women interested in promotion: preparatory seminars for women interested in promotion, providing precise information about the kinds of responsibilities to be expected (including theoretical discussion about why there are so few women in management positions, and discussion about legal options for dealing with discrimination); training in job application, with a view to producing a more confident performance in application procedures; training in public speaking; leadership; dealing with the male management-style; time management. (Reichert, 1995, p. 23)

The need for training opportunities for female heads – and also male heads – is pointed up in a survey carried out as part of an undergraduate dissertation-project in Hamburg: one of the main criticisms voiced by both men and women heads interviewed for this was that they had had to assume their new responsibilities without any preparation (Rotering-Steinberg and Wilhelm, 1993, p. 49).

In Lower Saxony in mid-December 1989, a one-week course for women heads, deputy women heads, and interested women teachers, on the theme 'School Management as a Task for Women', was held for the first time by the *Niedersächsische Lehrerfortbildungsinstitut* (NLI – Lower Saxony Institute of Advanced Teacher Training). Demand for the course was very great (Wirries, 1990, p. 4). In September 1990, there was a follow-up conference on the theme 'Women in Management Positions'. The education ministry planned four regional one-week courses for 25 participants over a period of four years, the aim of which was to provide preparation for assuming headship positions (Wirries, 1991a, 1992a, b). A BLK pilot scheme was then developed,[13] entitled 'School Management as a Women's Task' (Decken-Eckardt *et al.*, 1994). In November 1995 the closing conference on the theme 'The Effects of the Orientation Courses "School Management as a Task for Women" on the Structure of Schooling' took place. The orientation courses were generally conducted by teams of three people – a woman head acting as course leader, plus one departmental adviser from the education authority and one from the school psychological service. The course consisted of a number of basic units combining factual information with hints for personal reflections. The core components were:

- career profile of a woman head,
- responsibilities for structuring,
- legal and administrative framework,
- application procedures, career planning.

Scientific observation of the pilot scheme was conducted by Luise Winterhager-Schmid. In her view, the project can be considered a

> great success, in that lasting networks of women were formed who supported each other in the pursuit of their managerial aspirations. Not all of them want to become heads, but the majority of the participants are determined to 'break cover' and take the structuring of schooling into their own guiding hands. One striking fact is that many of these women are already amply qualified to do this . . . In other words, it is clear that a not insignificant number of women teachers (including some younger ones!) want to go beyond the standard 'ideal' of the women teacher and are manifestly so well qualified that they are capable of assuming institutional responsibility in leadership positions. Astonishingly, many of these (younger) women have children and families. (letter of 7 November 1995 from Luise Winterhager-Schmid)

However, this phase of orientation and qualification is not of itself sufficient to ensure that more women make their way into managerial positions, or to make any marked difference to the statistics as they currently stand. As early as 1991, Ingeborg Wirries predicted that 'If more doesn't happen, there is a danger that there will be a kind of bottleneck of qualified women on the job market' (Wirries, 1991a, p. 9; see also Wirries, 1995). It is up to the decision-makers to show that the argument that 'women would like to, but are not allowed to' really does not apply any longer. To achieve this goes beyond legislative changes. More important, in my opinion, is the existence of more and more women's support networks which might begin to break the circle, described by Anne Ratzki in 1989, whereby men in administration promote men into management positions by using the old boy networks. It is women themselves who must provide strong instruments in changing gender relations.

NOTES

1. In Berlin and North Rhine-Westfalia it is 10 years.
2. Of 15- to 20-year-olds many more young women stayed on in the educational system in 1990 than in 1961, and of the 60- to 65-year-olds more retired early.
3. This item was stated as follows: 'Der alte Ausspruch "die Frau gehört ins Haus und zur Familie" ist im Grunde richtig, und es sollte auch so bleiben.'
4. Even the existing empirical studies on education authorities provide no statistical data, let alone any indication of gender distribution. If one takes as an example the *Jahrbücher der Schulentwicklung*, which have

been published at two-yearly intervals since 1980 and adopt a critical stance favouring equality of opportunity and educational reform, even here one will search in vain for some mention of the subject of 'women in educational management'. The most recent issue does contain an article on educational authorities, but the gender question does not figure in it (Burkard and Rolff, 1994).

5. There have been some older publications giving some data, but they were mostly limited to one *Land* (see Bunz, 1987, Lührig, 1989c). The most recent collection of data about women in the educational system is Horstkemper in 1995, but this gives no data on the administration.

6. The current national average shows an even greater female preponderance of the new *Länder*: in the school year 1993, 62 per cent of teaching staff in general schools in the old and new *Länder* were female (Bundesministerium für Bildung und Wissenschaft, 1994).

7. Anne Ratzki cites the following figures for women in education authorities in North Rhine-Westfalia in 1986: in regional government, 18 per cent of education authority staff were women; at municipal and local level the proportion was 10.7 per cent in 1983 and had risen slightly by 1986 (Ratzki, 1989, p. 135). The unpublished paper from the Ministry does not contain comparable figures but concludes overall, that the rise of women in such employment was still only a slight one.

8. Karin Flaake's research is based on interviews which she made with 162 male and 55 female teachers in *Hauptschulen* and *Gymnasien* in Hesse in 1982. Heidemarie Krüger and Charlotte Röhner carried out several interviews with women teachers in Kassel and female school heads in Frankfurt/Main and Wiesbaden, but their articles do not state the exact number of interviews.

9. Haller and Wolf relate from their experience in training teachers since 1972, that most male teachers also do not aim for management positions (Haller and Wolf, 1995, p. 137). This is a realistic view of the teaching profession, which provides only relatively few career positions.

10. These reports are based on personal experience, which creates difficulties in establishing the frequency of discrimination or changes in its extent. The promotion process is not a very transparent one: the *Schulrat* usually inspects a lesson of a person who wants to become a head. After that there is an interview with a commission but the criteria for the selection are not made public. There is a wide discussion about the necessity to change this (see Bildungskommission NRW, 1995).

11. Apparently this school still has a teaching week of six days. Most schools in most *Länder* rearranged the school week in such a way that Saturday is not a teaching day any more.

12. To my knowledge this example of job-sharing is the only documented one at the level of a *Gymnasium* headship. However, it may function as a model for other women who want to job-share such positions.

13. The BLK – *Bund-Länder-Kommission für Bildungsplanung under*

Forschungsförderung (Federation-States Committee for Educational Planning and the Promotion of Research) comprises representatives from the federal government (Ministry of Education) and the individual *Länder*. Amongst other things, it supports pilot schemes in individual *Länder* with a view to their findings being used as guidelines for all the *Länder*.

REFERENCES

Arbeitsgruppe Bildungsbericht am Max-Planck-Institut für Bildungsforschung (1994) *Das Bildungswesen in der Bundesrepublik Deutschland. (Strukturen und Entwicklungen im Überblick)* (completely revised and expanded edn.) Reinbek.

Bellenberg, Gabriele and Klemm, Klaus (1995) Bevölkerung und ausgewählte Familiendaten, in Böttcher, Wolfgang and Klemm, (eds.) *Bildung in Zahlen. (Statistisches Handbuch zu Daten und Trends im Bildungsbereich)* Weinheim, pp. 17–25.

Bildungskommission NRW (1995) *Zukunft der Bildung – Schule der Zukunft. (Denkschrift der Kommission 'Zukunft der Bildung – Schule der Zukunft' beim Ministerpräsidenten des Landes Nordrhein-Westfalen)*, Neuwied.

BMBFT (ed.) (1995) *Grund – und Strukturdaten (1995/96)* Bonn.

BMFJ (ed.) (1992) *Frauen in der Bundesrepublik Deutschland*, Bonn.

BMBW (ed.) (1994) *Grund – und Strukturdaten (1994/95)* Bonn.

Böttcher, Wolfgang (1995) Schule und Unterricht, in id. and Klaus Klemm (eds.) *Bildung in Zahlen. (Statistisches Handbuch zu Daten und Trends im Bildungsbereich)*, Weinheim, pp. 40–62.

Bunz, Angelika (1987) Frauen als Schulleiterinnen – noch immer eine Ausnahme, *päd.extra*, no. 5, p. 16.

Burkard, Christoph and Rolff, Hans-Günter (1994) Steuerleute auf neuem Kurs? (Funktion und Perspektiven der Schulaufsicht für die Schulentwicklung) in Hans-Günter Rolff *et al.* (eds.) *Jahrbuch der Schulentwicklung*, Vol. 8, Weinheim, pp. 205–265.

Collignon, Gisela (1991) Lehrerinnen und Führungsaufgaben, *Forum Lehrerfortbildung* H. 20, pp. 44–49.

Decken-Eckhardt, Christa-Maria von der, Heide Niemann and Petra Behrens (1994) Kursangebote für Lehrerinnen – eine Benachteiligung für Lehrer?, *Schulverwaltungsblatt für Niedersachsen*, no. 5, pp. 164–6.

Flaake, Karin (1987) Das Peinliche der eigenen Wünsche, *päd.extra*, no. 5, pp. 4–8.

Flaake, Karin (1988) Weibliche Identität und Arbeit in der Schule: Das unterschiedliche Verhältnis von Lehrerinnen und Lehrern zu ihrem Beruf, in Sigrid Giesche and Dagmar Sachse (eds.): *Frauen verändern Lernen*, Kiel, pp. 180–6.

Flaake, Karin (1989a) *Berufliche Orientierungen von Lehrerinnen und Lehrern. (Eine empirische Untersuchung)*, Frankfurt/Main.

Flaake, Karin (1989b) Die Angst vor der eigenen Stärke. (Zum ambivalenten Verhältnis von Lehrerinnen zu Macht und Autorität), in Maria Anna Kreienbaum (ed.) *Frauen bilden Macht (Documentation of the Seventh German National Congress on Women and School)*, Dortmund, pp. 121–31.

Flaake, Karin (1990) Geschlechterdifferenz und Institution Schule. (Das unterschiedliche Verhältnis von Lehrerinnen und Lehrern zu ihrem Beruf), *Die deutsche Schule*, Suppl. 1, pp. 160–71.

Hahn, Roswitha and Weiß-Hennerici, Mechthild (1995) Job-Sharing in Funktionsstellen – Frauen als Partnerinnen in der Schulleitung, in Landesfrauenausschuß der GEW Baden-Württemberg (ed.) *Durchbruch zu einer feministischen Bildung. (Frauen für die Demokratisierung der Geschlechterverhältnisse.) (Documentation of the Ninth German National Congress on Women and School)*, Bielefeld, pp. 198–201.

Haller, Ingrid and Wolf, Hartmut (1993) Berufsspezifische Ausprägungen von Führungshandeln im Arbeitsfeld Schule, *Forum Lehrerfortbildung*, no. 23, pp. 50–65.

Haller, Ingrid and Wolf, Hartmut (1995) *Führung in Gesellschaft und Schule zwischen Tradition und Emanzipation. Auf dem Wege zu dialogischer Kompetenz*, Landesinstitut für Schule und Weiterbildung, Soest.

Hanesch, Walter (1995) Soziale Ungleichheit und soziale Problemlagen, in Wolfgang Böttcher and Klaus Klemm (eds.), *Bildung in Zahlen. (Statistisches Handbuch zu Daten und Trends im Bildungsbereich)*, Weinheim, pp. 258–74.

Horstkemper, Marianne (1995) Mädchen und Frauen im Bildungswesen, in Wolfgang Böttcher and Klaus Klemm (eds.), *Bildung in Zahlen. (Statistisches Handbuch zu Daten und Trends im Bildungsbereich)*, Weinheim, pp. 188–216.

Jacobs, Elisabeth and Münch, Hans H. (1992) 'Weibliche' Schulleitung, *Schulmanagement*, Vol. 23, no. 5, pp. 21–33.

Kriszio, Marianne (1995) The Situation of Women in East German Universities after Reunification, in C. Färber and A. Henninger (eds) *Frauenförderung an Europäischen Universitäten*, Freie Universität Berlin

Krüger, Heidemarie (1986) Über die Qual der Wahl – Lehrerin oder Schulleiterin? in FIF *et al.* (eds.) *Frauen Macht Schule*, Frankfurt/Main, pp. 87–97.

Krüger, Heidemarie and Röhner, Charlotte (1985) Schulleitung: doch ein Amt für Frauen?, *Grundschule*, Vol. 17 no. 2, pp. 38–41.

Lührig, Marion (1989a) Lehrerinnenfortbildung – Schulleitung als Frauenberuf, *Friedrich-Jahresheft (Feminin – Maskulin)* VII, pp. 28–30.

Lührig, Marion (1989b) Schulleitung – nur ein Männerberuf?, in Maria Anna Kreienbaum (ed.) *Frauen bilden Macht (Documentation of the Seventh German National Congress on Women and School)*, Dortmund, pp. 139–50.

Lührig, Marion (1989c) Schulleitung als Frauenberuf, *Pädagogik*, no. 11, pp. 20–5.

Lührig, Marion (1990) Karrierehindernisse auf dem Weg zur pädagogischen Führungskraft, *Die deutsche Schule* Suppl. 1, pp. 172–84.

Lutzau, Mechthild von / Metz-Göckel, Sigrid (1996) Wie ein Fisch im Wasser – Zum Selbstverständnis von Schulleiterinnen und Hochschullehrerinnen, in id. and Angelika Wetterer (eds.) *Vorausdenken – Querdenken – Nachdenken. Texte für Ayla Neusel*, Frankfurt/Main, New York.

Niedersächsisches Kultusministerium (1991) *Aufstieg für wen? (Beförderungsämter im Schulbereich. Wie hoch ist der Anteil der Frauen?)*, Hannover.

Ratzki, Anne (1989) Schulleiterin in einer Männerwelt, in Maria Anna Kreienbaum (ed.) *Frauen bilden Macht (Documentation of the Seventh German National Congress on Women and School)*, Dortmund, pp. 132–8.

Reichert, Barbara (1995) Gymnasiallehrerinnen mit gemischten Gefühlen, *Profil*, no. 1–2, pp. 20–4.

Rotering-Steinberg, Sigrid and Wilhelm, Monika (1993) Stärken von Frauen in leitenden Positionen, *Forum Lehrerfortbildung*, no. 23, pp. 43–59.

Statistisches Bundesamt (ed.) (1995) *Datenreport 1994. Zahlen und Fakten über die Bundesrepublik Deutschland,* Bonn.

Terhart, Ewald (1995) Lehrerprofessionalität, in Hans-Günter Rolff (ed.) *Zukunftsfelder von Schulforschung,* Weinheim, pp. 225–66.

Terhart, Ewald, Czerwenka, Kurt, Ehrich, Karin, Jordan, Frank, Schmidt, Hans Joachim (1993) *Berufsbiographien von Lehrern und Lehrerinnen. (Abschlußbericht an die DFG),* Institut für Schul – und Hochschulforschung, Lüneburg.

Wirries, Ingeborg (1990) Frauen als Schulleiterinnen, *Schulmanagement,* Vol. 21, no. 2, pp. 4–5.

Wirries, Ingeborg (1991a) Schulleitung als Aufgabe für Frauen, *Schulmanagement,* Vol. 22, no. 1, pp. 7–10.

Wirries, Ingeborg (1991b) Gibt es einen weiblichen Führungsstil?, *Schulmanagement,* Vol. 22 no. 4, pp. 4–8.

Wirries, Ingeborg (1992a) Schulleiterin – ein Beruf? Plädoyer für eine Professionalisierungsdiskussion, *Schulmanagement,* Vol. 23, no. 2, pp. 24–8.

Wirries, Ingeborg (1992b) Lehrerfortbildung im Blickpunkt – Chance für eine bessere Konzeption, *Schulmanagement,* Vol. 23, no. 4, pp. 30–3.

Wirries, Ingeborg (1995) Die untere Schulaufsicht in der Diskussion – Anmerkungen zu einer empirischen Untersuchung, *Schulmanagement,* Vol. 26, no. 3, pp. 34–8.

5

Greece

Georgia Kontogiannopoulou-Polydorides and Evie Zambeta

Women across the world have traditionally occupied positions in the labour market corresponding to professions and occupational activities which offer no prospect of development or mobility. As Patricia Niedzwiecki (1993) points out, the majority of women are to be found at the bottom of the hierarchical and salary ladders, where there is also a plethora of words to describe them. This is certainly the case in education, a source of employment which especially in Greece serves as a stronghold as well as an occupational shelter for women.

The problem of discrimination against women in education in Greece has been identified and studied either in terms of limited access to higher education and particular fields of study, or in relation to the unequal division of labour between the sexes (Eliou, 1978; Kontogiannopoulou-Polydorides, 1991; Fragoudaki, 1985). Access to administrative and managerial positions is open to experienced teachers in all education including at the tertiary level. It is in this sense that gender differences in these positions have to be studied in close relationship to access to teaching.

WOMEN AND EMPLOYMENT

The participation of women in the labour force has increased in Greece during the past fifty years. Although the percentage of the population in the active labour force has declined, from 60 per cent in 1983 to 57 per cent in 1991, this does not seem to have directly affected women. While the percentage of men in work fell from 82 per cent to 76 per cent in the same period, women's participation increased from 39 per cent to 40 per cent (Dedousopoulos, 1994).[1] It would be wrong to assume from these figures that the situation in the labour market is favourable to women. On the contrary, empirical evidence suggests that women are the ones most affected by unemployment, especially the younger generation.

In spite of the fact that women's access to the labour market has improved, the professed intention of the OECD countries, of wanting to integrate women into the labour market, and of ensuring equality of treatment and opportunity, is far from being achieved (OECD, 1990). One of the most obvious indicators of the hierarchical division of labour between the sexes can be seen in the restricted access of women to high status jobs in national institutions.

Women began to play a more active role in Greek politics after 1974, when parliamentary democracy was re-established following the fall of the junta. Today, only one parliamentary party (the KKE, the Communist Party of Greece) is led by a woman; another party (representing the political Left) has had a woman leader from 1988–1993, and a woman European Commissioner was appointed from 1989–1993. However, these examples are only promising exceptions to the general rule of restricted participation by women in political institutions. Although they constitute 51 per cent of the population, women only account for 5.6 per cent of the members of the National Parliament and for just 16 per cent of Greek MEPs. Given these figures, it is not surprising that women's participation in the various governments between 1981 and 1993 never rose above 12 per cent (General Secretary for the Equality of the Sexes (GSE), 1995). Fifteen per cent of the Greek Diplomatic Corps are women; in practice only men are eligible to gain access to the two highest levels of the service.

The role of women in regional and local government is also very limited. Only 7.4 per cent of prefects and 2 per cent of mayors are women (GSE, 1995). Women in rural areas are excluded from the political system to a greater extent than women in cities, where higher levels of education and wider acceptance of women in the labour market has led to a revision of traditional ideas and attitudes.

Employment opportunities for women are increasing faster than for men, especially in the fastest growing areas of economic activity (banking and services). At the same time, women lose their jobs more quickly in areas of economic decline, which could be seen as supporting the view that women are used as a reserve source of labour. It seems that women are the first to be made redundant in times of economic recession, and the first to be taken on when the economy improves. In addition research suggests that women continue to find employment in those areas where they have traditionally found work, indicating that there is no trend towards women replacing men in the workplace, but that women's opportunities reflect traditional ideas about the sexual division of labour (Mousourou, 1993; Dedousopoulos, 1994).

Female employment is concentrated mostly in the service industries, and in some sectors, such as education, medicine, and dentistry, women are in a majority (Mousourou, 1993).[2] This can be attributed to two main factors. Firstly, over the past 40 years there has been a serious decline in the agricultural labour force, and a movement of women as well as men to seek social integration and work in the urban centres. Secondly, there has been a significant rise in the percentage of women working in science-based industries, from 34 per cent in 1981 to 43 per cent in 1991 (GSE, 1995). Education is arguably the most important mechanism women have for gaining social mobility, which is why it is such an important route into the labour market.

Despite women's increased employment in the service sector, they are underrepresented in top grades. In 1994 women made up 41 per cent of all civil servants and accounted for just 24 per cent of heads of department and 10 per cent of directors, a fact which underlines their limited access to top jobs (GSE, 1995). The legal right of women to take 'early retirement' is one of the reasons given to explain this imbalance, but it is also a reflection of traditional attitudes, also held by women, towards their role in the workplace, their ability to compete with male colleagues, and their professional aspirations. It has been argued that women's choice of profession, and their mobility, are determined by their 'family strategy', and that their own earnings are only to be considered as a supplement to the family income (Mousourou, 1993).

Maternity (and paternity leave) provision is modest in comparison with other European countries. Statutory maternity leave lasts 14 weeks on full pay and an additional 3 months' unpaid leave is available to each parent. Furthermore, new mothers are entitled to a work schedule which is by law reduced by two hours per day in the first year and one hour per day in the second year of the baby's life. Child care provision, though improving, remains inadequate. The public day care centres (*paediki stathmi*) catering for children from birth to 6 years are very limited, especially in small towns and rural areas. The shortage of available places leads working women to look for alternatives such as private child care centres and privately hired nannies, who also assume household duties. The high expenses involved mean that lower income working women have to rely on the members of the extended family. A more recent development, but of limited impact, includes cooperatively organized child care centres in the workplace. With a comparatively short school day of 4 to 5 hours' duration, after-school care can also present problems.

Today, the most important factor in the sexual division of labour is not direct discrimination (i.e. in pay) but indirect discrimination related to social and cultural practices. This issue will be discussed more thoroughly with regard to the position of women in the teaching profession.

THE GREEK EDUCATION SYSTEM

The Greek education system is a highly centralized one. Responsibility for the Educational Acts, the recruitment of teaching staff, in-service training and assessment, school timetables and last but not least, the National Curriculum rests with the Ministry of Education. Moreover, the National Curriculum is based on a single textbook for every subject area, the choice of which is also the Ministry's responsibility.

General education consists of nine years of compulsory schooling starting from the age of six and of three years of upper secondary education which is optional. Almost all the schools are co-educational. About 5 per cent of the students attend private schools whilst in public schools education is offered free of charge.

- *Preschool education* which is under the authority of the Ministry of Education provides for two years of schooling starting at the age of four and remains optional.
- *Compulsory education* is divided into six years of primary education and three years of lower secondary education.
- *Upper secondary education* lasts three years and is provided in various types of *Lycea* (grammar schools) and technical and vocational schools.
- *Higher education* is provided in universities and technological educational institutes. University education lasts at least four years, whilst the minimum duration of technological education is three years. Universities in Greece are publicly funded and there are no tuition fees. The institutional framework of higher education is the Ministry of Education's responsibility but the university retains its academic freedom.

Enrolment from one education level to the next is free except in the case of higher education where entrance is regulated through nationwide examinations, and governed by a *numerus clausus*. The organization of the above exams rests with the Ministry of Education.

Teachers for all the educational levels are university graduates and their appointment is regulated by the Ministry of Education through long waiting lists by subject area.

The modernization of the curriculum and pedagogy throughout all educational levels is a question always present on the educational political agenda during the last two decades. However, some attempts towards this target have taken place regarding institutional modernization and democratization, new subject areas in the curricula and revision of teaching methods. Those attempts nevertheless present a slow rate of development. Some explanations for this state of affairs include the so-called resistance to change, which is particularly strong in a centralized educational system, the slow rate of further training and recruitment of new teaching personnel and last, but not least, a lack of resources. This has offered grounds for a neoliberal attack on the public character of the Greek education system. Although limited to the level of debate at present, privatization issues are placed at the top of the political agenda, especially regarding universities.

The dilemma which faces Greece, as other countries, can be summed up as: equality or efficiency, social heritage or consumerism, public control or market forces?

WOMEN IN TEACHING

It has been pointed out that we are witnessing a process of feminization in the teaching profession in all developed countries, and that this is an indication of a downgrading of the social status of teachers (Vasilou-Papageorgiou, 1995). It is also assumed that this 'decline' explains why men are leaving the profession.

We can observe these trends in Greece. Preschool teaching had traditionally been considered the preserve of women, to the extent that men were not only excluded from that area of schooling, but from the colleges which prepared preschool teachers. These restrictions were removed in 1982.

Tables 5.1 and 5.2 illustrate the gender ratio of primary and secondary school teachers over the past twenty years. Table 5.1 shows that women primary school teachers are now in the majority. Although this was not the case as recently as two years ago, women's participation in this field was considerably stronger than in other areas of employment. At secondary level, women teachers have been in the majority from 1974 to the present day. The decline in the academic year 1980–81 reflected the expansion of secondary technical schools, where men are strongly represented.[3]

Table 5.1   Primary education: teaching staff by gender, 1974–96

Academic Year	Total	W	% W
1974–1975	27,543	12,683	46.0
1980–1981	34,738	16,411	47.2
1995–1996	38,706	19,527	50.4

Source: ESYE, Education Statistics, Academic Years 1974–75, 1980–81, Ministry of Education (1995–1996), unpublished data.

Table 5.2   Secondary education: teaching staff by gender, 1974–96

Academic Year	Total	W	% W
1974–1975	16,060	8,587	53.5
1980–1981	45,720	21,544	47.1
1995–1996	60,890	32,863	54.0

Source: ESYE, Education Statistics, Academic Years 1974–75, 1980–81, Ministry of Education (1995–1996), unpublished data.

Although evidence from other European countries shows that an increase in the number of women working in education leads to a gradual transformation in the pattern of employment in this sector, the picture in Greece at first appears to be quite different, with a much lower percentage of women engaged in teaching. However, a more thorough examination of the figures shows that this is not the case. Table 5.3 shows the ratio of men to women in primary and secondary education in relation to years of teaching experience. The data show a significant increase in the proportion of women in teaching, with noticeably more (68 per cent) in the younger age group at primary level than in secondary (59 per cent). The comparatively low figures for women teachers at secondary level could be due to the introduction of new subjects into the curriculum, such as technology and computer sciences, to which women seem to have restricted access. However, the overall rate of increase in women's employment is almost the same for both primary and secondary education (approximately 0.8 per cent per year).

Table 5.3   Primary and secondary education teaching staff by gender and age group, 1990

Years of teaching	PRIMARY EDUCATION			SECONDARY EDUCATION		
	M	W	% W	M	W	% W
0–5	546	1,161	68.0	2,799	3,998	58.8
5–10	3,596	5,527	60.6	2,871	3,820	57.1
10–15	4,060	4,309	51.5	4,429	5,595	55.8
15–20	3,260	3,122	48.9	5,394	7,091	56.8
20–25	2,999	2,366	44.1	4,821	5,880	54.9
25–30	2,214	1,744	44.1	3,293	3,624	52.4
30–35	2,358	1,188	33.5	1,623	1,471	47.5
35+	146	110	43.0	2,797	1,384	35.0
TOTAL	19,179	19,527	50.4	28,027	32,863	54.0

Source: Ministry of Education, unpublished data.

The trend of feminization in women's employment is confirmed in the student ratios in university faculties offering teacher training courses. In the academic year 1992–93, 95 per cent of those studying for preschool education were women, while in faculties which train primary teachers, women represented 76 per cent of the student body, the patterns of subject study and higher education overall remaining the same.

In secondary education, gender ratios by specialization show that women are 'overrepresented' in most of the humanities (English, French, and Greek language and literature, for instance, but not theology[4]), well represented in music and fine arts and 'underrepresented' in sciences (mathematics and physics). Indeed, there has been a decline in the number of women teachers and lecturers in the latter subjects, despite an increase in the percentage of women studying these subjects, from 10 to 15 per cent in the last 20 years.

Women's participation in the French and English language faculties rose to 91 per cent of the student population, and in the faculties of Greek language and literature (philology[5]) to 83 per cent. At the same time, in fields formerly considered to be male preserves, such as mathematics and physics, women's participation is improving (to 36 per cent and 28 per cent respectively) (Ministry of Education, Department of Statistics and Operational Research, 1995). While it cannot be assumed that every woman graduating from these faculties will enter the teaching profession, it is very likely that this changing trend in the gender ratio of secondary school teachers will continue in the same fashion, indicating a potential increase in the proportion of women teachers.

There has also been a general decline in the number of women choosing a career in physical education. This can partly be attributed to the growth in professional athletics and private centres of training which have been encouraged by government policies. Both are established in the competitive private sector, a fact which discourages non-career-oriented working women. University trained women engineers constitute 24 per cent of the teachers in secondary (mainly technical) schools. Given that women constitute 12 per cent of the engineering student body, it is clear that women engineers are overrepresented in the teaching profession. This fact reflects in part, at least, the difficulty they find in being considered for better paid, higher status jobs in the private sector. Women engineers trained in technical colleges (non-university tertiary education) account for 15.6 per cent of teachers in secondary (technical) education.

WOMEN IN EDUCATIONAL ADMINISTRATION

The centralization of administrative planning and decision-making is one of the enduring characteristics of the Greek educational system (see Dimaras, 1978; Kazamias, 1978; Kontogiannapoulou-Polydorides, 1978). Even now, in spite of the educational reforms of 1976 and 1985, top appointments in education are made at ministerial level.

The Ministry of Education and Religion is the central administrative body responsible for legislation and for the implementation of the institutional framework of the educational system. It is responsible for all local and regional administrative institutions, curriculum planning, the selection of teaching materials, and sets the standards and procedures for assessing student performance. All teaching staff, managers, and administrative personnel are ultimately accountable to the Ministry. The Ministry also controls the Pedagogical Institute, which advises on school curricula, in-service teacher training and the standardization of teaching materials.

Directors are appointed by the Minister of Education to perform routine functions at prefecture level, with responsibility for teaching and administrative personnel. They have differentiated but often complementary responsibilities from the heads of primary and secondary education local offices. School advisers at regional level are responsible for giving guidance to teachers, and monitoring school performance. All three types of top level appointments are drawn from the ranks of senior teachers (Zambeta, 1994).[6]

Although women have made some progress towards equality within the teaching profession, with some exceptions they have made fewer inroads in educational administration at management level. In the Ministry of Education women represent 11.5 per cent of directors. Their relative success in accounting for 50.6 per cent of heads of department reflects the fact that, while there is a 'glass ceiling' that limits the promotion of women beyond certain positions, they are relatively well represented in the civil service as a whole, and in the Ministry of Education in particular. The same cannot be said for the Pedagogical Institute, where although women account for the overwhelming majority of staff (see Table 5.4), no woman has been appointed to the most senior rank of counsellor (who mainly deals with curriculum planning and book content decisions). This fact serves to highlight the highly influential Pedagogical Institute's overall views on the role of women in education, its political approach to appointments generally, and the ideological bias it exercises on educational policies.

Table 5.4   Pedagogical Institute: personnel by level and gender, 1996

	M	%	W	%
Counsellors	15	100.0	0	0.0
Assistants (permanent)	4	57.2	3	42.8
Consultants	58	78.4	16	21.6
Teachers on secondment	55	40.7	80	59.3
Administrative Staff	4	17.4	19	82.6

Source: Pedagogical Institute, unpublished data.

The situation in local education is similar, as Table 5.5 illustrates. At the time of writing, all 57 directors of primary education are men; all but 4 of the 134 heads of primary education offices are men, and only 8 per cent of general primary school advisers are women. This contrasts sharply with the overall predominance of women teachers in the primary education sector from which all managerial appointments for this educational level are drawn.

Table 5.5   Primary education: educational managers by gender, 1996

	M	%	W	%
Heads of Regional Administrative Seats	57	100.0	0	0.00
Heads of Education Offices	130	97.0	4	3.0
School Advisers in Primary Education	247	96.9	8	3.1
School Advisers in Special Education	15	100.0	0	0.0
School Advisers in Preschool Education	0	0.0	37	100.0

Source: Ministry of Education, unpublished data.

The representation of women in the administration of secondary education is a little better, as illustrated by Table 5.6. In secondary education 3 out of a total of 55 directors and 5 out of a total of 64 heads of education offices are women. There are no women heads of the technical and vocational education offices, and only 5 heads of offices for physical education. Among secondary school advisers, only 29 out of 194 are women.

A similar pattern emerges when data on the representation of women as school advisers to individual subject areas are examined, as Table 5.7 shows.

Table 5.6   Secondary education: educational managers by gender, 1996

	M	%		%
Heads of Regional Administrative Seats	52	94.5	3	5.5
Heads of Education Offices General Education	59	92.2	5	7.8
Heads of Education Offices Technical–Vocational Education	3	100.0	0	0.0
Heads of Education Offices Gymnastics	48	90.6	5	9.4
School Advisers	165	85.1	29	14.9

Source: Ministry of Education, unpublished data.

Table 5.7   Secondary education: gender ratio of teaching staff and of school advisers by subject area, 1996

Subject Area	TEACHING STAFF			SCHOOL ADVISERS		
	M	W	% W	M	W	% W
Theology	2,024	1,267	38.5	14	0	0.0
Philology	4,549	14,745	76.4	58	10	14.7
Mathematics	6,172	2,131	25.7	26	2	7.1
Physics and Chemistry	5,538	2,554	31.6	23	2	8.0
French	90	1,970	95.6	2	6	75.0
English	318	3,175	90.9	5	6	54.5
Fine Arts	231	467	66.9	0	1	100.0
Economics	568	540	48.7	0	1	100.0
Gymnastics	2,563	1,400	35.2	13	0	0.0
Engineering	727	226	23.7	13	0	0.0
Law	183	377	67.32	1	0	0.0
Medicine	304	277	47.7	1	0	0.0
Home Economics	5	913	99.5	0	1	100.0
Music	321	682	68.0	2	0	0.0
Engineering (teachers with non-university education)	1,898	350	15.6	6	0	0.0
Total	28,027	32,863	54.0	165	29	14.9

Source: Ministry of Education (1996a, b, c), unpublished data.

Although most teaching staff are women, this is not reflected in the gender ratios of the school advisers. Some fields, such as French and English, have women advisers even though men are very much in the majority. In other areas, such as religious studies, physical education, and engineering, there are hardly any women school advisers. This unequal situation places severe limits on women's promotional prospects within educational management.

Women in primary education appear to expect an even lower rate of promotion in the management of educational administration than their secondary school colleagues. Selection outcomes for primary managers are strongly biased against women, with male teachers being 39 times more likely to move into management positions than women. Among secondary teachers, male teachers are 6 times more likely to move into similar promoted positions.

Closer examination of the figures shows other inequalities. As women teachers are in a majority in the humanities, it might be expected that they would gain easier access to the top of the hierarchy in that field than, for instance, in sciences, which are still largely male-dominated. However, the highest inequality involves philologists, and the lowest mathematicians. Of the three main teaching groups, (mathematics, philosophy, and physics) which represent some 60 per cent of secondary teachers, it seems that the extent to which women are able to work as school advisers affects their chances of progressing higher in the management chain.

This unexpected evidence is in complete contrast to everything we know about the social characteristics of teachers, and leads to another hypothesis, which has yet to be verified through fieldwork. This suggests that women who decide early on that they want to make a career in a traditionally male-dominated profession are more likely to be determined to fight for their future and for their career. When obstacles to promotion occur, therefore, they are more likely to have developed the skills with which to cope with them.

Inequality is slightly lower for women teachers in English and French than for those teaching Greek language and literature (philology), perhaps due to the fact that the socio-economic background of foreign language teachers is higher. It is also likely that women teaching languages tend to have had a more open, multicultural education which might help counteract the effects of professional traditions and conservatism to some extent.

Many disparities of opportunities relate to geography, i.e. to whether the prospective manager is based in the centre or in the regions. Women primary teachers, in particular, do not opt for positions in rural areas; they are, in fact, more likely to gain access to top positions in the capital, as Table 5.8 illustrates. Access to jobs in educational management is so severely restricted in any case that it would be difficult to make an analysis of geographical disparities. However, it is noticeable that the 13 women primary school advisers appointed in the perfecture of Attiki (including the Athens area) are distributed as follows: Athens (4), East Attika (4), Piraeus (2), and West

Table 5.8 Primary and secondary education: gender ratio of staff in educational management in Attiki and the rest of the country, 1996

	Attiki				Rest of the Country				Total			
	M	%	W	%	M	%	W	%	M	%	W	%
PRIMARY EDUCATION												
Guidance	62	93.9	4	6.1	200	98.0	4	2.0	262	97.0	8	3.0
Administration	32	100.0	0	0.0	153	97.5	4	2.5	185	97.9	4	2.1
SECONDARY EDUCATION												
Guidance	59	81.9	13	18.0	106	86.9	16	13.1	165	85.1	29	14.9
Administration	35	89.7	4	10.2	127	93.4	9	6.6	162	92.6	13	7.4

Source: Ministry of Education (1996a, b), unpublished data.

Attika (3). Given that the first two are the most prosperous middle and upper-middle class districts, and the other two industrial working-class districts, it could be argued that the distribution of opportunities for women reflects and reinforces the social division of labour.

Little research is available on the situation of women headteachers. However, in 1994–95 36 per cent of secondary headteachers were women, as compared with 53 per cent of secondary staff. Recent figures for primary education have not been found (Laemers and Riujs, 1996).

ELIGIBILITY FOR MANAGEMENT POSITIONS

Promotion to top positions in educational administration and management (as identified in the previous section) is open to senior teaching staff with at least 12 years of experience. There are 3 categories of criteria for selection: scientific qualifications, teaching experience, and experience of working in educational management and the advisory services. Each applicant's CV is evaluated by a special committee according to a points system established by presidential decree. Candidates who satisfy these requirements are called to interview for final selection by a committee appointed by the Ministry of Education. The committee tends to be made up of top executives from the Ministry of Education, with some of the Minister's advisers, representatives of the teachers' unions, and various other educational experts, mostly university academics. The Minister's ideological and party political control over the committee, and thus over the selection process, is quite often manifest.

The criteria for selection are not always consistent. An applicant with a PhD, for instance, might be considered less well qualified than another without a postgraduate qualification, but who had attended a number of seminars and in-service courses. Some of the criteria are subjective, being based on vague estimates of the candidate's 'depth of knowledge of educational problems', or 'ability to implement scientific and pedagogical knowledge', which also leaves room for discrimination. Other criteria relating to experience in educational management (which count for 35–40 per cent of the total 'score') effectively require that the applicant should already be an education manager.

The present criteria perpetuate the prevailing sexual division of labour in teaching, and leave room for political manipulation of the selection procedures. The fact that women are largely excluded from political manoeuvring clearly leaves them at a serious disadvantage. The effects can be seen by contrasting the figures for women appointed to jobs in educational administration with those who join the advisory services. These show that when the decision is largely based on qualification criteria (as in the latter case) women candidates are more likely to be successful.

It could be argued that the relative lack of promotion prospects is due to the fact that women teachers still tend to be less qualified academically than their male counterparts. However, the differential is small, and declining, so cannot be used to justify their exclusion from the highest ranks of management. As Table 5.9 shows, the female/male ratio for further education qualifications is 1 woman to 1.1 men, while the ratio for appointments to primary and secondary teaching, including administration and advisory services, is 1 woman to 14.4 men.

Table 5.9 Teaching staff with further qualifications as percentage in total by gender (%)

EDUCATION LEVEL	TOTAL		In-service training				Further training abroad		Second university degree		Postgraduate degree			
			2 years		1 year						Masters		PhD	
	M	W	M	W	M	W	M	W	M	W	M	W	M	W
Primary Education	29.01	21.7	8.3	3.7	12.8	9.0	1.0	0.6	0.6	8.0	0.2	0.3	1.0	0.1
Secondary Education	20.01	16.8	–	–	15.1	13.7	0.8	0.5	2.2	1.4	1.3	0.8	0.6	0.4

Source: ESYE, Education statistics, 1992–93.

If women are not being refused promotion because of their qualifications, other explanations must be sought. Whether this stems from direct discrimination based on traditional ideas about the sexual division of labour, and a lack of confidence in women's ability to manage, or from indirect discrimination based on women's more limited professional aspirations, and lower levels of self-esteem, leading to 'self-exclusion' from promoted posts, remains open to question. In either case, the results of discrimination are clear.

There are no official records on the gender ratio of applicants. Off-the-record explanations for this provided by the Ministry of Education amount to the view that 'most of the time, women don't even apply for management jobs'! Even if this were the case, the obvious question remains 'Why not?'.

WOMEN IN UNIVERSITY TEACHING

University teaching has a special status, giving academic staff a place at the top of the educational hierarchy. Teaching staff are paid more at this level than their colleagues in schools, though much less than they would earn for doing the same work in other parts of Europe, or as MPs, lawyers, or other professionals.[7]

Until recently university teaching had a notoriously strict hierarchical structure.[8] This was designed to place power in the hands of a limited number of professors, and position the lower teaching staff as their assistants who could have no say in management or curriculum planning, or in staff assessment. This situation was changed dramatically by the 1982 Education Act, which ended the regime of the university chair and established instead four levels of academic personnel: lecturers, assistant professors, associate professors, and professors. All university teaching staff are now required to have a doctorate.

Table 5.10 shows the relative positions of senior to junior teaching personnel in 1981 and, in particular, after the 1982 reforms. The effects on women's careers were two-fold, and contradictory. While they were able to increase their representation in senior grades from about 7 per cent in 1981 to 22.5 per cent in 1996, the percentage of women in all grades fell over the same period from 35 per cent to 26.5 per cent. This development was due to the fact that women in the lower grades got promoted over the years, and also to the fact that in the upgrading of the lower ranks the newcomers (e.g. assistant professors) comprised more men than women (Table 5.11). The percentage of professors who are women, at 7.6 per cent of the total, remains low.

Table 5.10   University teaching personnel, 1974-96. Percentage women and ratio of senior to junior ranking personnel

Years	TOTAL	% W	SENIOR Total	% W	JUNIOR Total	%W	Ratio senior:junior
1974-75	5,466	35.9	987	12.6	4,479	41.1	18:1
1980-81	6,924	35.3	1,411	6.7	5,513	42.6	20:4
1995-96	8,015	26.5	6,456	22.6	1,559	42.7	80:5

Source: ESYE, Education statistics 1974–75 and 1980–81. Data for 1995–6 calculated from university catalogues.

Table 5.11   University teaching personnel by academic level and gender, 1996

Academic Level	Total Men	Total Women	% Women
Professors	1,200	98	7.6
Associate Professors	864	159	15.5
Assistant Professors	2,063	687	25.0
Lecturers	870	515	37.2
Assistant Teaching Personnel	894	665	42.7

Source: Data calculated from university catalogues.

Women have had more access to academic posts since 1982, despite continuing restrictions, which have resulted from economic recession and cuts in public funding and which have ended the expansion of tertiary education. Demand for higher education in Greece is very intense, but while this is reflected in educational policies, government gives scant regard to improving, or even maintaining standards. While student numbers rose by 111 per cent, and 77 new faculties were created, an increase of 74 per cent between 1975 and 1996, the number of academic staff increased by just 46 per cent (ESYE, 1975; Ministry of Education, 1995).

Within the country as a whole, proportionately more women hold posts in universities in the Athens area, notably in the Pantion University of Political and Social Sciences, and in the National and Kapodistrian University of Athens, where they account for 32 per cent and 26 per cent of academic staff respectively. As discussed, most women academics are employed in the lowest grades, and it is here, especially in the traditional stronghold of the humanities, that the trend of feminization can be observed.

Management in universities, however, remains, with few exceptions, an all-male affair. All but one of the rectors of the country's 18 universities are men, and this sets the tone for those employed lower down in the system. Again, further research is needed into the question of whether this is due to overt exclusion or covert social exclusion (so-called 'self-exclusion').

RANK AND LANGUAGE IN EDUCATION

The feminization process began much earlier in education than in most other fields of employment. This is reflected in the terminology used for teachers, which allows a masculine as well as a feminine form for the primary school teacher, the secondary school teacher, and the primary school headmaster (*daskalos, daskala; kathigitis, kathigitria; diefthintis, and diefthintria,* respectively).

Further up the hierarchical scale, from the job of secondary school headteacher upwards, only masculine forms are found, reinforcing the tradition of male-exclusiveness. Thus professionally-ambitious women find themselves 'surrounded by masculine symbolism, constraining accordingly the verbal consciousness of women, so that women respond by refusing even attempting to gain power' (Niedzwiecki, 1993, p. 21).

Another, similar division exists in the terminology used for educational qualifications. The same expression is used to refer to male and female graduates from primary and secondary schools (*apophitos* and *apophiti*). Although women have been studying in universities for 100 years, and have been in a majority since 1980, references to holders of first degrees (*diplomatouchos* and *ptychiouchos*) and of doctorates (*didactor*) continue to have masculine forms only. The absence of a feminine form, which is a denial of that reality, reflects, albeit unconsciously, another reality – of the enduring hierarchical gap between men and women graduates.

SOME FURTHER REMARKS

In Greece the teaching profession does not offer exciting career prospects, and is not well paid, but it continues to offer stable and secure employment. For young women of rural background, who represent the majority of teachers, especially at primary level, it offers the prospect of social mobility and a move to the city. Historically there has always been a gap, in terms of academic qualifications and socio-economic status, between teachers in primary and secondary schools, to the point that the former are referred to as *daskali* (teachers) and the latter as *kathigetes* (professors). This divided view of education has serious repercussions on the profession's social and cultural character, and is reflected in its hierarchical structure.

Until 1985 the training of primary teachers was vocational, and took place over a period of 2 years in post-secondary teacher training colleges (*pedagogikes academies*). These schools had low educational standards, semi-qualified teaching personnel, and no academic freedom.[9] Most of the male students recruited came from an agricultural background, while female students came from middle-class rural families. In one of the most important reforms of the 1985 Education Act, carried out under pressure from the teachers' union, the PASOK government brought primary teaching within the ambit of university education, and thus in line with secondary school teaching, which had always recruited teaching staff from graduates of subject disciplines.

In some areas of educational management, disparities in career opportunities for women seem to match disparities in university faculties attributable to socio-economic factors. Women teachers are least advantaged in primary education and, at secondary level, in religious studies, physical education, and engineering. Empirical evidence shows that teachers working in these areas (with the exception of engineering[10]) come from approximately the same socio-economic backgrounds. Research into the careers of 939 teachers who started their careers in primary and secondary education in 1978 showed the following results: 86 per cent of primary teachers, 93 per cent of teachers of religious studies, and 72 per cent of physical education teachers came from rural areas; the highest percentages of those drawn from Athens and Piraeus were teachers of foreign languages and physics (Demetriadou, 1982[11]).

Analysis of teachers by their fathers' occupation showed that 79 per cent of primary teachers, 71 per cent of religious studies teachers, and 61 per cent of physical education teachers had fathers who were manual or agricultural workers. Those most likely to have fathers in professional employment were teachers of foreign languages (47 per cent) and physics (45 per cent) (Demetriadou, 1982).

A similar picture emerges on examining the social stratification of university students in faculties which correspond to school subject areas. Those with the lowest socio-economic backgrounds were training to be preschool or primary teachers, or studying physical education or religious studies, while those at the higher end of the scale were studying music, engineering, French and English.[12]

Students from an agricultural background chose to study the same subjects, and were least likely to be studying music, foreign languages, mathematics, engineering, or physics. The same survey showed a noticeable decline in the overall representation of such students, not just in general, but specifically in those subject areas to which they had traditionally gained access. These changes are thought to be due to the selective approach taken in higher education, the trend towards urbanization, and the proletarization of people from agricultural areas.

Evidence presented in this chapter leads to the following conclusions:

1. In Greece, as in other countries, teaching is increasingly becoming a feminine profession: overwhelmingly so in some fields, such as preschool education, home economics, and the humanities.
2. In spite of being in a majority in the teaching profession, women are generally denied access to management positions.
3. The 'glass ceilings' are more obvious in the regions than in and around the capital, and in administration more than in the advisory services, i.e. wherever political pressures are strongest. While there is a widely-accepted view that women find it easier to advance their careers in areas such as the humanities where they are well represented, the available empirical evidence suggests that the reverse is actually the case. (The exceptions to this are English and French language, reasons for which need to be further investigated.) Women are found to gain promotion more readily in the male-dominated subject areas of mathematics and physics.
4. Most women academics, working on the lowest rank of the academic ladder, have not benefited as much from the 1982 reforms as male lecturers.
5. It is argued that this difference cannot be justified in terms of academic qualifications, and is in fact the result of institutionalized gender discrimination. It is further argued that direct and indirect discrimination are closely connected to social and cultural characteristics of the teaching profession and the social context, including the division of labour in society.

As argued elsewhere, women are not able to make a free choice of university career, having to take account of 'feedback from the division of labour and the division of sex roles in society' (Kontogiannopoulou-Polydorides, 1991, pp. 109–10).

Access to particular fields of study at tertiary level is related to the degree of literacy which individuals achieve. Polydorides (1995) indicates that culture, social status, and gender are all reflected in the individual's type and level of literacy. Literacy also plays an important role in social and cultural reproduction, and is associated with the active efforts of different social groups to maintain positions of power in specific social contexts. The data suggests that in this process men are more successful in overcoming the mechanisms of cultural and social reproduction, since women are more strongly focused on factors concerned with the family and the home (Kontogiannapoulou-Polydorides, 1996).

In spite of the trend towards the feminization of the teaching profession, the reinforcement of sex roles and the sexual division of labour can be observed in educational management. This is particularly true in the fields (the humanities), and subject areas (mathematics and physics) dominated by students from a relatively low socio-economic background. Those women who have gained most access to male-dominated areas of study, such as mathematics and physics, and who have acquired higher self-esteem, tend to come from middle-class families living in urban areas. Their socio-economic backgrounds have helped them survive in the aggressive environment of intra-professional mobility.

Those who have followed the academic paths traditionally open to women mostly come from rural areas and relatively deprived social origins, and are more likely to come up against social barriers and sexual discrimination. One reason for this may be their own low expectations, which lead them to adopt traditional roles, and to accept that the scales will be weighed against them if they seek promotion. Perhaps this is the reason why they 'don't even apply' for management positions, together with a feeling that teaching is compatible with marriage and motherhood, provides a respectable contribution to the family income, and in general suits their 'family strategy'.

It can be safely assumed that as long as tradition and change co-exist, the process of women's emancipation and the abolition of discrimination by gender will be mediated predominantly by socio-economic factors.

NOTES

1. Part-time workers in the labour force are represented in small numbers and are decreasing. Although 63 per cent of part-time workers are women, only 7 per cent of women worked part time in 1991 (Plantega, 1995).

2. Mousourou (1993, pp. 86–89) states that women represent the majority of the employees in the service sector (as in education, medicine and dentistry). We believe that this applies to all personnel levels.

3. The decline in the percentage of women recorded in the year 1980–81 is due to the expansion of secondary technical education, in which male teachers are in the majority as a result of the professional specializations they cover which correspond to male dominated fields.

4. Philologists in Greece graduate from the university faculties of philosophy. The curriculum includes Ancient and Modern Greek language and literature, Latin, history, philosophy, psychology and educational sciences. Specialization is offered in the above fields and the graduates are permitted to teach any of these subjects.

5. The fact that women are the minority among theology teachers (although this is part of the humanities) is a result of the recruitment of these secondary school teachers from both departments of theology as well as schools of divinity. In the latter women are represented in smaller numbers (around 40 per cent) since the orthodox church does not allow women to serve as priests. University pastoral schools exist in which clergymen have preferential access. Today in faculties of theology 54 per cent of the students are women while in pastoral faculties women consitute 41 per cent. Graduates from both faculties may enter the teaching profession.

6. In Greece, almost every education administrative and guidance district includes schools of both urban and rural areas. This fact means that in terms of positions in local educational management there is no clear division between urban and rural areas. Of course there are certain management positions which are in charge of urban schools only and this is particularly the case in the prefecture of Athens.

7. On average, professors in Greece have a salary of about 60 per cent of the average in the EU (not accounting for cost-of-living differences).

8. For a more detailed analysis of the social characteristics of the academic profession in Greece, and the place of women, see Eliou, 1988.

9. These former teacher training institutions enjoyed none of the privileges of self-management and academic freedom reserved for the university level departments, such as the appointment of teaching staff, curriculum planning and decision making, textbooks and self-government which were all in the full responsibility and control of the Ministry of Education.

10. Engineers who graduate from university polytechnic schools tend to have a particularly high socio-economic background. Since we do not have empirical evidence on the socio-economic background of those who enter the teaching profession we cannot estimate their situation.

11. Findings from this project are particularly relevant to this analysis, since the research population is eligible for promotion to educational management positions.

12. At the time of writing, the Greek public education system still does not offer advanced level courses in foreign languages in secondary schools. This means that anyone wishing to read English or French at university will have to have studied privately over many years; clearly not an option for students who live outside urban areas, or whose parents cannot afford to pay school fees.

REFERENCES

Dedousopoulos, A. (1994) Institutions and Policies in the Greek Labour Market 1974–1994, Athens (unpublished, in Greek).

Demetriadou, K. (1982) *Greek teachers' criteria for choice of profession. An empirical research*, Thessaloniki, Kiriakides (in Greek).

Dimaras, D. (1978) The Movement for Reform: A Historical Perspective, *Comparative Education Review*, 22, 1, pp. 11–20.

Eliou, M. (1978) Those Whom Reform Forgot, *Comparative Education Review*, 22, 1, pp. 80–93.

Eliou, M. (1988) Women in the academic profession: Evolution or stagnation? *Higher Education*, 17, pp. 505–24.

Frangoudaki, A. (1985) *Sociology of Education*, Athens, Papazeses.

General Secretary for the Equality of the Sexes (1995) *The Situation for Women in Greece in the decade 1984–1994*, National Report for the 4th United Nations Conference for Women, Athens: GSE (in Greek).

Kazamias, A. (1978) The Politics of Educational Reform in Greece: Law 309/1976, *Comparative Education Review*, 22, 1, pp. 21–45.

Kontogianopoulou-Polydorides, G. (1991) Greece, in M. Wilson, (ed.) *Girls and Young Women in Education. A European Perspective*, Oxford: Pergamon Press.

Kontogianopoulou-Polydorides, G. (1996) The Influence of Culture, Society and Educational Contexts, in H. Wagemaker, K. Taube, I. Munk, G. Kontogianopoulou-Polydorides and M. Martin, *Are Girls Better Readers?* Amsterdam: IEA.

Laemers, M and Riujs, A. (1996) Statistical Portrait, in *Context*, no. 12, pp. 7–15.

Ministry of Education (1995) Department of Statistics and Operational Research Data.

Ministry of Education (1996a) Directorate of Primary Teaching Personnel Data.

Ministry of Education (1996b) Directorate of Secondary Teaching Personnel Data.

Ministry of Education (1996c) Directorate of Computerization Data .

Mousourou, L. (1993) *Women and Employment*, Athens, Gutenberg (in Greek).

National Statistical Service of Greece (ESYE) (1978) *Statistics of Education 1974-1975*, Athens: ESYE.

National Statistical Service of Greece (ESYE) (1986) *Statistics of Education 1980–1981*, Athens, ESYE.

National Statistical Service of Greece (ESYE) (1994) *Statistics of Education 1984–1985*, Athens, ESYE.

National Statistical Service of Greece (ESYE) (1996) *Statistics of Education 1993–1994*, Athens, ESYE (unpublished data).

Niedzwiccki, P. (1993) *Women and Language*, Cahier de Femmes d'Europe, 40, Brussels: European Commission.

OECD (1990) *Labour Market Policies for the 1990s*, Paris: OECD.

Polydorides, G. (1978) Equality of Opportunity in the Greek Higher Education System: The Impact of Reform Policies, *Comparative Education Review*, 22, 1, pp. 80–93.

Polydorides, G. (1995) *Educational Policy and Practice*, Athens: Greek Letters (in Greek).

Plantega, J., Labour Market Participation of Women in the European Union, in Doorne-Huiskes, A. van, Hoof, J. Van and Roelofs, E. (1995) *Women and the European Labour Market*, London: Paul Chapman Publishing.

Vasilou-Papageorgiou, V. (1995) Education and Sex: the gender dimension in primary teaching personnel, in A. Kazamias, M. Kassotakis, (eds.) *Greek Education: Restructuring and Modernization Perspectives*, Athens: Serios, pp. 495–514 (in Greek).

Zambeta, E. (1994) *Education Politics in The Greek Primary Educational System (1974–1989)*. Athens: Themelio (in Greek).

6

Hungary

Eva Széchy

The slow process of women's emancipation in Hungary began with the defeat of fascism at the end of the Second World War, yet essentially feudal attitudes towards the position of women can still be found in the workplace, and in society as a whole. Changes in the character of women's employment, and in their role in the family, were observable from 1945. Until then Hungary had been a semi-developed agro–industrial country: 25 per cent of the working population were employed in industry, one-third of them women. Most were employed in semi-skilled work in light industry, where they earned substantially less than their male counterparts. The service sector accounted for 10 per cent of the workforce. This gave women a more equitable share of the wage bill, for example in trade, office work, or kindergartens, but overall pay was much lower than in industry.

The great majority of upper- and middle-class women were housewives who employed maids and other domestic servants. The majority of other women at that time were married to agricultural workers, and were housewives, but a large proportion of them were also forced to take seasonal low-paid employment in addition to their own domestic work.

During the same period the proportion of women who belonged to the intelligentsia was less than 5 per cent overall. Rather more were employed as teachers in nurseries and in the public health sphere, were self-employed, or so-called 'freelance' intellectuals. Women who came to occupy leading positions usually did so in exceptional circumstances – as outstanding artists, intellectuals or educators – though even here, for example in the running of girls' schools, they were underrepresented (Pölöskei, Gergely and Izsák, 1996).

The general condition of cultural backwardness in the period leading up to the Second World War is reflected in the fact that only 50 per cent of children completed the first six classes of primary schools; rates of underachievement and illiteracy were considerably higher among girls. Far fewer women than men entered professional schools or high schools, and an even smaller proportion of them – well below 10 per cent – were accepted into universities and other institutes of higher education (Pölöskei, Gergely and Iszák, 1996).

Since 1945, successive waves of modernisation have brought about ·a profound transformation in the education and employment prospects of women, and in their overall role in society. Although there have been standstills, reverses, and contradictions in this process, by the end of the 1980s 80 per cent of women available for work were in employment. With a policy of full employment and comparatively generous childcare provisions, only 3 per cent of Hungarian women worked part time, in contrast with many European countries. Paid maternity leave of 24 weeks, an income-related childcare allowance for up to 2 years, and widely available creches, nurseries, and after-school care enabled women to participate in the labour force (Eberhardt, 1991). Apart from the areas in which women traditionally found work (in the textile industry, as seamstresses, as teachers in kindergartens, and as nurses) women's participation in the service sector has increased to 60 per cent and in trade and commerce to 66 per cent, while the proportion of self-employed women in agriculture is now 35 per cent and in industry 40 per cent. In several professions which called for higher education training – teaching, medicine, pharmacy, law, etc., women had become the majority, even if they mostly held subordinate roles. The number of women holding senior positions has continued to grow, but they are still underrepresented at the highest levels in the various professional hierarchies. This is the case in general and higher education, and in educational science and management. Men also earn on average 146 per cent of the gross average female wage (Pölöskei, Gergely and Izsák, 1996).

THE HUNGARIAN EDUCATION SYSTEM

Education is currently compulsory between the ages of 6 and 16 in Hungary. The general education standard of Hungarian girls is equal to that of Hungarian boys and, in the younger age groups, is actually better. In Hungary today only one child in a hundred receives no formal education. Figure 6.1 illustrates the structure of the public education system in Hungary.

Typical education routes part after primary schooling. At present, about one half of pupils aged 14+ study in secondary schools; 48 per cent of enrolments are in the *Gymnasien* (grammar schools, which prepare for university entrance), 27 per cent are in secondary vocational schools, and about 25 per cent in technical schools, which currently offer professional qualifications rather than a final examination. The proportion of girls attending secondary schools equalled that of the boys by the mid-1970s, and they now account for 56 per cent of all students in secondary schools. Sixty-five per cent of girls attend grammar schools. Those who attend technical schools tend to opt for courses in economics, health, trade, mechanics, administration, catering, and nursery school teaching. The remainder of this age-group attend various vocational training courses, where boys account

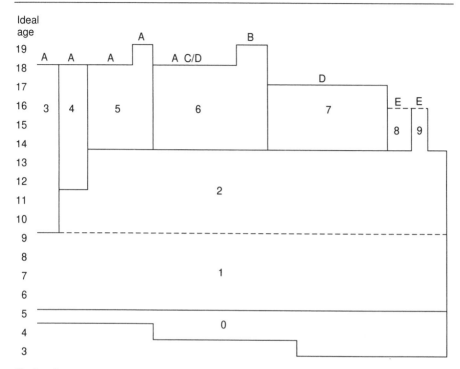

Explanation:
Grades of education
0   Nurseries
1   General primary school lower grade
2   General primary school higher grade
3-5 Grammar school education
6   Secondary vocational school education
7   Technical education
8-9 Special profession school education
Certificates, exams
A   Certificate of final examination
B   Technician exam
C   Secondary professional exam
D   Technical exam
E   Lower grade technical qualification

Figure 6.1   The Hungarian public education system

for two-thirds of students, mainly pursuing courses related to heavy industry or the building trades. These are an increasingly popular option (Köpeczi, 1986; Széchy, 1987; Pölöskei, Gergely and Izsák, 1996). Table 6.1 shows the distribution of males and females in the Hungarian education system.

At the age of 18 or 19, young men or women may opt for higher education. The sector currently comprises 91 institutions, with a total of 150,000 students. The higher education sector comprises state and denominational colleges and universities and some private and foundation colleges. There are two basic

Table 6.1   Enrolment percentages in full-time education

| | 1980/81 | | | 1985/86 | | | 1993/94 | | |
	Males	Females	Total	Males	Females	Total	Male	Female	Total
Primary Schools	98.6	99.1	98.8	97.7	98.7	98.2			
Apprentice Schools	40.2	19.9	30.4	38.8	20.5	29.9	33.4	17.8	25.8
Secondary Schools	32.9	47.8	40.1	32.9	47.4	40.0	42.2	56.0	48.9
Higher Education	9.0	9.4	9.2	9.1	10.7	9.9	12.3	13.9	13.0

Source: United Nations Fourth World Conference on Women (1995).

types of institution; colleges, offering 3–4 year courses and universities, offering 5–6 year courses. In 1996, the age-participation rate of 18–22 year olds in full-time higher education was 13 per cent. The proportion of male to female enrolments had equalised by 1980. Female students now comprise 51 per cent of the total number of students in full-time higher education, 73 per cent of those in part-time higher education, and 53 per cent of correspondence course students. Although women students comprise only 21 per cent of engineering students, they account for 43 per cent of students of the sciences, 49 per cent of medical students, and 56 per cent of law students (Ministry of Education and Culture, 1996). The changing enrolment patterns of male and female students in higher education are illustrated in Table 6.2.

Table 6.2   Breakdown of full-time higher education students by gender and area of studies (%)

| Area of studies | 1980 | | 1985 | | 1993 | |
	Males	Females	Males	Females	Males	Females
Technical/Engineering	82.1	17.9	83.1	16.9	78.2	21.8
Agriculture	66.6	33.4	66.6	33.4	55.5	44.5
Veterinary	85.0	15.0	83.2	16.8	68.6	31.4
Medical	43.5	56.5	44.4	55.6	51.1	48.9
Health care	8.5	91.5	4.9	95.1	9.8	90.2
Economics	38.5	61.5	33.2	66.8	42.4	57.6
Law	50.3	49.7	42.3	57.7	44.2	55.8
Humanities	27.5	72.5	24.2	75.8	26.8	73.2
Sciences	54.5	45.5	52.1	47.9	56.4	43.6
Teacher training at college	24.6	75.4	27.6	72.4	30.4	69.6
Special education	8.9	91.1	6.7	93.3	9.0	91.0
Physical exercise/sport	54.3	45.7	54.3	45.7	57.6	42.4
Primary school teacher training at college	11.5	88.5	12.4	87.6	11.4	88.6
Nursery school teacher training at college	0.4	99.6	0.8	99.2	1.9	98.1
Arts	48.2	51.8	45.9	54.1	45.2	54.8
Divinity					66.4	33.6
Other					94.8	5.2
Total	50.1	49.9	47.7	52.3	48.1	51.9

Source: United Nations Fourth World Conference on Women (1995).

The structure of the Hungarian system is going to be changed considerably according to the Act on Education, passed in 1993 and amended in 1996. The main changes will be:

- an extension of basic schooling to the age of 16;
- a new school leaving exam to be introduced at 16;
- complete autonomy of the universities;
- the introduction of a new national curriculum, which will specify objectives and minimum requirements, but leave individual schools to adopt their own textbooks and syllabi (subject to approval);
- encouragement of foreign language teaching;
- an extension of the school year;
- a restructuring of the system of higher education to a 3-year college, 5-year university system.

The state will continue to set the framework of the national curriculum for schools, and to set standardised examination requirements. However, schools will have considerably more control to determine their educational objectives and over their internal organisation, with implications for the role of the headteacher (Szebenyi, 1992).

Since a degree of liberalisation of the education system in 1988, all headteacher appointments have nominally had to meet with the approval of the teaching staff concerned. However the Education Act of 1993, while still requiring consultation of teachers in the appointment process, excludes them from the final decision in headteacher appointments. The local government body maintaining the school has the exclusive right to appoint headteachers, who in turn have the right to appoint teaching staff. The appointment of all teachers, headteachers and university staff takes place by competition. The formal requirement for teaching pupils of lower secondary age (10–14 years) is a 4-year teacher training diploma and for pupils of upper secondary age (14–18 years) a 5-year university diploma. Candidates for the post of headteacher should have at least 5 years practical experience in a school.

Academic staff in universities and colleges are required to hold a PhD. and a further degree, the *Habilitation*, which can only be awarded by some specially accredited departments. Since 1996, teachers working in the public sector in schools and universities have had to pass an examination every 10 years in order to continue teaching.

WOMEN IN TEACHING AND EDUCATIONAL MANAGEMENT

Teacher training currently comprises a 4-year college course or 5-year university degree, with very little practical experience. Enrolments to college courses are low, despite attempts to change their status by law. In Hungary, there are about 90,000 primary school teachers, of whom 85 per cent are women. Despite this, male teachers occupy about one-third of senior positions at this level. (Gazsó, 1994; Ministry of Education and Culture, 1996). At the level of secondary education, 97 per cent of grammar school and 60 per cent of vocational school teachers are women, while the proportion of women deputy heads and headteachers in these schools is 40 per cent and 30 per cent respectively (Ferge, 1995; Okker Education Office, 1995a). Subject divisions are also strong: women account for about half of all teachers of theoretical subjects and only one-fifth of teachers of applied subjects at this level.

There are almost 6,000 women teaching in higher education centres, who constitute 37 per cent of all lecturers. Women lecturers are in a majority in teacher training faculties and in the medical and business colleges. Only 3 per cent of them are university or college professors, 15 per cent are readers, and 35 per cent are senior lecturers (Okker Education Office, 1995b). Table 6.3 gives the proportion of male to female academic staff, according to rank. Women are seriously underrepresented in relation to their qualifications in the ranks of rectors, directors, deans, and heads and deputy heads of department. Far fewer women than men are admitted to scientific bodies. It is characteristic that among the 33 members of the University Council of the most important Hungarian university, the Eötvös Loránd Scientific University, there are only 6 women: 2 lecturers or researchers, 3 out of the 11 student representatives, and 1 administrator, although more than half of the students are women, and the proportion of women lecturers is more than one-third. Similarly among the 20 top positions at the University (rectors, deans, directors, etc.) only one is occupied by a woman, while among Heads of Department and of Research Units there are no women (Széchy, 1996).

Table 6.3 Number of teaching staff according to teaching rank

Total	Prof.	Reader	Assoc. prof.	Assist.	Lang. t.	Phys. ed. t.	Coll. t.	Total
No.	2,525	4,205	6,276	4,141	1,390	342	223	19,103
%	13.22	22.01	32.86	21.68	7.28	1.79	1.17	100
of which Female No.	203	918	2,148	1,650	935	79	41	5,974
%	3.28	14.83	34.70	26.65	15.10	1.28	0.61	100

Note:
Of teaching staff, the proportion of female teachers is 35.64%.
Source: Statistical information: Higher Education 1994/95, Budapest, 1996, Ministry of

Reasons for the underrepresentation of women in senior positions

There are both objective and subjective reasons why women are pushed to the background in connection with the leading positions in state education. Mention must first be made of the serious lack of recognition accorded to the moral and material importance of the teaching profession. In general, the Hungarian National Report (1995) to the 4th World Conference on Women in Beijing concluded that: 'the wages of teachers are the lowest among educated professionals' (Beijing Statement, 1996). In 1993 the average wage of a man working in state education was 38,654 Hungarian Forints (HuF) per month; the average wage of a woman doing the same job was 29,364 HuF per month (at that time equivalent to less than US$300). This was approximately 40 per cent less than the average wage of other educated professionals, and 60–80 per cent less than the average wage of white collar workers in the financial and industrial sectors. In 1993–4 men working in state education received a 7.7 per cent rise on their wages for the previous year, but women received only 6.3 per cent, while inflation was running at over 20 per cent. At the same time men in other academic professions received a 20.4 per cent wage rise, and women 19.8 per cent. In 1993 women in state education earned 36.6 per cent less than men doing the same job. Since then, the situation has grown worse, since the real value of teachers' salaries has fallen still further. These factors reduce the attractiveness of the profession to those best qualified to practise it, which weakens teachers' dedication to their job, and increases the chance of them seeking another career (UN Fourth World Conference, 1995).

Objective factors militate against women white collar workers keeping up with their male colleagues in private study, creative experiments, and professional competition, especially in higher education and scientific research work. These include having children, doing household work, and the increasing cost of services which make a woman's work easier. The traditional division of labour within families resulted in a dual burden for working women, who continue to bear the brunt of household duties, apart from home repairs (Eberhardt, 1991). In addition, women, especially those with outstanding talent and achievements, are not given the help they need (scholarships, study leave, study tours, etc.) to compensate for their patently disadvantageous circumstances (Ferge, 1995).

The subjective prejudices that work against the appointment of women who have or expect to have children are especially strong where senior positions are concerned, and even the best qualified women find it difficult to fight for recognition of their ability. The complex tasks of family, profession, further study, and public appearance, demand increased energy from women. The above-mentioned prejudices make it difficult for them to win promotions or new appointments in competition with men, to obtain *Habilitation* or further academic degrees in order to gain tenure and to secure personal and professional acceptance.

In the wider political arena, the constitutional equality of women is not matched by reality. Since multiparty elections were introduced in 1990, fewer women have been nominated as candidates, or elected to Parliament, than in the 1980s. In 1985, 25 per cent of MPs were women, and by 1990 this had dropped to 7 per cent. The Hungarian Women's Council was the only women's organisation of the ruling party before the 1990s. Since then, it has become disenfranchised as the Alliance of Hungarian Women and some newer women's organisations have been founded. At present their effects have yet to be felt (Eberhardt, 1991).

All this must be seen in a context where the overall economic conditions of family life and of the education system are under serious threat.

THE EFFECT OF RECESSION AND CHANGES IN THE SYSTEM

The world economic crisis that began in the mid-1970s and continued to be felt into the next decade halted economic development in Hungary and in the whole of Europe's Central Eastern region. It led to the depression and grave socio–political crisis which eventually brought about a change in the entire system. Amongst other effects, such as a profound shift in cultural values and the freezing of scientific development and investment, the result of the so-called 'transformation crisis' was a worsening in the economic and educational prospects for the population at large. There is an urgent need for educational reform, not just in response to this crisis, but also to meet the new expectations which have led to the modernisation of education throughout the world.

The move from a centrally planned to a market economy has had profound effects, particularly in terms of high inflation and zero economic growth. Hungarian production has fallen by 20 per cent since 1989 as a consequence of the economic crisis, and some two-thirds of the population have suffered a rapid decline in their living standards. The unemployment rate amongst women has increased by 20 per cent – greater than that of men. With a very low level of unemployment before 1989, this has had a strong psychological effect on the workforce (Eberhardt, 1991). On average, male manual workers are paid 30–40 per cent more than women, while male white-collar workers enjoy a 50–60 per cent pay advantage over their female colleagues. The social security system that was designed to help women, mothers, and their families, is in a state of collapse. Unemployment is higher for young women starting out in their careers than for men; unskilled women are the first to be dismissed, and the early retirement system has been used chiefly against women (UN Fourth World Conference, 1995).

The impoverishment of large numbers of women has become one of the gravest problems facing Hungary today: the image of the family with two wage-earners is no longer typical, since over half of all families either have one wage-earner or none at all. This contrasts with the 1980s, where many wage-earners had second jobs, such as taxi-driving, in order to earn enough for a flat or a car. This resulted in very long working hours and stress on family life (Eberhardt, 1991). This phenomenon continues to exist today, mostly among the middle classes, who take on extra work in order to compensate for the decline in the real value of their earnings and social status. The participation of the unemployed in the black economy also places them in a vulnerable situation, with uncontrolled working hours and conditions. This rapid deterioration of the economic foundations of family life is having serious effects on the upbringing of children, the relationship between women and men, and the incidence of divorce.

Women's health is rapidly deteriorating as a consequence of all these socio-economic changes. The birth rate has fallen to among the lowest in Europe (at 1.7 live births per 1,000 people), and population is in absolute decline (UN Fourth World Conference Report, 1995). Almost half the country's crèche places have been closed. Nursery schools have not lost so many places, but parents have to pay more for them, as they do for school meals. A significant proportion of impoverished families are unable to pay for these services. The situation of mothers who have to care for children on their own is especially difficult. The spectre of the starving child is reappearing in Hungary (Ferge, 1995).

Before the 1990s, 70 per cent of nurseries were provided by the state and 30 per cent by companies; now many workplace nurseries have been closed. The present lack of places affects families living in suburbs and small outlying villages in particular, where the need for social and educational help is greatest. A number of denominational, charitable foundation, and private nursery schools have appeared on the scene, but they are very few in number and the private schools are in any case designed to educate the children of a wealthy élite.

Although public sector daycare remains free of charge, after-school provision now reflects the market orientation of education, with the introduction of charges for meals, sports and cultural activities. As Ferge comments, the increasing role of the market has had the effect of separating a formerly integrated system into institutions serving the wealthy and the poor, in the fields of education and health, from the earliest age on (Ferge, 1995).

The new educational legislation is designed to promote a network of schools in the public, municipal, church, and foundation sectors at compulsory school age as well. Such schools are often selective, and can charge fees which are not affordable by the poorer sections of the community. Because of rising unemployment, the number of students in academic secondary schools is increasing. There is also some evidence that the rate of enrolment in higher education is increasing too, particularly in those areas where women are well represented (e.g. law and medicine) because of economic pressures (Hrubos, 1996). This will in turn present problems for teacher supply.

The economic crisis presents a lasting threat to the development of public education. For well over a decade the real value of budget subsidies for education has stagnated. Schools have been merged, jobs have been lost, and many teachers have left the profession, because of lowered wages.

CONCLUSION

In the field of state education in Hungary there is a *de jure* right which guarantees that women have equal rights where a promotion to a senior position has to be made. However, the *de facto* achievement of this right is part of a longer socio-historical process, for which the necessary social, cultural, moral, and, in many cases, legal conditions do not exist. The two most important requirements for achieving equality for women are the stabilisation of our economy, and further modernisation of basic areas of our social life.

The further development of equal rights for women also requires opportunities for women to carry out further study in every field of education; for example, the provision of scholarships and study leave for talented women to develop their creative work.

The specific role of women demands the best possible social support for preparing for family life, for accepting and bringing up children, and for the creation of a new family model, in which the household duties can be fairly shared. It is therefore vital to introduce family allowances into a more just taxation and income distribution system. Likewise, the large-scale development and provision of the family support services and of a fair price system for household appliances, convenience foods, canteen meals, laundry services, etc. is also crucial.

A greater degree of proportional representation and more active participation by women in top educational jobs are also essential. In order to create the adequate objective conditions for this, we have to find reasonable solutions to harmonise professional and family life, and subjective prejudices and obstacles relating to the wage system have to be overcome. The work of women's organisations dedicated to defending the specific interests of women in the workplace, in local government, and in every other sphere of public life should be encouraged. In turn, equality of women may develop dynamically in response to political change.

REFERENCES

Beijing Statement (1996) Fourth World Conference on Women, *Social Review* (Társadalmi Szemle), Vol. 51.

Eberhardt, E. (1991) *Women of Hungary*, Brussels, Commission of the European Communities.

Ferge, Z. (1995) *Challenges and Constraints in Social Policy. Question Marks; the Hungarian Government, 1994–5* (in Hungarian), Budapest, Korridor Research Centre on the Political Sciences of the Scientific Academy of the Hungarian Republic.

Gazsó, F. (1994) *Public Education and the Labyrinth of Power. Government on the Scales, 1990–1994* (in Hungarian), Budapest, Korridor Research Centre on the Political Sciences of the Scientific Academy of the University of Budapest.

Hrubos, I. (1996) Education and Professional Qualifications of Women in Hungary (in Hungarian), *Social Review*, Vol. 51, pp. 55–8.

Köpeczi, B. (1986) *The Road to Hungarian Culture 1945–1985*, Budapest, Kossuth.

Ministry of Education and Culture (1996) *Report on Hungarian Public Education, 1995* (in Hungarian), Budapest.

Okker Education Office (1995a), *Statistical Information: Lower grade education 1993–4*, Budapest.

Okker Education Office (1995b) *Statistical Information: Nursery schools 1993–4*,

Budapest.

Okker Education Office (1996) *Statistical Information: Higher education 1994–5*, Budapest.

Pölöskei, F., Gergely, J. and Izsák, L. (eds.) (1996) *The History of Hungary 1918–90* (in Hungarian), Budapest, Korvina Publishing House.

Szebenyi, P. (1992) State Centralization and School Autonomy: Processes of Educational Change in Hungary, *Oxford Studies in Comparative Education*, Vol. 21, no. 1, pp. 57–70.

Széchy, E. (1987) The Problems of Female Education in Hungary, *Comparative Education*, Vol. 23, no. 1, pp. 69–84.

Széchy, E. (1996) Nök az Eötvos Loránd Tudományegyetem Vezetésében, (unpublished manuscript in Hungarian).

United Nations Fourth World Conference on Women (1995) Budapest: National Report of Hungary.

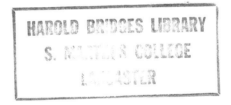

7

Ireland

Kathleen Lynch

The position of women in Irish society is changing. Changes are occurring across all institutions, including the law, employment and education.This chapter analyses the position of women in the Republic of Ireland. Northern Ireland is part of the UK and has quite a different system of educational management. Where data refer to Northern Ireland, this is made clear in the text.

WOMEN, POLICY AND THE LAW

Under the Irish Constitution (Article 40.1) all persons are equal before the law. Yet there is no clause which explicitly promotes equality between women and men such as there is in the Basic Law of Germany (Article 3 (2)). Indeed, if one were to assess the position of women in Irish society by examining the provisions relating to women within the Constitution, a bleak traditional picture emerges. Under the Constitution drafted in 1937 (under the considerable influence of the Roman Catholic hierarchy at the time) a woman's place was defined as being in the home. Not only does Article 41.2 assign to women a domestic role as wives and mothers, it implicitly suggests that womanhood and motherhood are synonymous: 'In particular, the State recognises that by her life within the home, woman gives to the State a support without which the common good cannot be achieved. The State shall, therefore, endeavour to ensure that mothers shall not be obliged by economic necessity to engage in labour to the neglect of their duties in the home.'

This provision is now regarded as dated and it has been criticised severely in recent years. Consequently the recent Report of the Constitution Review Group recommended that the original article be deleted and that it be replaced by a gender neutral statement which would value the importance of caring in society without assigning the responsibility for it to any particular gender group (Constitution Review Group, 1996).

In spite of the traditional constitutional status assigned to women, major changes have been occurring in the legislative spheres which have benefited women. While some of these have been introduced due to internal pressures from the women's movement and other social groups, such as the legalisation of divorce in 1996, most of the changes in employment law have resulted from EU directives.[1] It was Ireland's accession to the UN Convention on the Elimination of All Forms of Discrimination Against Women in 1985 that precipitated the enactment of the Irish Nationality and Citizenship Act, 1986, and the Domicile and Recognition of Foreign Divorces Act, 1986, both of which gave greater rights to married women.

One of the areas where there has been some advancement is in the establishing of structures, and in the formulation of policies at a centralised government level to promote greater equality between women and men. Two Commissions on the Status of Women have reported. The first Commission (1972) paved the way for the formation of the Council for the Status of Women (CSW) in 1973. This body is now reconstituted as the National Women's Council of Ireland. The latter functions to co-ordinate the work of women's organisations, to examine and contest discrimination against women, and to consider legislative proposals. It is actively involved in negotiating at central government level on behalf of women.

The Second Commission on the Status of Women reported in 1993. A Monitoring Committee was set up to review the implementation of its recommendations and its first report was presented in 1994. Some legislative changes have been implemented on foot of the recommendations of the 1993 report [2] Others are at the draft Bill stage, such as the new Employment Equality Bill (1996) and the Equal Status Bill (the full text of which is yet to be published).[3]

The Employment Equality Agency was another body established (in 1977) to promote greater equality for women in employment. It has done much to promote the awareness and practice of equal opportunities policies in the workplace. However, its powers and capacities are limited by the nature of the equality legislation drawn up in the 1970s which many regard as weak liberal legislation, only addressing the more obvious forms of direct discrimination but not addressing indirect discrimination effectively (Connelly, 1993).

On the political front there have also been a number of important changes. The election of Mary Robinson as President and Head of State in 1990 was a major boost for the status of women in Ireland. As a well known feminist, socialist and highly respected human rights lawyer, she symbolised a new era of politics and change, not only for women but for many other marginalised groups. Yet change in political structures facilitating women has been slow; only two of the smaller political parties operate a quota system for women in the selection of candidates for election (the Green party and Democratic Left) and significantly fewer women than men contest elections. Currently just 12 per cent of both *Dail* (the national parliament) and local government members are women although their representation in the European parliament is better with one-third of the 12 MEPs being women. An encouraging development in 1982 was the appointment of a Minister of State at the Department of the Taoiseach (the Prime Minister) who is responsible for promoting action on women's affairs. This junior ministry was subsequently changed to a full ministerial post in the early 1990s and is now the Ministry for Equality and Law Reform. It is not exclusively concerned with equality for women however, as it has responsibility for all types of equality issues including disability, race, ethnicity, sexual orientation, etc.

At the policy level, the government has formally adopted policies for promoting equal opportunities between men and women in employment, legislation and education. Prior to the formation of the current government, an agreement was reached between the coalition members that all government-appointed boards and bodies would have at least 40 per cent women (and men). The government has been generally consistent in operating this principle and it has radically altered the composition of certain public boards. It has, of course, met with opposition, and one of the consistent problems which the government faces is that bodies with a right to nominate members to public boards such as employers and trade unions, for example, have not always honoured the gender quota principal. Consequently a review of publicly appointed boards in 1996 found that just 33 per cent of all appointees were women.

WORK AND EMPLOYMENT

Like most women elsewhere, Irish women work long hours, very often in areas of work where the value of their labour goes unrecorded (Lynch and McLaughlin, 1995). The largest single area of work for women in Ireland is that of full-time homeworker although this is officially recorded as 'home duties'(sic) and is not regarded as being part of the 'labour force'. In 1995, there were almost 618,000 women recorded in the Labour Force Survey as being on 'home duties' (i.e. full-time unpaid at home) while just 502,000 were in the so-called labour force (i.e. in the paid labour market). This means that only 36.5 per cent of women over fifteen years of age in Ireland are in the labour market compared with 70 per cent of men (see Table 7.1). There are indications however that the participation of women in the paid labour force is increasing at a considerably faster rate than that of men, although much of this increase is in the more casualised (part-time and/or temporary) areas of employment in the services sector especially (Employment Equality Agency, EEA, 1995).

The proportion of employed women who are in part-time jobs has grown steadily over the last ten years, from 13.4 per cent in 1987 to 23 per cent in 1995. Yet, only 5 per cent of men in paid work are in part-time employment (Employment Equality Agency, EEA, 1995; CSO, 1996). Overall, women comprise 72 per cent of all part-time employees (CSO, 1996).

Table 7.1 Principal economic status of women age 15 and over, 1995

	Women		Men	
	N*	%	N*	%
At work	454,800	33.0	778,800	59.0
Unemployed	47,900	4.0	142,000	11.0
Student	169,300	12.0	163,300	12.0
Work at home	617,600	45.0	9,900	1.0
Retired	56,100	4.0	173,300	13.0
Unable to work	18,800	1.4	43,400	3.3
Other	12,900	0.6	13,200	0.7
TOTAL	1,377,300	100.0	1,324,000	100.0

*Figures are rounded.
Source: Central Statistics Office, CSO, 1996.

Not only are women more likely to be part-time workers than men, they are also heavily concentrated in particular fields of employment. Currently women comprise 78 per cent of clerical workers and 58 per cent of service workers (CSO, 1996). Textile and clothing workers are also predominantly female (58 per cent) while just over half of all professional and technical workers are women (mostly nurses and teachers). In contrast, 70 per cent of production workers are men and 92 per cent of farmers (CSO, 1996). This pattern has not changed since 1987 (EEA, 1995:12). The horizontal segregation of women is also accompanied by a vertical segregation, both in terms of status and power within occupations, and in terms of income.

Only 13 per cent of all self employed people and 16 per cent of all employers are women, although women comprise 43 per cent of all employees (CSO, 1996). Moreover, data for the industrial sector shows that women's average hourly earnings were only 70 per cent of men's in 1993 (EEA, 1995).[4] Although there has been no major study of the reasons for gender differentials in income across the different sectors of employment, the available data would suggest at least three reasons. First, differentials would seem to arise from the gender segregated nature of the labour market through which women are heavily concentrated in low wage areas such as the cleaning, catering and other general service sectors (Combat Poverty and ICTU, 1990). A second factor contributing to gender differences in earnings is that women, within both higher paying sectors such as the professions, and highly wage differentiated fields such as the civil service and private business, are less likely to occupy senior posts than men (EEA, 1995). Finally, the fact that women are often less available to undertake extra overtime work due to their caring and domestic commitments also contributes to lower earnings. Caring and domestic commitments also affect their promotional prospects in other fields as they lack the availability (for study and extra work) and visibility which is required.

Women's participation in employment also varies with their marital status, particularly if they have children. While there is evidence that women are staying on in employment after marriage (married women now comprise 45 per cent of all women working compared with 30 per cent in 1981) there is considerable evidence that the nature of their participation changes when children are born. The fact that their participation pattern changes is borne out by aggregate data on employment patterns for women of different ages and for married as opposed to single women. While just over 50 per cent of married women aged from 20–34 were active in the paid labour force in 1993, only 36 per cent of married women aged 35–44 were participating (EEA, 1995). Figures for the labour force in 1995 show that while 41 per cent of all single women were in the paid labour force, just 30 per cent of married women were (the comparable figures for men were 70 per cent and 59 per cent). Interestingly the participation rates for separated and widowed women is very similar to that of men (CSO, 1996).

One of the factors which still militates against women's successful participation in the paid labour market is their unequal responsibility for childcare. The limited data available shows that women carry a disproportionate responsibility for childcare even when they are in full-time employment (Lynch and McLaughlin, 1995). In addition, there is no state-supported childcare service except in certain areas of high socio-economic disadvantage (McKenna, 1988). What this means, in effect, is that women with dependent children find it very difficult to work especially if they are in low paid employment. The cost of childcare is often too high relative to their disposable income. Unless they are in a position to avail of family support for childcare, lowly paid women with young children often simply cannot afford to work! Women also take a disproportionate responsibility for other forms of care, including care of dependent older persons, and lack of support services in this area also militates against women staying within, or re-entering, the labour market (Lynch and McLaughlin, 1995).

Thus, while several legislative changes have guaranteed Irish women equal rights with men, these legislative changes have precipitated limited changes in the socio-economic status of the majority of women; men have maintained their comparative advantage. Women still constitute a majority of those in the part-time labour market and of those engaged in unpaid home work. They are far less likely to be employers, or to own land or other productive property, than men. And those who are employees tend to earn less per hour than their male colleagues. The latter occurs due to both horizontal segregation (concentration in those areas of employment which have lower pay) and vertical segregation (being located on the lower rungs of the occupational ladder within a given field).

The high concentration of married women working in the home, is one of the features of Irish society which distinguished it from other European countries. While there is no doubt that married women in Ireland are more financially dependent on their spouses than in many other European countries, this pattern is changing fast. A recent Labour Force estimate for the first half of 1996 claims that the number of women at home had dropped dramatically in the previous twelve months, while a study of almost 1,600 second-level students in twelve different centres throughout the country (in 1995) would confirm this trend. Just over 58 per cent of the students said their mothers had jobs (29 per cent full-time and 29 per cent part-time) which is far above the national recorded figures for women with dependent children at work (Lynch and Lodge, 1997). One reason for the difference in the official (see Table 7.2) and the unofficial figures could be the operation of the so-called 'informal economy' which has been documented in Northern Ireland but which has not been systematically analysed in the Republic (Leonard, 1994).

To suggest that the position of women in Irish society is one of unbridled subservience to men would, therefore, be far from true. Over the last 25 years, major social and economic changes have occurred in Ireland which have advantaged women in several ways. The most obvious economic development was that Ireland changed from being a predominantly rural society, largely dependent on farming, to being a highly educated, urban-industrial society increasingly dependent on manufacturing and service industries. Industrial expansion led to increased job opportunities for women. Married women, in particular, became much more active in the labour force. From Table 7.2 one can see that women comprise a noticeably larger proportion of the labour force in 1995 (35 per cent) than they did 17 years previously (26 per cent) (and our own research noted above would indicate that is a significant underestimate of the number of married women at work). Even if one accepts official figures on married women's participation in the paid labour force, though still low by international standards, their participation rate is much greater in 1995 than it was in 1971: while married women comprised only 14 per cent of the female labour force in 1971, they constituted almost 51 per cent in 1995. With greater labour force participation came greater financial independence – at least for those who were in paid employment.

Table 7.2 Changes in women's (paid) labour force participation from 1971 to 1995

Labour Force (paid)	1971	1981	1988	1995
Total*	1,125,000	1,272,000	1,309,800	1,423,500
Total women	289,300	370,000	399,500	502,700
Women as % of total	25.7	29.1	30.5	35.3
Married women** in paid labour force	39,200	112,000	164,800	254,400
Married women as a % of the paid female labour force	13.6	30.2	41.3	50.6

*Figures are rounded.
**Includes separated and divorced women.
Sources: John Blackwell (1989) Women in The Labour Force, Dublin: Employment Equality Agency, 1989, Table 3.1 and Central Statistics Office, Labour Force Surveys 1988 and 1995, Dublin: Central Statistics Office (CSO, 1989, 1996).

THE IRISH EDUCATION SYSTEM

Most Irish children start their schooling in the infant classes of the national (primary) system at age four and complete eight years later at age 12. Eighty per cent of the age cohort go on to complete second level over six years at age 18 (approx.) with 40 per cent of the age cohort going on to higher education. The aim is to increase the completion rate at second level to 90 per cent by the year 2000 and to have 50 per cent of all school entrants transferring to higher education (Department of Education, 1995a). While there are some fee-paying institutions in all sectors of education, over 90 per cent of students at each level attend schools, colleges and universities which do not charge fees, up to and including undergraduate education.

Preschool education is for children under 4 years. Preschools are only state aided in designated disadvantaged areas and even in these areas, preschool education is not consistently available across the country. There is also a growing further, adult and community education sector which is highly diverse but in receipt of limited state aid.

There are 3,203 primary schools in Ireland and these cater for just over half a million pupils. These are known as National Schools although all but 12 of them are in fact denominationally-run, 92 per cent being Roman Catholic. All National Schools receive well over 90 per cent of their funding from the state; the remaining funds have to be raised locally (by the Church, parish or community) to help with the day-to-day running of the school. This practice arose in the context of the denominational character of the schools. It is a practice which penalises schools in low income communities. There are a very small number of fee-paying primary schools, mostly in the larger cities, but these cater for less than 2 per cent of all primary pupils (Department of Education, 1995b).

There are 782 second-level schools catering for 371,000 students. Four different types of second-level school exist: secondary schools are the most common comprising 59 per cent of all second-level schools. Almost one-third (32 per cent) are vocational while the remaining 9 per cent represent a combination of community schools and colleges, and comprehensive schools (Department of Education, 1995b). While secondary schools were traditionally the most academically-oriented, all second-level schools now prepare students for the same public examinations although vocational schools generally tend to have more technologically-oriented subjects than secondary schools. Fee-paying schools (including day schools and boarders) cater for approximately 10 per cent of all second-level students.

Third-level education is divided into a number of different sectors, with the largest and most powerful being the university sector. However, over the last 20 years there has been a rapid expansion in the non-university sector with the building of 11 Regional Technical Colleges and the amalgamation into one body of a range of Dublin colleges to form the Dublin Institute of Technology. The Teacher Education Colleges, which educate primary teachers, represent another sector although they are currently becoming closely affiliated to two separate universities. A range of private third-level colleges, most of which are offering the 'chalk and talk' subjects especially business and accounting, have also been developed in the last 10 years as the demand for higher education continues to grow. There are almost 100,000 students in higher education and there are no fees for undergraduate courses except in some of the private colleges.

Ireland does not have a well developed further education sector although this has begun to change in the last 5 years especially. There are now almost 22,000 students attending further education courses annually, mostly Post-Leaving Certificate courses. These are run in second-level (especially vocational) schools as further education colleges have not been built. (There is spare capacity in many schools now as the birth rate has declined steadily since 1980.) In addition, 5,000 long term unemployed people were involved in the Vocational and Technical Opportunities scheme in 1995, which is essentially a second-chance education scheme. There is also a very vibrant adult and community education sector (70 per cent of attendees are women), although it is poorly resourced with many courses being self-funding in terms of direct staff costs. Adult and community education has developed on an *ad hoc* basis with neither systematic planning, funding nor accreditation (Coolahan, 1994). New structures are now being put in place however, at both regional and national level, to address these problems.

Undoubtedly one of the changes which most benefited women in Ireland in the last 25 years has been the expansion and development of the education system. From the late 1960s onwards, formal education became the principal medium through which privilege and occupational advantage could be attained or retained. Ireland moved from being a society in which 40 per cent of the adult population were self-employed in the early 1950s (mostly on farms, small shops and businesses – which were almost invariably inherited by a male member of the family) to being an employee society where occupational opportunity was closely correlated with educational credentials. Surveys of school-leavers over the last 10 years show that there is a strong correlation between employment opportunities and the level of the educational credential obtained: the higher the credential, the higher the opportunity of obtaining employment. Cultural property, in the form of educational credentials, has become crucial in mediating the relationship between class origins and destinations (Breen *et al.*, 1990). Women, particularly middle class women, have benefited from this shift to cultural property as a tool in determining occupational opportunity.

Over the years women have had slightly higher retention rates in second-level education than men although the gap has narrowed recently: in 1992, 52 per cent of all of those who took the Leaving Certificate Examination (the final examination at the end of second level education for all students) were women. Women's performance in public examinations is also higher than that of men in both the Leaving Certificate and the Junior Certificate (age 15 approx.) examinations (Department of Education, 1995b).

Within higher education, women's entry rate is now almost equal to that of men (49 per cent of all entrants in 1992) and it has been rising steadily for the last 15 years. Women comprise a higher proportion of new entrants to the university sector (53 per cent) although they comprise a lower proportion of new entrants (43 per cent) in the technological sectors (Clancy, 1995).

It must be noted however, that among both women and men, it is people from middle class backgrounds who have benefited most from the great educational expansion of the last 25 years. While women of all social classes are significantly better educated than they were 20 years ago, in common with so many other countries, liberal equal opportunities policies have benefited the relatively advantaged within each gender group (Blossfeld and Shavit, 1993; Lynch, 1996).

WOMEN IN TEACHING

Research conducted on the hidden curriculum of Irish second-level schools (Lynch, 1989) shows that there is a dualism at the heart of Irish educational and cultural thought about the position of women in work. On the one hand women are socialised in schools to be highly successful academically. The achievement orientation in all-girls schools, as measured in terms of practices and procedures undertaken by the school itself to reward and encourage high academic attainment, was found to be higher than in all-boys schools (Lynch, 1989). On the other hand, girls are still socialised, both in and out of schools, to play very traditional roles as the carers and bearers of society in a way that boys are not (Hannan et al., 1996). Both past (Lynch, 1989) and ongoing research (Lynch and Lodge, 1997) suggests that girls are socialised simultaneously into two strong sets of cultural identities, as high achievers on the one hand, and as carers on the other. The socialisation of boys is much more singular and career-focused with relatively little attention being paid to their future roles as carers.

Thus while women are increasingly expected to work, and to be qualified for work, they are also expected to be the principal carers in society. Men are not socialised strongly to be equal partners in caring. When care responsibilities arise, particularly with children, male attitudes are still a major barrier to equality for women. While such attitudes are by no means culturally exclusive, what compounds the difficulty for women working outside the home in Ireland is the lack of adequate supports for childcare. There is no state-supported childcare system except in a small number of low income communities (McKenna, 1988).

Teachers, especially primary teachers in Ireland, are widely regarded as an occupational group which experiences relatively low levels of conflict between their occupational and their family/caring roles. The reason for this is simply that the working day for teachers is the same as the children's school day. This is not to say that teachers do not have preparation and correction work to do after school; they do, especially in second-level, but this work can be undertaken at home. What generally happens therefore is that once a child is old enough to attend primary school at age 4, the teacher's working day is the same as the child's school day. While this is more true of primary than second-level teachers (most second-level schools do not finish until 4 p.m. while primary schools finish, on average, one hour earlier) teachers are in a much better position than almost any other occupational group to combine childcare with employment. Moreover, teachers, in common with civil and other public service workers, can avail of a range of different types of leave arrangements to accommodate their care work (including up to five years unpaid career break). They may then return to their jobs if they wish.

Thus while women teachers are no different to other women in terms of the strong cultural expectation that they will be the principal carer in the household, the fact that teaching accommodates this role much better than other jobs, gives them greater scope to stay on at work after children are born. Although there are no national data available on the proportion of women who continue to teach full time after the birth of their child(ren), circumstantial evidence would suggest that the proportion is high by comparison with other occupations.

TEACHING IN IRELAND

The working conditions of teachers in the three sectors (primary, second-level and third-level) where salaries are paid entirely by the state, are generally good and secure. Within these sectors, there are, however, a minority of teachers and lecturers, especially in the universities, who are part-time and/or temporary whose working conditions are far from ideal. There has, in fact, been a growing casualisation of university teaching in recent years (IFUT, 1996). Almost all teachers in the further, adult and community sectors of education are temporary, and mostly part-time. Many work for hourly rates with all the insecurity and unpredictability that this entails.

Teaching (at primary and second-level) is now regarded as a secure and safe occupation rather than an exciting high-paying one. It is an increasingly feminine profession, especially at primary level, where 90 per cent of entrants to primary teacher education colleges are women (Clancy, 1995). At second-level, 63 per cent of all new teachers registered with the Teacher Registrations Council in 1993/94 were also women (Department of Education, 1995b). It is only within higher education that men outnumber women. Although the precise figures for new appointments across higher education are not available, data for the universities show that 21 per cent of all academic staff are women, although the proportion of junior lecturers who are women was 39 per cent in 1993/94 (it must be noted however, that while many of these are new entrants, not all are), up from 24 per cent in 1983/84 (Smith, 1996).

The proportion of women teaching in the technological sectors of higher education is slightly lower than in the universities, at just over 19 per cent in the Dublin Institute of Technology in 1995 (see Table 7.3). Although the complete figures for all the colleges in different sectors is not available, estimates suggest that just 25 per cent of all academic posts in the eleven Regional Technical Colleges (RTCs) are held by women (Burke, 1996). These women are by no means equally divided across faculties however. Data from nine RTC colleges shows that 37 per cent of those employed at lecturer level or above in the Business/Professional/ Management faculties are women, while women comprise only 5 per cent of those in the engineering schools (Burke, 1996).

Table 7.3   Proportion of women in teaching posts, principalships and senior management (%)

School Type	Teachers	Principals	Ratio of Female Teachers to Principals/Heads
Primary (1995) (1,2)	78.0	46.0	1.7:1
Second Level (1995)	54.0	29.0	1.9:1
of whom			
Secondary(3,4,5)	58.2	43.2	1.3:1 (all)
		14.7 (lay) 28.5 (religious)	4.0:1 (lay)
Vocational (6)	47.0	11.0	4.3:1
Community/Comprehensive	49.6	8.5	5.8:1(all)
		6.1 (lay) 2.4 (religious)	8.1:1 (lay)
Regional Technical (1995)	25.0	6.1 (Head of Department)	4.1:1 Colleges
Dublin Institute (1996)	19.4	9.0 (Senior Lecturer Grade 2):	2.2:1
of Technology Colleges		this is the Grade for heads of schools which is a more senior post than head of department	
University (1995)	21.0	5.0 (Professors and Associate Professors)	4.2:1

Notes:
1. Almost 90% of female primary school principals are lay.
2. Just over 95% of male primary school principals are lay.
3. 34% of all female secondary school principals are lay.
4. 74.1% of all male secondary school principals are lay.
5. 42% of principals in all types of secondary schools are lay men and 14.7% are religious men or priests i.e. 56.7% overall are men.
6. Almost all teachers and principals are lay persons in vocational schools.

Sources: Department of Education for all levels: Personnel Departments of the Universities and other higher education institutions; Higher Education Authority, Irish National Teachers Organisation, Association of the Secondary Teachers, Ireland, Teacher Union of Ireland and O. Egan (ed.) (1996) *Women Staff in Irish Colleges*, Higher Education Equality Unit, Cork.

Teachers in Ireland have traditionally had high status (Coolahan, 1981). This was true in rural areas especially, where, until the 1960s, teachers were often the only people in a rural community with third-level education, apart from the priest and the doctor. In a society which valued education, but where education was a scarce resource, teachers had high standing. After the introduction of free second-level education for all students in the late 1960s (primary was always free from the foundation of the State) and the expansion of higher education in the 1970s and 80s, the status and influence of teachers changed. While they are still respected, they are now just one of the many groups with higher education in a given community. Indeed several people, even in rural areas, may not only have greater exposure to higher education than teachers, they may also have higher paying jobs. Teachers have become just one of a host of professionals working in the public and private sectors.

Another factor which has influenced people's views on teaching is the high level of stress reported among second-level (but not primary) teachers. Over the last 10 years, the teacher unions have undertaken a number of studies highlighting the stress levels of second-level teachers especially. One of the main reasons for increasing stress is the pressure on teachers to ensure that students get high grades in their Leaving Certificate Examination so that they can compete successfully for entry to higher education.[5] The fact that second-level schools are now serving almost the entire youth population up to 17 or 18 years of age, and that teachers themselves are an ageing work force may be contributing also to the increase in stress.[6] The students attending second-level schools are far more heterogeneous than they were 25 years ago, and many teachers find the adaptation to a more diverse (and sometimes disinterested) student body a difficult adjustment to make.

Despite recent developments, teaching is still regarded as a good secure occupation, especially for women. The hours of work are regarded as ideal for child rearing (which is still regarded in practice as primarily a woman's responsibility). For men, primary and second-level teaching is not as highly regarded as it was traditionally, unless men enter managerial positions within schools. However, the fact that teaching (at all levels) is permanent and pensionable gives it high standing, especially in the context of a global economy where the casualisation of labour is the norm at all occupational levels. One of the annual indicators of the status of teaching is the Grade Point Average(GPA)[7] required in their Leaving Certificate to enter primary teacher education colleges; in Ireland, the GPA required for teacher education is still high relative to other degree programmes indicating the continued high status of teaching. Moreover, there is also keen competition at the postgraduate level for entry to the Higher Diploma in Education programmes (the programme which qualifies one to teach at second level).[8]

While the status of Irish teachers has changed with the expansion of professional employment opportunities in both the public and the private sectors, the power of their unions has not waned. Ireland has three major teacher trade unions and almost all teachers are union members.[9] By international standards, teacher unions in Ireland are well funded and highly organised. A review of Irish education by the OECD suggested that the teacher unions were the most powerful force in Irish education (OECD, 1991). There are a number of reasons why the teacher unions are powerful. First there is a long history of trade union organisation: the primary teacher union (the Irish National Teacher Organisation) was formed in 1848 and has been very active ever since then. Secondly, all three teacher unions work collaboratively through a loose federation agreement established in the 1980s. Third, education is regarded as a crucial asset in Ireland's economic development and teachers are regarded as central to that project.

Ireland has a centralised bargaining system for establishing the general parameters for wages and salary agreements. A series of national 'Programmes for Government' and 'Wage Agreements' have been negotiated every three or four years over the last 20 years, and the teacher unions have been key players in making such agreements, working through the umbrella trade union body, the Irish Congress of Trade Unions.

Primary and second-level teacher salaries are comprised of basically three elements: (1) the basic salary; (2) special qualification allowances, based on the level and nature of degrees and other relevant qualifications; and (3) allowances granted for posts of responsibility in schools. Salaries for teachers are regarded as quite good for younger teachers but only average for more senior teachers, especially for those who hold senior managerial positions as principals and vice-principals. From October 1st 1996, the starting salary (point 1 on the scale) for a teacher with an honours degree is approximately IR£15,500 while the top point of the 26 point scale for the same teacher without a post of responsibility is IR£28,411 (ASTI, 1996). Given that it can take several years to reach the top point on the scale, many teachers do not regard teaching as a particularly rewarding career financially. It is widely known, although not researched, that male teachers, especially those who have not been promoted to managerial positions, often have work-interests outside of teaching including farming, business, writing etc.

Salaries for school principals (head teachers) are only a few thousand pounds above those of classroom teachers at the top end of the scale (between IR£4,000 and IR£5,000 for the principal of an average size secondary school) (ASTI, 1996). Consequently there is a general belief that the salary of a principal does not take proper account of the longer hours and considerable responsibility and hassle which the principalship involves. This is certainly the belief at second level where a principalship is regarded as a particularly onerous job. While there is a series of reasons why salary scales for school principals are not that high, one reason is undoubtedly the fact that the principalships of most second-level schools have, until about 20 years ago, been the prerogative of religious personnel for whom salary scales were not an issue; there was no pressure built up to pay heads of schools salaries commensurate with their work load. Sixty per cent of Irish second-level schools are still owned by religious orders and other religious bodies, and it is only in the last 10 years especially that lay people are being regularly appointed as principals in such schools. The drop in entrants to religious life has made the option of retaining principalships in religious hands untenable. The historical legacy of relatively low salaries for principals, and limited promotion to middle management positions, is an inheritance therefore from the days when religious bodies owned and ran schools without any outside involvement from either teachers or parents. While religious bodies still exercise huge power over education in Ireland, only a small number of principals are now religious (see Table 7.3).

Salaries for lecturers in the higher education colleges and the universities are higher than those of teachers once one enters the career grade of college lecturer (starting salary of IR£21,065) although the starting point for a junior assistant lecturer is actually the same as that of a teacher in a second-level school. Salaries for professors range from IR£33,786 to IR£50,000 at the apex of the top professorship scale. It must be remembered that professorships in Irish universities are very limited in number being tied mostly to headships of departments. Permanent lecturers in the universities are not called professors unlike many mainland European countries. Only 20 per cent of all full-time university appointments are professorial and one-third of these are associate professors (Smith, 1996).

WOMEN'S POSITION IN EDUCATIONAL MANAGEMENT

Gender differences in the distribution of senior management posts in Irish education are marked at all levels of the education system (see Table 7.3). Representation at senior management levels is best at primary level and worst in the universities and other institutes of higher education. In addition, almost all the senior administrative posts in the Department of Education are held by men although women are in the majority in the civil service: in 1991, for example, the five assistant secretaries and the departmental secretary were all men (and still were in 1996); only 10 per cent of principal officers and 16 per cent of assistant principals were women (Drudy and Lynch, 1993). Within the inspectorate only 9 per cent of the posts from senior inspector upwards are held by women (INTO, 1995).

Primary and Second-Level Education

Women comprise 78 per cent of the teachers and 46 per cent of the principals in Ireland's 3,203 national primary schools. At second level, 29 per cent of all 782 school principals are women, although it must be noted that over half of these (57 per cent) are actually religious women who did not have to compete for jobs under open competition. As the women's own religious order ran the school, they had the authority to nominate one of their own members for the post subject to the approval of the Department of Education. Almost all religious principals (female and male) are in religious-run secondary schools.

There are three different types of schools at second level, each with its own traditions and administrative structures. Promotional opportunities for women (and men) are quite different across the school types. Secondary schools comprise the single largest category of school with 59 per cent of all schools being of this type. Secondary schools are not owned by the State.

They are owned and run by various bodies (mostly Catholic religious orders and diocesan clergy). The teachers are appointed by the school on the approval of the State Department of Education, and teachers in these, as in all schools, have their salaries paid directly or indirectly by the central exchequer via the Department of Education. While lay women comprise 54 per cent of the teachers in secondary schools only 14.7 per cent of the principals are lay women. In contrast, religious women constitute about 4.3 per cent of all teachers but they hold two-thirds of the female-held principalships. In vocational schools, where 47 per cent of the teachers are women, 11 per cent of the principalships are held by women, while in the community and comprehensive schools although half of the teachers are women only 6.1 per cent of principalships are held by lay women (see Table 7.3)

While the position of women at vice-principalship level, and in other senior posts is more favourable than it is at principalship level, it is still far from satisfactory (see Table 7.4). In primary and secondary schools, women are well represented at vice-principalship level; however, it must be remembered that within these schools such posts (and A and B promotional posts) are not filled by open competition but by seniority.[10] Thus the favourable representation of women cannot be attributed to their success in open competition. However, in those schools where senior posts are filled by competition, women tend to be seriously underrepresented, although not as seriously as is the case with principalships. Only one in four vice-principals in community and comprehensive schools are women, and somewhat less than one in four in vocational schools. The position with regard to A posts is also very unfavourable in these schools. While women's position in relation

Table 7.4 Gender differences in the distribution of vice-principalships and other promotional posts (%)

School Type	Vice-Principals		A posts		B posts	
	women	men	women	men	women	men
Primary (1995)	82.6	17.4	68.9	31.1	76.0	24.0
Secondary (1995)	41.3	58.7	47.3	52.7	54.1	45.9
Vocational (1996)	22.8	77.2	32.1	67.9	47.4	52.6
Community/Comprehensive(1995)	26.0	74.0	34.2	65.8	50.0	50.0

Higher education sector – percentage of posts held by women

Dublin Institute of Technology (1996) Senior Lecturer 1
18.0
Regional Technical Colleges (1995) Lecturer 2
16.5 (data available for only 6 of the 11 colleges)
Universities (1995) Senior/Statutory Lecturer
12.0

Sources: Department of Education for all levels: Personnel Departments of the Universities and other higher education institutions; Higher Education Authority, Irish National Teachers Organisation, Association of the Secondary Teachers, Ireland, Teacher Union of Ireland and O. Egan (ed.) (1996) *Women Staff in Irish Colleges,* Higher Education Equality Unit, Cork.

to B posts is slightly better than at other grades in vocational and community and comprehensive schools, it must be remembered that these are the lowest grade promotional posts. Moreover, women are heavily concentrated in the lowest points in the teaching scales in all types of second-level schools. While this is partly a function of the fact that even second-level teaching is becoming feminised (75 per cent of teachers under 30 years of age were women in vocational schools, 92.5 per cent of those under 30 years were women in the secondary sector, and 95 per cent in community and comprehensive schools in 1996; data received directly from the Teachers Union of Ireland) it is also a function of the failure of women to get promotion to more senior grades.

The fact that women are not getting promotion to middle management in proportion to their overall numbers when open competition exists, suggests that the so-called 'merit' system of promotion is far from favourable to women. It is rather ironic that it is only when promotional posts are given on the basis of seniority that women are likely to be adequately represented! Women's underrepresentation at middle management level means that they are significantly disadvantaged when it comes to seeking principalships as they may not be seen to have the relevant experience (Kellaghan and Fontes, 1985). Indeed, in some cases it is known that short lists for interviews for principalships and vice-principalships are drawn from A post holders only. Such practices, though they may be legally correct, indirectly discriminate against women, as women in community, comprehensive and vocational schools especially are significantly less likely to be A post holders than men.

Third-Level Education

Although the majority of teachers at second level are women, women are poorly represented in teaching in higher education. No more than a quarter of the lecturers in higher education colleges are women in any given sector. However, the proportion of junior lecturers who are women has risen significantly in recent years particularly in the universities where 39 per cent of all assistant lecturers were women in 1994 compared with 24 per cent in 1984 (Smith, 1996). Viewed in proportion to their representation in the teaching force, women are no better represented in senior posts in third-level education than they are overall in second level with the representation of women in senior professorial posts in the universities being particularly poor. Within the higher education sector, women's promotional rate is best in the Dublin Institute of Technology (DIT) Colleges and poorest in the universities.

The reasons for women's poor representation in teaching in higher education is related to a wide range of factors including the fact that much of the expansion in higher education in the last 20 years has been in the technological field where women are still poorly represented at undergraduate and graduate level; the availability of alternative well-paid and secure employment in science-related and other fields has also meant that well qualified women simply do not apply for university posts. The fact that, proportionately speaking, women are still underrepresented in doctoral programmes (both inside and outside Ireland) across most disciplines also means that they are often not in a position to compete for certain academic posts. Despite of all these considerations, however, one cannot discount the influence of male-dominated interview and selection boards. There are no legal or monetary sanctions imposed on the higher education colleges if they fail to have gender balanced boards of assessors.

Both appointments and promotions in the higher education sector are based on open competition. The general practice is for a given college to appoint a board of academic assessors which nominates candidates for posts and/or for promotion. Although no major study has been conducted on job selection and promotion practices, it is widely accepted within the university sector that while one's research and publications record is important at the selection stage, it is of overriding importance when it comes to promotion. Smith and Burke's (1988) study of women academics within University College Dublin suggested that one of the reasons that women might not fare as well as men in promotion is because they often lacked the necessary research profile, often devoting more of their time to teaching and administration, both of which counted for much less than research and publications.

APPLICATIONS AND APPOINTMENTS TO PRINCIPALSHIPS

A study of female primary teachers in the mid-1980s found that only 16 per cent of women who were in a position to apply for promotion intended to do so (Kellaghan and Fontes, 1985). The corresponding figure for men was 50 per cent. A survey of second-level teachers by the Teachers Union of Ireland a few years later indicated that there was an even lower level of interest in principalships among second-level teachers as only 3 per cent of the women surveyed aspired to be principals. However, roughly comparable proportions of women (38 per cent) and men (44 per cent) were actively seeking promotion (TUI 1990). Research by the Association of Secondary Teachers (ASTI) confirmed earlier findings regarding women's relative lack of interest in principalships; while 16 per cent of the men surveyed had actually applied for a principalship, only 5 per cent of women had done so (Gleeson, 1992).

More recent information received from the Secretariat of Secondary Schools (1993) confirms the survey findings among teachers. Their data suggests that only one in twelve of the applicants for principalships in the three years 1990–92, inclusive, have been women. Table 7.5 shows the more up-to-date pattern of appointments to principalships from 1991–1995 inclusive, although data is not available on the number and gender of applicants per place for those years.

Table 7.5   Appointments in secondary* schools: 1991–1995

	All Boys Schools N	All Boys Schools %	All Girls Schools N	All Girls Schools %	Co-educational Schools N	Co-educational Schools %
Women	0	0.0	13	62.0	6	23.0
Men	19	100.0	8	38.0	20	77.0
Total	19	100.0	21	100.0	26	100.0

*Secondary schools represent 59% of the 782 second-level schools. Total number appointed = 66: total women = 19 (29 per cent): total men = 47 (71%)
Source: Association of Secondary Teachers, Ireland (ASTI) *Report of the Equality Committee*, 1996.

There were 66 new principals appointed in the five years from 1991–1995 of whom 71 per cent were men. While eight men were appointed principals in girls' schools, no women were appointed principals in any of the boys' schools. The most revealing figure from Table 7.5 is that 77 per cent of the principals appointed in co-educational secondary schools were men. While it is not clear from the data available whether women applied for posts in either co-educational or single sex schools at the same rate as men, what is clear is that it was only in girls' schools that women were more likely to be appointed principals than men.

The application and appointment rates for women at primary level are somewhat better; female applicants outnumbered males in three out of the four years from 1989 to 1992 inclusive, and in both 1995 and 1996. However, women are still not applying in proportion to their representation in the teaching population (see Table 7.6). When one examines the number of female and male applicants for 1994/5 and 1995/6 combined, a slightly higher

Table 7.6   Primary school principalships: applications and appointments from 1983–1996

Year	Applicants Women (%)	Applicants Men (%)	Applicants N	Appointments Women (%)	Appointments Men (%)	Appointments N
1983/4	29	71	656	37	63	123
1984/5	38	62	483	44	56	80
1985/6	32	68	677	42	58	97
1986/7	32	68	558	45	55	89
1987/8	47	53	1422	45	55	112
1988/9	54	46	606	58	42	55
1989/90	48	52	754	55	45	82
1990/1	52	48	632	67	33	91
1991/2	51	49	473	51	49	100
1994/5	51	49	871	58	42	165
1995/6	52	48	630	56	44	127

Note: 1983/84–1985/86 inclusive there were 596 female and 1,220 male applicants; this represents a female:male (F:M) ratio of 0.49:1. The appointment ratio (F:M) for those years was 0.68:1. For 1989/90–1991/92 the female:male application ratio was 1:1 while the appointment ratio was 1.35:1. For 1994/5-1995/96 inclusive there were 773 female and 728 male applicants representing a female:male ratio of 1.1:1. The appointment ratio (F:M) for these years was 1.34:1.
Source: Equality Officer, Irish National Teachers Organisation (INTO).

proportion of women (773) to men (728) applied, giving a ratio of 1.1:1. This compares favourably with the 1989–1992 period when the ratio was 1:1, and with the earlier three year period, 1983–1986, when the ratio of female to male applicants was only 0.49:1. Thus, the ratio of female to male applicants has increased, albeit slowly, over the past decade. However, while the trend for women interested in positions of authority can be viewed as more positive, it must be borne in mind that 78 per cent of primary teachers are women.

One of the questions which is raised in the literature about principalships, and what is clearly an issue at second level, is the proportion of women who obtain principalships in co-educational schools. From Table 7.7 it is clear that women are quite well represented in principalships in co-educational primary schools in Ireland: almost 44 per cent of the principals in co-educational primary schools are women while 46 per cent of *all* principals are women. The only schools in which women are really poorly represented in principalships are in senior co-educational schools. These are the schools which teach senior primary classes only. These represent only a very small minority of all co-educational primary schools.

Table 7.7 Principalships in co-educational primary schools, 1995/96

Type of School	Women N	Men N	Total N	Women %
Junior co-ed.	86	18	104	82.6
Senior co-ed.	11	52	63	17.5
Special schools	74	49	123	60.2
Full co-ed	992	1394	2386	41.6
Total	1163	1513	2676	43.5

Source: Department of Education, 1996.

It would be interesting to see what proportion of the recent female appointments to principalships were in co-educational schools and in larger schools. Unfortunately, the data is not available at the time of writing on this. However, given the fact that all new primary schools built in recent years are co-educational, and that women's appointment ratio per application exceeds the male rate for the last 13 years, it does seem that women are being appointed to principalships in co-educational primary schools. Further research is necessary to confirm this however.

Overall, women's appointment ratio exceeds their application ratio every year since 1983 with the exception of 1987/88. This means that women who apply are more likely to be appointed than men. Although this might suggest some positive discrimination in favour of women, what is more likely true, and what the limited data available suggest, is that women are less likely to apply for posts than men if they think they lack all the necessary qualifications. Thus the pool of women applying is likely to be more qualified than the male pool accounting for their better appointment ratio (Kellaghan and Fontes, 1985).

COMPARING THE REPUBLIC OF IRELAND AND NORTHERN IRELAND

It is interesting to compare the position of primary teachers in Northern Ireland with the Republic. In both the controlled (state run and predominantly Protestant) and maintained (state aided and predominantly Catholic) primary sectors in Northern Ireland, women are neither applying nor being appointed at a similar rate to men. Although women comprise 79 per cent of primary teachers, men outnumbered women applicants for principalships by over 2:1 and by 1.4:1 in appointments in 1991/92. Although it is clear that women's appointment ratio is significantly ahead of their application ratio in Northern Ireland, this does not compensate for their low application rate. Tables 7.7 and 7.8 show that this is not the pattern in the Republic where more women are applying for primary principalships than men; also, their appointment rate is either just above, or equal to, their application rate.

Table 7.8 Primary school principalships: applications and appointments, 1991/1992

| | Northern Ireland | | | Republic of Ireland | | |
	Female	Male	Ratio (F:M)	Female	Male	Ratio (F:M)
Applicants	183	451	1: 2.5	242	231	1.05: 1
Shortlist	122	258	1: 2.2	not available		
Appointments	34	47	1: 1.4	51	49	1.05: 1

*The data are collated from the INTO Equality of Opportunity Reports for 1993. The Northern Ireland data relates to data provided by four of the Education and Library Boards (which oversee controlled schools) and the Catholic Conference of Maintained Schools

Further research is necessary to understand why women seem to be so poorly represented in appointments to principalships in Northern Ireland. However, it is clear from existing appointments patterns in the North that women do not tend to be appointed principals in co-educational primary schools (Lynch and Morgan, 1994). This could help explain the difference between the Republic and the North as women are almost as strongly represented among principals in co-educational primary schools in the Republic as they are in schools generally (see Table 7.5). Why such a difference exists needs to be more fully explored however, as does the impact of school size and the nature of administrative control on applications and appointments (North and South) in co-educational schools especially.

Data on second-level applications and appointments to principalships suggests that, as is the case in the Republic, the pattern of applications and appointments is even more gender biased than at primary level in Northern Ireland (INTO, 1993). In the two Education and Library Boards where information was available (the Belfast and Western Boards), no applications were received from women for the two principalships in the Belfast area, while only one of the twelve applicants for one post in the Western area was a woman; the three posts went to men. As these are all co-educational schools, it is clear that women are not applying for principalships in this type of school. In the maintained system, where there are still a large number of single sex schools, the application rate is slightly better for women: in 1992 there were 41 male applicants and 6 female applicants for 7 posts. Three of the seven eventual appointees were women. Unfortunately it is not clear from the INTO report if the women were appointed in girls' schools, although it is quite likely to have been the case.

Because the precise application and appointment rates for different school types is not consistently available, either in Northern Ireland or in the Republic, it is hard to draw definitive conclusions. However, at second level, there appears to be a pattern of very low application rates for principalships from women, especially in boys' schools and co-educational schools in both parts of the island. While the ratio of female:male applications and appointments in the higher education sector is not available, what is evident is that women are also poorly represented in this sector at management level, especially in the universities.

WOMEN, EQUALITY AND MANAGEMENT

Liberal and voluntaristic principles underpin equality policies in Ireland to date, especially in the field of education (Lynch, 1996). For example, while the Employment Equality Agency has published guidelines for employers on promoting equality between the sexes – through such practices as appointing gender-balanced interview panels and selection boards – the guidelines are voluntary rather than mandatory. Thus, school boards and college selection panels can, and do break the guidelines without fear of sanction. Interview boards are still strongly male dominated (Kellaghan and Fontes, 1985; Teachers Union of Ireland, 1990; Irish National Teachers Organisation, 1993). Male dominance of the selection and promotion procedures makes women feel uncomfortable about seeking promotion (TUI, 1990; Gleeson, 1992). That women know they are disadvantaged in seeking promotion is shown in an ASTI survey of second-level teachers. It found that 77 per cent of both women and men believed it was helpful being a man when seeking promotion, while only 17 per cent thought it would be an advantage to be a woman (Gleeson, 1992). It seems reasonable to hypothesise therefore that there may be indirect discrimination against women occupying senior posts in education, particularly senior posts in large co-educational institutions at second-level as their rate of appointments in these schools is especially low. The survey by the Teachers Union of Ireland (TUI, 1990) lends support to this hypothesis as it shows that a number of those involved in selecting staff for senior administrative posts in second-level schools operate out of a traditional hierarchical and masculine view of management. Much more research is necessary however to either confirm or contradict the hypothesis regarding the extent and nature of indirect discrimination at all levels of education.

On the positive side, it must be noted however, that the recently published Employment Equality Bill (1996) prohibits indirect discrimination in employment on gender (and other) grounds. How the courts will interpret the provisions outlawing indirect discrimination remains to be seen.

The evidence of indirect discrimination does not, in itself, explain the difference in the application rates for promotion between women and men, although there is no doubt that the knowledge that the entire process is male dominated can, in itself, be a disincentive for women to apply. The limited research evidence available suggests however that women's multiple role responsibilities may also be an important explanatory variable. As noted above, the pay and support available to school heads in Ireland are far from adequate. Women, especially those with heavy caring and/or domestic responsibilities, often do not regard the extra rewards of a principalship or headship of a university department as being worth the extra effort and hassle required (Egan, 1996). Kellaghan and Fontes' national study of primary teachers (1985) found, for example, that there were significant differences in the types of women who intended applying for principalships: over twice as many single women without children intended to apply for principalships compared with married women. A small study of second-level principals identified a similar trend: of the nine women principals in the study, five were single with no children; one was married with no children; while the three remaining had children, only one had a child under 18 years of age (Daly, 1989). Although other factors may explain the differences between single and married women especially, such as the greater mobility of single women, the unequal responsibility which women take for caring and domestic work in households is undoubtedly a very important explanatory variable in understanding the differences between women's and men's promotional prospects.

CONCLUSION

The socio-economic position of women in Irish society has changed radically over the last 25 years. More women than men are now successfully completing second-level education, while just under 50 per cent of all higher education entrants are women; 53 per cent of university entrants being women. Women's participation in postgraduate programmes continues to rise each year although it has not yet equalled the male rate. There is also a vibrant adult and community women's education sector even though it is poorly and insecurely funded in comparison with other sectors of education. Women are the principal participants in adult and community education (Inglis *et al.*,1993).

The growth in women's participation in education has been paralleled by their rising participation in paid employment. Although Irish women's employment rate remains low by European standards (only 35 per cent of the paid labour force are women, see Table 7.2) the proportion of women in employment is rising steadily each year. The most notable change has been in the participation of married women in the paid labour force: they now comprise 51 per cent of all women in paid work compared with 30 per cent in 1981. Moreover, recent data from research on school-going pupils suggest that many more women may now be working than is officially being recorded in Labour Force Surveys (Lynch and Lodge, 1997).

Increased participation in employment has not given women parity of income or status with men. While there are a minority of professional women who earn roughly comparable salaries to men, women are still disproportionately represented among the junior grades of professional occupations, including teaching. Moreover, they comprise the majority (72 per cent) of part-time workers and of low paid workers. They are disproportionately represented in relatively low wage occupations in the services sector including cleaning, catering, shop assisting and clerical work, while only 16 per cent of all employers are women (CSO, 1996).

Relative to men, female teachers in Ireland occupy a very similar position to women in other occupations. However, while they tend to occupy the lower rungs of the educational ladder, they are better represented in management posts than women in occupations such as banking, insurance or the civil service. Moreover, if viewed as a corporate entity compared with other female dominated occupations such as civil servants, nurses or general service workers, teachers remain relatively highly paid with good conditions of employment. The fact that they have been members of a powerful set of (male dominated) trade unions has protected them and left them the most highly paid teachers within the OECD in 1996.

Women are most strongly represented in senior management in the primary sector and least well represented in the university sector. In 1995 the ratio of women teachers to women principals was 1.7:1 in the primary sector and 4.2:1 in the universities. Women were most poorly represented however, at top management within the community and comprehensive second-level schools (i.e. when religious principals are excluded) with a ratio of 8.1:1 women teachers to principals. The ratio was 4.0:1 in the secondary schools (see Table 7.3). The position of women in other senior management posts (vice-principals, A posts and B posts) is also best in the primary sector, although it must be noted that these posts are not based on open competition; they are given on the basis of seniority in both primary and secondary schools. Promotion in the other second-level schools (vocational, community or comprehensive) is based on competition as it is in the higher education sector. When promotional posts are given on the basis of open competition, women fare considerably less well than men see Table 7.4).

There is much commentary in Ireland on the status of women and the fact that women are not obtaining senior posts at the same rate as men. Within the teaching profession there has been a deliberate attempt by the teacher unions in particular to promote greater equality for women. Each of the three main teacher unions now have full-time equality officers and the monitoring of the position of women teachers, as well as promoting greater equality of opportunity in employment, is part of their brief. The primary teachers union, The Irish National Teachers Organisation (INTO), has been particularly active in this regard. Catholic educational authorities have also indicated an interest in promoting women as principals. They organised a conference on Women in Leadership in Education in 1993 and published both the Conference papers and their policies subsequently (Conference of Religious of Ireland, 1994). In the higher education sector, the setting up of the Higher Education Equality Unit which monitors all equality issues in higher education, has been a significant advancement in promoting an awareness about the lack of equality in the promotional prospects of women. However, while awareness of equality issues has increased, the practices within institutions have not changed radically to facilitate women's promotional opportunities. While a range of educational authorities have made concessions by developing equality policies, many of these are more impressive on paper than in practice.

If the position of women in teaching is to change so that they are more equitably involved in senior management, not only must promotional and selection procedures become more open and egalitarian, so also must the attitudes of male partners. Caring work is a fundamental part of the work of society; if women carry a disproportionate responsibility for such work, then they simply cannot compete equally with men for senior posts without seriously damaging their own health through overwork. The same issue arises with domestic work.

What is equally essential is a radical restructuring of the organisation of power and authority within work organisations. Collegial structures, power sharing and rotating responsibility at senior levels would greatly facilitate women (and men) who may wish to manage, but who also wish to attend to equally important tasks in their personal lives. Unfortunately certain schools, especially second-level schools, in Ireland have tended to adopt the more 'aggressive chief executive' model of management in recent years thereby signalling to many women (and men) who do not adhere to this model that senior management is not for them. A move away from a hierarchical to a more egalitarian style of management structure is essential for the promotion of equality for women in educational management (Lynch, 1994).

NOTES

1. The Anti-Discrimination (Pay) Act, 1974, the Employment Equality Act, 1977, The Unfair Dismissals Act, 1977, and The Social Welfare (No. 2.) Act, 1985, were all passed in response to EU Directives (Department of The Taoiseach, 1987: 25)
2. This law ensures that the feminine gender shall be construed as also importing the masculine gender unless the contrary intention appears.

Moreover the government have decided that in general all future bills and statutory instruments should be drafted in gender neutral language as far as possible. Under Stillbirths Registration Act, 1994, birth certificates can be issued for babies who are stillborn.

3. These two pieces of legislation are complementary as they involve the prohibiting of both direct and indirect discrimination against women (and a wide range of other groups not covered heretofore) in both the employment and the non-employment areas.

4. As the data on earnings in Ireland is only calculated systematically for the industrial sector, and as only 17 per cent of all female employment is in this sector, the findings on earnings must be interpreted with caution.

5. While there are approximately 30,000 places for new entrants to higher education each year, there are almost 60,000 undertaking the leaving certificate examination. The number of applicants far exceeds the number of places available so competition for places is keen. Entry to all colleges is determined by open competition based on the grade point average attained in the leaving certificate examination.

6. The birth rate in Ireland has declined steadily since 1980. This has led to a decline in teacher recruitment at both primary and secondary levels with the consequent effect of raising the age profile.

7. All entrants to universities and other higher education colleges are selected on the basis of the number of 'points' they obtain in the Leaving Certificate Examination, that is their grade point average in the examination. As Ireland has a larger cohort of school leavers wanting to enter higher education than can be accommodated, competition for higher education places in degree programmes is very keen; the qualifying standards of entry have risen considerably over the last 10 years. Teaching is still an occupation for which there is keen competition for places, especially among women.

8. There are two basic routes to qualify as a teacher in Ireland. Primary teachers undertake a three year degree (B.Ed.) programme combining the subject of education with another academic subject of their choice. All primary teachers are educated in Teacher Education Colleges affiliated to different universities. Most second-level teachers only enter teacher education programmes (the one year full-time Higher Diploma in Education course) after they have completed their primary degree in the field of their choice, be it in the sciences, economics, arts, languages etc. Certain specialist second-level teachers such as those in home economics, the visual arts, physical education and technology are educated to degree levels on separate programmes in a range of colleges affiliated to the universities.

9. The Irish National Teachers Organisation (INTO) represents all primary teachers while second-level teachers are represented by two unions, the Association for Secondary Teachers, Ireland (ASTI) and the Teachers Union of Ireland (TUI). The Teachers Union of Ireland also represents

lecturers in the technological sectors of higher education, that is in the Dublin Institute of Technology Colleges and in the Regional Technical Colleges. University lecturers are mostly represented by the Irish Federation of University Teachers (IFUT) although some lecturers are members of the Services, Industrial and Professional Trade Union (SIPTU) which is currently the largest trade union in the country. Trade union participation among university lecturers is much lower than among both primary and second-level teachers.

10. Although this may seem strange in an age of so-called meritocracy, promotion on the basis of seniority is a practice which has been steadily protected by the teacher unions. It has however been a contentious issue both among teachers and between teachers, management and the Department of Education.

REFERENCES

Association for Secondary Teachers, Ireland (ASTI) (1996) 'New Pay Scales from October 1st 1996', ASTIR: *Journal of the Association for Secondary Teachers, Ireland*, Vol. xxvi, no. 2, October.

Blackwell, J. (1989) *Women in the Labour Force*. Dublin, Employment Equality Agency.

Blossfeld, H.P. and Shavit, Y. (1993) 'Persisting Barriers: Changes in Educational Opportunities in Thirteen Countries', in S. Shavit and H.P. Blossfeld (eds.) *Persistent Inequality*. Oxford, Westview Press.

Breen, R., Hannan, D., Rottman, D. and Whelan, C. (1990) *Understanding Contemporary Ireland*. Dublin, Gill and Macmillan.

Burke, M.R. (1996) 'Women Staff in the RTC (Regional Technical College) Sector', in O. Egan (ed.) *Women Staff in Irish Colleges*. Cork, Higher Education Equality Unit.

Central Statistics Office (CSO) (1996) *Labour Force Survey 1995*. Dublin, Government Publications Office.

Clancy, P. (1995) *Access To College: Patterns of Continuity and Change*. Dublin, Higher Education Authority.

Combat Poverty and the Irish Congress of Trade Unions (1990) *Low Pay: The Irish Experience*. Dublin Combat Poverty/ICTU.

Commission on the Status of Women (1993) *Report to Government of the Second Commission on the Status of Women*. Dublin, Government Publications Office.

Conference of Religious of Ireland (Education Commission) (1995) *Women for Leadership in Education*. Dublin, Conference of Religious of Ireland (CORI).

Connelly, A. (ed.) (1993) *Gender and the Law in Ireland*. Dublin, Oaktree Press.

Constitution Review Group (1996) *Report of the Constitution Review Group*. Dublin, Government Publications.

Coolahan, J. (1981) *Irish Education: History and Structure*. Dublin, Institute of Public Administration.

Coolahan, J. (ed.) (1994) *Report on the National Education Convention*. Dublin, Government Publications Office.

Daly, M. (1989) The Under-Representation of Female Post-primary Teachers in

Promotional Posts. M.Ed. Thesis, UCD Education Dept.

Department of Education (1995a) *Charting Our Education Future: White Paper on Education*. Dublin Government Publications Office.

Department of Education (1995b) *Tuarascail Staitistiuil 1993/94: Statistical Report*. Dublin Government Publications Office.

Department of the Taoiseach (1987) *United Nations Convention on The Elimination of all Forms of Discrimination against Women: First Report by Ireland*. Dublin, Government Publications Office.

Drudy, S. and Lynch, K. (1993) *Schools and Society in Ireland*. Dublin, Gill and Macmillan.

Egan, O. (1996) *Women Staff in Irish Colleges*. Cork, Higher Education Equality Unit.

Employment Equality Agency (EEA) (1995) *Women in the Labour Force*. Dublin, EEA.

First Report of the Monitoring Committee on the Implementation of the Recommendations of the Second Commission on the Status of Women (1994) Dublin, Government Publications Office.

Gleeson, J. (1992) *Gender Equality in Education in the Republic of Ireland. Second Report of the Third Joint Oireachtas Committee on Women's Rights*. Dublin, Government Publications Office.

Hannan, D.F., Smyth, E., McCullagh, J., Oleary, R. and McMahon, D. (1996) *Coeducation and Gender Equality*. Dublin, Oaktree Press.

Inglis, T. *et al*. (1993) *Liberating Learning: A Report on Daytime Education Groups*, Dublin, AONTAS, National Association for Adult Education.

Irish Federation of University Teachers (IFUT) (1996) *Equality Issues*, Summer.

Irish National Teachers Organisation (INTO) (1993) *Equality of Opportunity Report in Educational Management*, Belfast, INTO.

Irish National Teachers Organisation (INTO) (1995) *Central Executive Report*. Dublin, INTO.

Kellaghan, T. and Fontes, P. (1985) *Gender Inequalities in Irish Primary School Teaching*. Dublin, Educational Company.

Leonard, M. (1994) *Informal Economic Activity in Belfast*. Aldershot, Avesbury.

Lynch, K. (1989) *The Hidden Curriculum, Reproduction in Education, A Reappraisal*. London, Falmer Press.

Lynch, K. (1994) 'Women Teach and Men Manage: Why Men Dominate Senior Post in Irish Education', Conference of Religious of Ireland (Education Commission) *Women for Leadership in Education*. Dublin, Milltown Park.

Lynch, K. (1996) 'The Limits of Liberalism for the Promotion of Equality in Education', in E. Befring (ed.) *Teacher Education for Equality*. Association for Teacher Education in Europe (ATEE), Oslo. Papers from the ATEE 20th Annual Conference Oslo, September, 1995.

Lynch, K. and Lodge, A. (forthcoming 1997) *Equality and the Social Climate of Schools*. Dublin.

Lynch, K. and McLaughlin, E. (1995) 'Caring Labour and Love Labour', in P. Clancy, S. Drudy, K. Lynch and L. O'Dowd (eds.) *Irish Society: Sociological Perspectives*. Dublin, Institute of Public Administration.

Lynch, K. and Morgan, V. (1995) 'Gender and Education: North and South', in P. Clancy, S. Drudy, K. Lynch and L. O'Dowd (eds.) *Irish Society: Sociological Perspectives*. Dublin, Institute of Public Administration.

McKenna, A. (1988) *Child Care and Equal Opportunities*. Dublin, Employment Equality Agency.

Organisation for Economic Co-operation and Development (OECD) (1991) *Reviews of National Policies for Education, Ireland*. Paris, OECD.

Organisation for Economic Co-operation and Development OECD (1996) *Education Indicators*. Paris, OECD.

Smith, A. (1996) 'Reviewing Breaking the Circle: A Pilot Project', in O. Egan, (ed.) *Women Staff in Irish Colleges*. Cork, Higher Education Equality Unit.

Smyth, E. and Burke, H. (1988) *Distant Peaks: A Study of the Relative Staffing Levels of Women and Men in University College Dublin*. UCD, Dublin 1988.

Teachers' Union of Ireland (1990) *Equality of Opportunity in Teaching*, No. 13, TUI Dublin.

8

Italy

Giovanna Campani and Anna Picciolini

In Italy, according to National Institute of Statistics (ISTAT) data for 1991, out of 1,398,069 people employed in the education sector, the vast majority of which are teachers, 940,537, that is, 67.35 per cent, are women. The feminisation of schools at the present time is a process which is both old and new. Indeed, the historical predominance of female teachers over male teachers in the primary or elementary sector has, in the last twenty years, extended to the number of female teachers overtaking that of male teachers in the secondary sector, first in the lower secondary schools and then, in the 1980s, in the upper secondary schools. According to data for 1989, compared with other European countries, Italy is the country with the highest degree of feminisation in teaching, not only in the elementary sector, but also in the secondary sector, both up to the end of compulsory schooling and beyond, with an average of 90 per cent of women teachers in the elementary sector and 60 per cent in the secondary sector (70 per cent in the lower secondary school sector) in 1990 (Ulivieri, 1996).

These figures suggest that school is 'a place of women', as has been defined by ISFOL (1992), but does this also mean that schools are in women's hands? Examining the quantitative data it emerges unequivocally that, in managerial roles and in places where knowledge is produced, such as the universities, schools are still definitely monopolised and run by men.

Among the managerial staff of the schools, headteachers in both elementary and secondary schools, the percentage of women is very low and drops as the level of teaching rises, in a pyramidal pattern. There are more female headteachers in the elementary sector than in the lower secondary sector and there are more (approximately twice as many) female headteachers at the lower secondary than at the upper secondary level, at 35 and 18 per cent respectively, figures which have changed little since the 1980s (ISFOL, 1992). Over 90 per cent of Italian elementary school teachers are female in comparison with 46 per cent of elementary school headteachers, while over 60 per cent of secondary school teachers are female in comparison with an overall proportion of 30 per cent (Laemers and Ruijs, 1995). 'The school sector is therefore characterised by a very high number of women, a real army which nevertheless has men in its key positions of command and coordination' (Ulivieri, 1996, p. 78).

In the university sector we find the same hierarchical pyramid. A large proportion of the lowest status areas of research are occupied by women. This proportion decreases among lecturers in the middle grades, senior lecturers, at 23.7 per cent, and falls alarmingly among staff in the top band, full professors, at 9.5 per cent.

How can we explain this male predominance at the highest managerial levels of the education system, which is without a doubt the public administration sector in which women occupy the highest proportion of posts? At managerial level, Italian women are generally underrepresented in all sectors of public administration[1], as in the private sector, in industry and in the service industries, not to mention politics, even though there are some women who are visibly successful[2], as we shall see in the following section. However, given the very high feminisation of the education sector, we might have expected to encounter different trends from other sectors. This is not the case: why?

It is precisely this question that we would like to answer in this chapter.

WOMEN AND MANAGERIAL ROLES – THE GLASS CEILING

Although women have entered the Italian labour force in increasing numbers, it is not on equal terms with men. Women comprised 25 per cent of the labour force in 1950 and 37 per cent in 1992. Although the proportion of part-time workers is low, at 10 per cent, in comparison with many other European countries, women are highly represented among part-time workers at 65 per cent in 1992. Women's gross hourly wages are about 80 per cent of the manual male rate and the female unemployment rate is about twice that of the male rate. Women constitute 70 per cent of service sector employees and also 70 per cent of low paid workers (European Commission, 1995). A European Commission funded research project called *Women and empowerment – the glass ceiling* carried out recently by the 'Network of Women and Decision-making Processes' presented recently to a convention in Turin, examined the position of female managers in the legal, health, finance and education sectors in Italy in 1995. Although women comprise nearly 50 per cent of professionals in Italy, this research revealed the general absence of women in management in all of these sectors, including education, in spite of its peculiarity of being a sector in which female employees are very much in the majority (Network donne e processi decisionali, 1996).

As far as the legal profession is concerned, out of 56,707 professional lawyers in Italy, only 10,666, that is 18.8 per cent, are women. In the National Council for Forensic Science there is only one woman. In the future it is, however, possible that this may change, as in the case of new recruits to forensic science, where the numbers of males and females are largely equal. In legal administration, women occupy 49.2 per cent of the posts, but the higher the grade, the rarer women become. For example, in the Courts of Appeal, no women occupy the posts of presiding judge, section president, procurator general and attorney general: the same situation is true for the presiding judges at the courts of justice. In the legal sector, women make up 55.3 per cent of the administrative staff, 30.1 per cent of the magistrature and only 24 per cent of the examining magistrates.

These figures are not very encouraging. However, it should not be forgotten that, in the legal sector, the profession of magistrate was only opened to women approximately thirty years ago. It was in fact the law of 9 February 1963, 'Admission of women to public office and to the professions' which allowed the actual application of article 51 of the Constitution on opening all careers to women. Article 1 of this law is worded as follows:

> Women may occupy any posts, professions and public offices, including the function of magistrate, in the various roles, careers or categories, without any limitation of tasks, except for under the conditions laid down by the law.

A keen scholar of the processes of female emancipation, Annamaria Galoppini, wrote of this law as though she were speaking of the storming of the Bastille: 'Shortly, owing to this last blow against the bastion of prejudice, we would see women magistrates, ministry heads, embassy counsellors, ships' captains, stationmasters, mechanics and assistant mechanics and communal secretaries etc' (Galoppini, 1980, p. 236).

However, Galoppini adds that the elimination of formal obstacles revealed the real problem of access of women to all careers: that of parity of working conditions and specific obstacles of a family or social nature, which even today prevent many women from freely choosing their career (Galoppini, 1980). Maternity leave provision at 5 months on 80 per cent of earnings, followed by an optional 6 months of parental leave at 30 per cent of earnings is comparatively generous. State-funded preschool provision is available for 95 per cent of 3–5-year-olds and the school day is comparatively long, at 8 hours (European Commission, 1995). Nonetheless, such constraints as family responsibilities and social attitudes appear to prevent women from obtaining managerial positions in the various sectors, not only in the 'newer' sectors which have recently opened up to women too, such as the law.

The situation in the health and finance sectors is even worse than that of the magistrature (and Italian women were not debarred from practising medicine, as they were from the magistrature). The seven general managers of the Ministry of Health are all men and the percentage of women among the general managers of the USLs (local health authorities which are responsible for public welfare services) is around a meagre 3 per cent: that is, six in the whole of Italy. Going down the scale of power, the percentages rise very slowly: the seventeen 'health directors' of the USLs only make up 8.4 per cent of the total.

There are very few women managers in the public sector; even in the state bank, the *Banca d'Italia*, there are no women on the board of directors or the board of auditors or among the general officials in central administration. A similar situation exists at the Ministry of Finance. In the world of insurance, most of the women (33.6 per cent) are employed in clerical work, whereas very few women succeed in becoming officials (6.3 per cent) or executives (2.7 per cent).

Let us now turn our attention to the education sector where the situation is not very different from the others, if not worse. As has already been mentioned, in the universities, the presence of women is concentrated in the lower grades (researchers). This lack of power is reflected in the Ministry of Universities where no Head of Department is a woman and in the CNU, the National Council for Universities, where the percentage of women is only 6.3 per cent. The situation improves slightly in the Ministry of Education, which is responsible for nursery schools, elementary and secondary schools where women managers number 14.4 per cent. In the National Council for Education, the percentage of women is 26.4 per cent.

Nevertheless, if we consider the overall percentage of women employed in the various categories and grades of the education system, these data are almost worse for the Ministry of Education than for the universities. Indeed, whereas in the universities (ISTAT data of 1991), women are in the minority of those employed (34,387 out of a total of 89,557), in the elementary and secondary schools women occupy 70 to 90 per cent of the posts, with the sole exception of vocational training.

The situation of women in Italian universities moreover mirrors a phenomenon which is unfortunately fairly generalised in the various countries of Europe with very few exceptions. The almost total absence of female management, even at elementary school level, seems to be paradoxical: a body of staff which is mainly if not exclusively female with male management. It is almost as though the women who work in the elementary or secondary schools do not know how to or cannot produce managers to represent them!

To explain this phenomenon, we should run through the stages of the 'feminisation' of schools in Italy, where we shall find a number of clues to the mystery of the poor female representation in the management of the education sector. We shall also refer to a number of recent studies on women teachers, carried out in various parts of Italy, which seek to understand what motivates them, their expectations and their impact as women on teaching and the teaching profession. We shall then analyse school establishments as an organisational system to see which obstacles exist in the hierarchical organisation itself, where women are concerned, and to examine the relationship between teachers and headteachers.

THE FEMINISATION OF ITALIAN SCHOOLS

In the feminisation process of Italian schools, it is useful to draw a distinction between the elementary and the secondary levels, in that, as has already been mentioned, the phases of the feminisation of the two levels of education are separate in chronological terms and occur in different contexts from the economic, social policy and cultural points of view. Furthermore, the feminisation of elementary schools has always been accompanied by a specific idea of the 'naturally female' characteristics of the teacher who has to educate small children below the age of ten (to a certain extent the idea of education as mothering), whereas the social perception, role and status of the teacher in the lower and upper secondary school have changed over time, also in line with the progressive lengthening of the period of compulsory schooling.

The phases of schooling in the Italian school system are, in brief:

- 6–11 years – elementary education;
- 11–13 years – compulsory secondary education;
- 14–18 years – optional secondary education in academic high schools, leading to the classical, scientific or technical *Maturità*; in technical schools, leading to various technical qualifications or to a technical diploma, which qualifies for university entrance; or in teacher training schools, which offer a 5 year elementary school teacher's diploma;
- at the age of 19 students enter higher education in universities or in technical institutes. Secondary school teachers are educated at university level.

The elementary school has always had a high proportion of women teachers, practically since the passing of the Casati Law which reorganised state schooling in the years following the unification of the country (1860) and created suitable schools for women teachers.

> The roots of the mass entry of women into elementary teaching and the feminisation of the teaching body in that sector lie in the contemporary emergence of the unified state and its need for lay staff to replace clerical staff, who were often hostile to the new political configuration of the country.
>
> (Ulivieri, 1995, p. 187)

This replacement did not occur without 'ideological' preparation. The task of women teachers was portrayed as a sort of lay vocation, almost a form of spiritual mothering.

During the first forty years after unification, female teachers therefore made up most of the teaching body in the elementary sector, whereas the secondary schools remained firmly in the hands of schoolmasters. The first female lecturers, trained at the *Istituti Superiori di Magistero Femminile* (female teacher training establishments) in Rome and Florence, found work mainly in the teacher training colleges and in female vocational schools, rather than in the *licei* (grammar schools), which were the stronghold of training for the future ruling class (male).

Nevertheless, the free state did not in fact debar the ascent of women into teaching or education (some even entered university teaching), but the examples are few in the face of a professional culture strongly dominated by men. The positions which female teachers managed to occupy in the teachers' and lecturers' associations were also very few. Even these few places were reduced by fascism which was decisively against women working. The fascists' policy was to combat male unemployment, giving men priority in job allocation and salaried work and trying to prevent a double salary entering a family by a series of measures intended to prevent women from entering employment. The task of the school and education was, among other things, to 'restore the subjugation of women by men'. It is clear that in this cultural climate room was found for legal provisions against women working and in particular against their connection with education, whether as pupils or teachers. For example in 1927 women were excluded from teaching the arts, philosophy and history in the grammar schools. The following year, female students had to pay double the fees in schools and universities and female teachers were debarred from competing for managerial posts in institutes of secondary education (Galoppini, 1980).

The feminisation of teaching, therefore, started with the very origins of schools in Italy, linking it with a view of the woman teacher, in vocational terms, as being in the role of a 'carer' rather than a decision-maker, excluding women from the production of knowledge. The fascist period demonstrated that feminisation cannot be regarded as a linear phenomenon in that political changes and/or economic problems can create reversals of trends which lead to the expulsion of women both from the job market as teachers and from the entire school system itself as pupils. It also damaged the status of women teachers, relegated even more to the 'natural' caring function. As Ulivieri rightly says (1995), although the fascist legislation was removed at the end of the Second World War, with the advent of democracy and the Republic, it continued to influence the model of the female teacher during the 1950s and 1960s. Almost all of the fascist school managers, after very short (or totally absent) periods of purging, were reinstated in their roles, keeping their own status and own ideology intact.

It is for this reason too that in the period after the Second World War and virtually up to the protests of the 1970s, which started in 1967–68, schools have appeared authoritarian in their centralised, bureaucratic and hierarchical approach, as recommended by the fascist philosopher Giovanni Gentile, author of the last global reform of the Italian education system, the general stamp of which can still be seen in the structure of the system and the content of study programmes today.

The Ministry of Education, moreover, firmly in the hands of the Christian Democrats, even during the various centre-left experiments, was to adhere for a long time to an educational policy, through programmes, directives and circulars, which established a strong hierarchy between teachers at the various levels (nursery school, elementary and the two secondary levels). This was a hierarchy which relegated the elementary sector, for which teaching is considered to be a vocational and female calling, to the lowest levels of qualification and remuneration. This view of the hierarchy, expressed by the Ministry of Education (for example, until 1977 men could not become nursery school teachers), promotes the idea of a division of roles between women and men in the education sector. In this way of thinking, feminisation therefore corresponds to the belief that women are better equipped to handle small children than men, whereas at the managerial level it is totally 'natural' that the posts should be occupied by men.

The entry of women teachers to the secondary school, first to the lower and then to the upper level, is therefore primarily due to the reduction in the number of men being attracted to a poorly paid profession in the years of economic expansion. To the increasing loss of prestige of the teaching profession for men, there corresponds a trend in schools of women socially drawn towards choosing courses of study which make it possible to reproduce the 'job of carer' in society. The role of women teachers is seen as being that of a 'custodian of knowledge', entirely parallel to the function of 'guardians of the home' (ISFOL, 1992).

THE 'VESTAL VIRGINS' OF THE SECONDARY SCHOOL

With the devaluation of the teaching profession, abandoned by men, and the lengthening of compulsory schooling, the male teacher is no longer the person who educates the ruling class but one who, at most, helps to preserve the existing order, that 'cultural system' made up of Catholic morals and *petit-bourgeois* values which the protests of 1968 were meant to sweep away. Here then are female teachers in the shape of 'vestal virgins of the secondary school' according to the famous definition of two sociologists, Maurizio Barbagli and Marcello Dei, authors of one of the first surveys on male and female teachers, published in 1969.

The theme they advance is that male and female teachers perform two substantially conservative functions; on the one hand the elimination from the school system of pupils from the lower social classes, or their diversion into non-institutional and less prestigious courses of study (vocational courses, etc.) and on the other hand, in a broader sense, the transmission of the cultural and behavioural values of the ruling class, with the aim of creating in pupils an educational habit made up of passivity, subordination and obedience to the existing social order.

The authors see a considerable difference between men and women as regards the profession practised, the motivational choices, the training received, the degree of professional satisfaction and the behaviour adopted as teachers. From a social point of view, for example, it would appear that male teachers come far more from families from humbler origins whereas their female colleagues are largely from the middle classes (white-collar workers, managers, the professions). Such women teachers coming from the middle to high bands have chosen to become teachers, whereas for the men, whose earning aspirations are higher, teaching is often a transitory working experience, an expedient profession which they hope to leave.

Even the faculties attended during their university studies vary between the sexes: female teachers largely study the arts and philosophy or teaching skills, male teachers study political sciences, the law, biological sciences and pharmacy, veterinary science, agricultural studies, geology and of course also the arts. The motivation for females choosing the profession starts early from the age of 14 to 16; most males, on the other hand, decide to turn to teaching after they have obtained their degrees, not least because of the difficulties with the job market and the greater number of teaching posts which came into being in the 1960s with the take-off of compulsory secondary schooling.

In some ways, young women can be seen to choose teaching first, and with more conviction, and in far higher numbers then their male counterparts. For them the choice is for a 'vocation'; but when we analyse the real, underlying reasons, the picture is very different. The 'choice' is brought about by their family and social circumstances. The teaching profession is better suited to women because, more than other professions, it leaves room for them to deal with their families.

These considerations recur frequently in the interviews referred to by Barbagli and Dei: 'I chose the Faculty of Arts and then teaching by a process of elimination and also for practical reasons. Of all careers, the one which combines best with a family for a woman is teaching, because it does not take up the entire day' (Barbagli and Dei, 1969, p. 23). Choosing the teaching profession for these reasons is the antithesis to choosing a career, even within the school itself, because this presupposes a greater task. The male teacher, on the other hand, who entered teaching for reasons of expediency, finds a way of escaping frustration (and a small financial improvement) by seeking advancement internally and, in this sector, he is therefore doubly motivated to seek a managerial role.

Even if it is becoming increasingly isolated, the type of mentality expressed by the female interviewee in 1969 still exists today, particularly in the older bands of teachers. But as we shall see, the reasons for choosing teaching and remaining at the lowest rungs of the career ladder now also have other motivations in a profoundly changed social context which has seen the student movement, the feminist movement and union struggles.

The school which produced the 'vestal virgin' ideology was in fact the subject of protests by the student movement and by a number of more politicised and socially-committed members of the teaching profession during and since the 1970s. The students accused schools of being elitist and the teachers of showing bias towards the ruling (economic and political) class, because of the selective system which tends to favour the elite. The unions' struggles have sought to reform a hierarchical and authoritarian structure with the introduction of opportunities for participation and democracy, which will open up schools to the outside. Measures introduced include the introduction of 'collegiate bodies' (to which the parents belong), the opening of regional centres running refresher courses, teacher-training centres which work in close collaboration with the local authorities and the non-governmental organisations, and the 150 hour compulsory schooling courses intended for workers but run within the school structures. At the same time, the feminist movement has again drawn attention to the sexist nature of the dominant culture which, as we shall see in the next section, has, among other things, led to the development of a difference in approaches to teaching between the sexes.

Finally, if we examine the process of feminisation in schools over the past twenty years, we can see that becoming the 'vestal virgins of the secondary school' did not prevent many women teachers from acquiring the tools to act as a basis for the search for a female professional and social identity, even if this arose within a structure resistant to change and relatively closed to outside influences. But in order for this to manifest itself externally, in the student movement, in the trade unions or in feminism, it was necessary to make the quantum leap seen in the 1970s.

THE FEMINISATION OF TEACHING OVER THE PAST TWENTY YEARS: SEGREGATION IN TRAINING

Becoming far more marked from the protest decade of the 1970s onwards, the feminisation of upper secondary school teaching, unlike that of the elementary school, occurred together with a combination of complex phenomena which fall within the context of general change in Italian society.

First of all, the increase in women teachers is a phenomenon which is closely connected with the increase in the period of female participation in schooling, and in higher education. Between 1970–71 and 1985–86, the levels of female participation in post-compulsory education between the ages of 14 and 18, rose from 36 to 57 per cent. It was precisely in the school year 1986–87 that the numbers of girls staying at school rose above those of boys (57 per cent as against 56 per cent) (Franci, Mapelli and Librando, 1987). In 1992, 70 per cent of girls and 67 per cent of boys completed secondary education (European Commission, 1995).

The numbers of girls at university also increased spectacularly after 1970, in line with an overall increase in participation in higher education. In 1970–71, the numbers of girls in education in the age band 19–24 were no more than 10 per cent, as against 17 per cent for males. As overall enrolments rose to about 25 per cent of the age group in the 1990s, the gap between them started to decrease until today when we have parity. At the beginning of the 1970s, girls made up only 35 per cent of university students; today they make up 50 per cent. This progressive increase in female enrolment at the upper levels of education was the result of a process of women's emancipation which accelerated rapidly in the 1970s and which sought to liberate women through the acquisition of 'culturally neutral knowledge' (Battistoni and Palleschi, 1992, p. 9).

However, the expansion of education to include women led to a crisis in understanding of male and female stereotypical cultures built on a rigid structure of capacity and ability, linked to a culture of 'know-how' and to unfavourable comparisons with the past when women were relegated to subordinate and marginal positions, on the basis of their presumed intellectual inferiority and their functional specificity in a social context connected with the 'laws of nature' (Battistoni and Palleschi, 1992). The feminist movement was to act as the spokesperson for a reassessment of knowledge 'differentiated by sex' which gives visibility to women as active authors of knowledge and self-representation.

The demand for knowledge, debates about male forms of knowledge and the search for knowledge differentiated by sex constitute a frame of reference which, although stimulating, has also produced crises in the professional identity of the teacher, and which ends by being perceived increasingly as 'evanescent', as shown by the most recent research (Battistoni and Palleschi, 1992; Ulivieri, 1996), especially given the ever greater loss of social prestige of the profession. It also should not be forgotten that the processes of female emancipation through study and work are in contradiction with the sexist structure of the job market and society in general.

The increase in the numbers of girls staying on at school is in fact more generally part of the development of a training system aiming to increase the acquisition of higher levels of qualifications. Even though, in Italy, the official school leaving age has remained at the age of 14, in the past twenty years we have seen a shifting upwards of the average levels of training required and the upper secondary school increasingly tends to assume the form, even if only informally, of a sort of compulsory school. It would therefore appear that there is an upward trend in the subjective requirements and in the training required to meet the demand for work, accompanied by an upward trend in the presence of women in the teaching profession. However, women are benefiting from what only appears to be a professional shift upwards, as they continue to be relegated to posts involving the dissemination rather than the production of knowledge, apart from those in which managerial groups are formed. As Sullerot wrote:

It is difficult to judge whether women really have or really have not made true progress as is usually maintained. Very often, they have only entered where men have wanted to let them in, because they no longer wish to defend this position and in fact are preparing to abandon it. This profession therefore of a male domain doggedly defended will become a female profession; not always, therefore, will it be a conquest, but more frequently a concession and sometimes even an abandonment, provided, however, that it leaves inviolate a number of other domains. Teaching has been closed to women for centuries; today we have seen that it is becoming feminised to a large extent, except in the upper echelons, which still retain the prestige connected with university posts.   (Sullerot, 1977, p. 319)

WOMEN AND MEN IN SCHOOLS – MOTIVATIONS AND EXPECTATIONS OF TEACHERS

Along with the increase in female participation in university education there is a corresponding phenomenon of the so-called 'segregation in training' which has seen a clear prevalence of women in some faculties, rather than in others. The faculties with the highest concentration of women are the arts, teaching and, to a lesser extent, biology. Eighty per cent of humanities graduates and 20 per cent of engineering graduates were female in 1992 (CISEM, 1988; European Commission, 1995). Many of the subjects chosen by girls lead mainly to teaching. Does this perhaps mean that these subjects are chosen beforehand due to the persistence of a female propensity towards professional care activities which make it practicable to reconcile the productive role and the reproductive role? Or is this also a kind of self-limitation, because in 'the place of women', which school is, it is not so necessary to face the disputes, competition or difficult scenarios which arise in other professional sectors?

But how can the choice, even during university studies, of a profession which now has little social prestige and low remuneration be motivated today? Clearly after years of feminist discourse, it can no longer be spoken of in terms of a 'natural' female 'vocation'. The idea of 'caring work' is in fact very different from that of a vocation; it presupposes first of all a social function, which is internalised, even in a positive way, compared with the roles and functions regarded socially as being male.

There still remains the motivation regarding teaching as a part-time job which leaves room for family responsibilities. If this motivation still arises, as we have mentioned, it is also very strongly questioned by the search for a new professional definition of the teacher, capable of recovering social and cultural prestige. It is here that the efforts of the most active and most heavily committed female teachers seem to be concentrated, engaged in the search for a new self-respect through union activities, experimental teaching, reflections on knowledge and the like. Their male counterparts, on the other hand, would appear to be interested in an internal career as headteachers, both in the lower and in the upper secondary school. This pressure towards an internal career explains the very high percentage of men in the position of headteacher, which is true in all types of upper secondary schools and in the teacher training colleges, where practically 100 per cent of students are female.

However, at this point, after having identified the limits of the feminisation of teaching compared with the loss of social prestige of the profession and after having explained the pressure on male teachers to occupy managerial roles, we have to try to understand the relations between women teachers and male managers, clarifying to a better extent the organisational structure of the school institution itself.

TEACHERS AND HEADTEACHERS

The school institution as an organised system is a structure with a very broad band of qualified and specialised staff at the same professional level (teachers), a very narrow base of white-collar and blue-collar staff (administrative staff, school caretakers), a single decision-making vertex (headmaster), flanked by a number of support structures (collegiate bodies), with functions of a consultative type.

At the level of the teaching staff there is no hierarchical differentiation: the role is the same for all. The only differences are of a remunerative nature, connected with the seniority of the role. In order to become an elementary school *Direttore* (Director), teachers have to take an additional 3 year course at university level after a long period in teaching and then participate in a state competition. Becoming a secondary school *Preside* (headteacher) also depends on experience and entry in a state competition, although this system is now under reform. Work in schools is carried out in an individual manner, with a high degree of autonomy; the career possibilities are limited. There are no formal relations between the teaching staff and the administrative and service staff. The latter staff report directly to the headteacher and have no hierarchical or functional relations with the teaching staff; the latter is in fact formally lodged in a hierarchically subordinate position to that of the headteacher (a role which involves the coordination of a complex structure), but upon which it does not appear to be functionally dependent.

What emerges is an organisational model of a professional type characterised by high autonomy, creativity and flexibility, which is precisely what is liked by teachers. In this context, the role of the headteacher, when it is positive, is a role involving coordination, direction, innovation and stimulus but, in many cases, it is a bureaucratic role, a role of obedience to the rules defined by central government and relating to management of the existing situation. Faced with bureaucratic headteachers, loathe to innovate, the teachers then wish for non-interference, which is very often the case. But autonomy also means being closed to new ideas, concentrating on the class and on relations with the pupils, rather than action within the structure, for innovation or planning.

Above the headteacher, the provincial education office (local body) and the Ministry appear to the teachers as distant bodies, substantially non-existent. 'In any case, they are bureaucratic chaotic organisations, the reports of which are viewed with uneasiness and anxiety, because they can cause difficulties for the performance of one's own job' (ISFOL, 1992, p. 26).

Recent research therefore shows that women teachers do not appear to recognise themselves as belonging to an organisational structure; they do not appear to be interested in taking on managerial roles; they do not seek collaboration or conflicts with the school authorities, but concentrate on the professional role in the classroom, on relations with pupils and on their own cultural development.

CONCLUSION

The feminisation of schools has been interpreted as a natural state of affairs for the lower levels (elementary), almost one of biological destiny (maternity), as a result of which it has been regarded as one more factor deterring male entrants to a profession which has gradually lost social prestige. Pursuing emancipation processes through study and work, women have realised that they were always at the lowest levels of the pyramid since as they gradually rose, the pyramid also rose.

Within school, which has become a 'place of women', the few men present have aimed at management, the only way in which to accept their role socially. Men have therefore accepted a highly bureaucratic managerial role within a structure which gives very few career (or economic) incentives. This role can no longer have a significant effect on the 'freedom and autonomy' of the teaching profession, which is one of the reasons why women teachers enjoy their work more.

Women teachers have, on the other hand, sought professionalism, once they had rejected the idea of being a teacher because of their natural gifts. The search for valid relations and for innovation did not, however, mean a true and proper innovation brought by women into the school. The same teachers oscillate between the propensity for stability and the search for change.

The feminisation of teaching continues not to mean that women have the opportunity to act and express themselves freely in schools. Women teachers appear to have been unable to present themselves as real innovators able to shake off the shackles of the organisational system of schools. The only changes which occur are brought about by individual actions; this can only lead to informal and circumscribed changes.

NOTES

1. In Italy, in the Chamber of Parliament, women make up 14 per cent of the members and 9.9 per cent in the senate. The situation is slightly better at local level with 23.8 per cent on the regional councils.

2. In Italy, there are three women ministers in health, social solidarity and equal opportunities; the latter two are ministers without portfolio, that is, not ministers, but officials in departments of the Presidency of the Council. The President of RAI, state radio and television, in the period 1994–1996, was a woman.

REFERENCES

Barbagli, M. and Dei, M. (1969) *Le vestali della classe media* (The vestal virgins of the secondary school), Il Mulino: Bologna.

Battistoni, L. and Palleschi, M.T. (1992) Introduction, in ISFOL (1992) op. cit.

CISEM (1988) *Donne e istruzione politecnica* (Women and polytechnic education), Franco Angeli: Milan.

European Commission (1995) *Women and Men in the European Union: a Statistical Portrait*, Office for the Publications of the European Community: Luxembourg.

Franci, G., Mapelli, F. and Librando, G. (1987) *Scolarizzazione e processi di crescita dell'identità femminile negli anni 70* (Schooling and growth processes of the female identity in the 70s), Franco Angeli: Milan.

Galoppini, A.M. (1980) *Il lungo viaggio verso la parità* (The long road towards equality), Zanichelli: Bologna.

ISFOL (1992) *Nuovi orientamenti e aspettative della professione docente: le donne insegnanti*, (New directions and expectations of the teaching profession: women teachers), Franco Angeli: Milan.

Laemers, M. and Ruijs, A. (1996) A Statistical Portrait, *Context*, no. 12, pp. 7–15.

Network donne e processi decisionali (1996) *Donne e empowerment. Il soffitto di cristallo* (Women's network and decision-making processes (1996) Women and empowerment. The glass ceiling) Turin.

Sullerot, E. (1977) *La donna e il lavoro* (Women and work), Bompiani: Milan.

Ulivieri, S. (1995) *Educare al femminile* (Education by women), Edizioni ETS: Pisa.

Ulivieri, S. (1996) (forthcoming) *Essere donne insegnanti* (Being women teachers), Rosenberg and Sellier: Turin.

9

The Netherlands

Ard Vermeulen and Annelies Ruijs

In the Netherlands considerable attention is paid to the position of women in educational management. The government places great importance on the proportional representation of men and women which is evident in the large number of measures taken in this field during the last ten years. A certain degree of modesty is appropriate, however, with regard to the results achieved. In spite of all the measures taken, the percentage of women headteachers and deputy heads is still one of the lowest in Europe. This chapter will offer some insight into the historical and current reasons for this situation and explain the various initiatives taken to improve women's representation in educational management.

WOMEN AT WORK

The Netherlands has the reputation of being a progressive, tolerant and prosperous country. This is confirmed by the 1995 Human Development Report of the United Nations Development Programme (UNDP, 1995). In the general index of 'human development' the Netherlands holds fourth place. However, the country drops to number 20 in a 'gender related index' on the position of women. The principal reason for this is the extremely unequal division of paid labour between women and men.

In 1981 only 30 per cent of women participated in the labour market, as compared with 85 per cent of men. However, there has been a substantial increase in the last decade and a half owing to fewer women leaving paid employment after their first child and married women re-entering the labour market. By 1995 the percentage for women had risen to 44 and for men had dropped to 79 (CBS, 1996).

Unlike in the 1980s, having a baby is for many women no longer an argument for stopping work. The participation of women in the labour market is now double what it was at the beginning of the 1980s. Only 1 in 14 women with a child under 6 worked in 1981; in 1995 that had risen to 1 in 7 (CBS, 1995).

Nevertheless, the Netherlands has one of the lowest percentages of working women worldwide. The reason for this state of affairs is partly historical. In the first half of this century, the ruling political parties campaigned for a living wage for men which would enable them to provide adequately for their families, thereby removing the need for women to work outside the home. The primacy which Dutch society placed on the woman's role in the family was indicated by a ministerial decision in 1924 to dismiss female civil servants when they married, and by legislation introduced in 1935 making the dismissal of married female school teachers mandatory. Changes did not occur until the 1960s when the demands of a newly flourishing economy could only be met by the employment of semi-skilled female workers (Noordenbos, 1994).

Some measures based on the principle of the single breadwinner are still in force, however, and do not make it particularly attractive for women with a working partner to participate in the labour market. The point at issue is the loss of the financial advantages of the single wage-earner if his wife goes out to work. This can have the effect that a part-time job of just a few hours for women, probably requiring low qualifications, can have a negative influence on the family income or mean that the family is only slightly better off. Paid employment is not attractive at all when childcare also has to be paid for. There is a great deal of criticism of these breadwinner advantages and the present government is in the process of abolishing them.

The majority of women work part-time; 60 per cent in comparison to 16 per cent of men in 1990. One in 5 working women works less than 12 hours per week. Nearly two-thirds work less than 35 hours, which is true of only 15 per cent of men (CBS, 1995). Fifty four per cent of all part-time workers are women.

The educational level of women is an important condition for equal participation with men in the labour market. Women older than 45 have a lower level of education than men. Below the age of 45, educational qualification are virtually the same. At the moment as many girls as boys are following higher or university education and girls even perform better than boys in higher professional education (Gordijn en Janssen, 1996). However, women and men choose very different types of courses. These differences are important as the choice of course has an enormous influence on their future position in the labour market. In spite of many measures and extensive information campaigns, such as the government campaign run from 1987 to 1989 to encourage girls to choose maths and science, women still mainly choose traditionally female courses at all levels of education which has a negative effect on their chances in the labour market (Dekkers, 1993).

Data from CBS (1995) show that more women with a higher level of education work, regardless of their own age and the age of their youngest child. The same category of women also makes use of childcare facilities more readily. Sixty per cent of mothers with a higher level of education work 20 to 34 hours per week in comparison to 40 per cent of mothers with a lower level of education. Maternity leave provision is available for 16 weeks at 100 per cent of earnings. Parents are entitled to reduced working hours for 6 months thereafter on an unpaid basis.

Working part-time has not contributed to improving women's position in terms of status and income. The part-time market is a predominantly 'women's market' typified by small, low-paid jobs in a limited range of occupations. This situation could change, however, in the near future. Legislation is being prepared at the moment which will give all employees the right to reduce their hours by 20 per cent.

The unequal position of women is manifest in their underrepresentation in higher positions. The percentage of women in top positions in the civil service varies with salary-scale. In 1995 women comprised 0.2 per cent of those on the highest grades (grade 18 and above), 0.9 per cent of those in the next band (grades 16 and 17), 5.8 per cent of those on grades 14 and 15 and 29.4 per cent of those on grades 12 and 13 (BIZA, 1996).

The situation is somewhat more favourable in politics. Since the last election, 48 of the 150 members of the lower house and 17 of the 75 members of the upper house are women. In the last government to be formed the number of women improved considerably. There are now 4 ministers and 5 women secretaries of state, the highest number ever achieved.

The number of women with a university education or higher professional education joining companies has increased considerably. Now that companies appoint more women and usually train them, they have an economic interest in keeping them. According to Tiedeman (1993) this points to

> more top women managers in the future. Idealism plays no role here; it is first and foremost a question of maximizing human capital. You do not need to be an economist to realize that it is a waste of money to train staff at great expense and then not utilize their knowledge and skills. Employers are also being forced to pay more attention to part-time work and, remarkably, it is slowly becoming accepted in the traditionally male sectors such as industry and higher management positions.
> (Tiedemann, 1993, p. 4)

Following the example of *Opportunity 2000* from England, a foundation known as *Opportunity in Bedrijf* was set up by the private sector and the government. The foundation's starting point is that a pluriform staff enhances the quality of the organization. On joining *Opportunity in Bedrijf*, companies commit themselves to improving the participation of women in the labour market both qualitatively and quantitatively. By 1997, 72 companies had joined the organization, including a community college and a university, and another university was considering membership.

UNPAID LABOUR

A distinct division of labour between the sexes is also characteristic of unpaid labour but the situation is the reverse to that in paid labour: 70 per cent of unpaid labour is performed by women and 30 per cent by men. Men's participation in unpaid work has indeed risen on average but this is mainly due to the increase in men living alone. In families with two working partners, women still spend almost twice as much time on housework and looking after the family as men, namely 17.7 hours per week in comparison to 9.4 hours. Compared with twenty years ago, working women now spend more than four hours per week extra on housework and looking after the family, whereas men spend less than three hours extra. Thus men now lag even further behind women in the number of hours spent on housework (SCP, 1996).

Public discussion of the combinability of paid labour and caring responsibilities shows that unpaid labour is becoming more highly respected and recognized as contributing to a better-functioning, more pluralistic society. A number of projections for the year 2010 focusing on the redistribution of paid and unpaid labour have been commissioned by the Ministry of Social Affairs. Of the four projections outlined, the 'combination scenario' is the most preferred. This comprises a package of family-friendly measures which enable the quality of care to be maintained while attaining an equal division of unpaid labour between women and men in the year 2010 (Commissie Toekomstscenarios Herverdeling Onbetaalde Arbeid, 1995).

The combinability of work and care is strongly influenced by the provision of childcare. Demand for childcare still outstrips provision even though the number of places has increased from 20,000 to more than 74,000. Subsidized childcare is available for only 5 per cent of children under the age of 4. Under this age, children of working parents attend part-time play groups, full or part-time day care centres or are looked after by childminders or relatives.

From the age of 4, children are taken care of at primary school. The school day used to be from 8.30 to 12 and from 2 to 4, with children going home to eat at lunch time. More and more schools are going over to a shorter school day, in particular by reducing the lunch break from two hours to one hour. Childcare provision during the lunch break is then easier, enabling children to be away from home for a longer unbroken period of time. About two-thirds of schools have introduced a 'continuous timetable' and provide childcare during the lunch break. About 50 per cent of children make use of this facility. Most schools finish at 3 o'clock but provision of after-school childcare between then and 6 o'clock is limited. Waiting lists are enormous in the larger cities and such facilities are non-existent in the smaller towns and villages (Dekkers, 1993).

Opinion polls show that conventional working patterns are poorly suited to the combinability of work and care. The high cost of childcare is also a serious obstacle. Many women and men find it difficult to arrange care for sick children (Spaans and Veldhoen, 1995).

THE DUTCH EDUCATION SYSTEM

Education in the Netherlands is compulsory from the age of 5 to 16. During their last year children only have to attend school part time. Nearly all children go to school at the age of 4. Practically all schools are co-educational. Education is administered in two ways:

- public authority education which is administered by the local authority,
- private education, i.e. schools founded and administered by private legal persons or entities.

Both types are funded 100 per cent by the state. The financial and judicial possibilities offered by this system (i.e. the right to and opportunities for an education of one's own persuasion) compare favourably with those of many other countries. They have made a considerable contribution to fulfilling the demand, historically very strong in the Netherlands, for religious and philosophical education which has resulted in a diversity of educational provision at all levels.

The Dutch education system comprises:

- primary education for 4- to 12-year-olds,
- secondary education for 12- to 16–18-year-olds,
- vocational training and adult education (community colleges),
- higher education at colleges of higher education (for professional education) and universities.

An important development in recent years has been the mergers that have taken place in all sectors, resulting in bigger and bigger schools. The heads of these schools have more and more become managers and are less involved in education itself. At the same time the way in which schools are funded has been changed. Schools are now increasingly responsible for their own budget and can no longer claim expenses from the ministry. They do, however, have a greater degree of autonomy in terms of policy and expenditure. All this demands very different skills of headteachers.

TEACHING AS A PROFESSION

Education is one of the largest employers in the Netherlands. The occupational group numbers 250,000 people which is almost 6 per cent of the working population. About 210,000 are teachers, the remaining 50,000 being ancillary staff. In total, about the same number of women and men are employed in education; although there are twice as many women in primary education as men, it is the reverse in secondary education and higher professional education (Commissie Toekomst Leraarschap, 1993) (see Table 9.1.).

After primary and secondary education, prospective teachers follow at least four years of teacher training. This training qualifies them to practise the profession to the full for the rest of their lives.

Table 9.1 Number of employees in education by sector and sex, 1996

	Primary education	Secondary education	Higher professional education
Men	29,113	59,898	13,735
Women	59,634	26,497	6,225
Total	88,747	86,395	20,060

Source: CBS, 1996.

Over the last 5 to 10 years the government has become increasingly concerned about the teaching profession. Teacher training courses are attracting fewer and fewer students. Health problems among teachers have become progressively more common. A special government commission and several studies have focused on the future of teaching (Commissie Toekomst Leraarschap, 1993). In comparison with other occupational groups in the Netherlands teaching clearly places an increasing psychological burden on its practitioners. This also applies to comparable groups in the health service and social services. Pressure of workload seems to comprise two elements: mental pressure and the enormous pressure of time.

During the last 10 years the teaching profession has in many respects become more demanding and wide-ranging. Patterns of interaction in the classroom have changed. Pupils are less amenable to authority and discipline than previously; they are more individualistic and mature than children were in the 1960s. Subject to many diverse kinds of pressure, they exhibit more behavioural and motivation problems which have an enormous influence on the atmosphere and order in the classroom. There have also been many changes in the curriculum and teaching methods in recent years. Moreover, since the 1970s the government has introduced a wide spectrum of new ideas on the structure and content of education. Government policy has been the cause of tension and concern as teachers consider the changes imposed from above to be inconsistent, educationally incorrect and a threat to working conditions. Lastly, looked at objectively, conditions of service in both the primary and secondary education sectors have deteriorated in the last 15 years. These conditions not only affect the pressure of workload, they make the profession less attractive (Commissie Toekomst Leraarschap, 1993).

In comparison with other countries, the workload of Dutch teachers is relatively high. The average number of pupils per class (22.4) in primary schools is one of the highest in Europe. In secondary education, a full-time job consists of 28 hours of teaching, which is considerably more than in many other countries. However, it was not until 1993 that agreements were reached in the Netherlands to increase starting salaries to make the profession more attractive. Currently, the salary of an experienced teacher just puts the Netherlands in the middle bracket of an international comparison (OECD, 1996). Primary headteachers are not paid much more than their classroom counterparts, although salary differentials are higher between promoted and non-promoted posts at the higher educational levels.

The pressure of workload is reinforced by the lack of possibilities for differentiation between jobs (horizontal transfer) and limited career opportunities (vertical transfer). Traditionally education has a flat structure with many people working at more or less the same horizontal level. The lack of career prospects in primary, secondary and further education was the reason for many looking outside the sector for career alternatives in the 1960s and 1970s. Increasing numbers of students and improved conditions for studying resulted in an expansion of higher professional and university education never experienced before. Teachers moved from primary education to secondary. Some went on to university and one or two even became professors. Depending on their interests and abilities, some teachers continued their careers in so-called 'teaching-related professions' at the National Institute for Educational Measurement, research institutes, and educational advisory centres and services. The result of this explosive growth within a period of just 10 years and the stagnation and cut-backs that followed was that the professional mobility of teachers became extremely limited.

Promotions are always made at school board level. Membership of school boards is voluntary, comprising parents and co-opted experts from business and finance. Procedure and policy are overseen by elected representative advisory councils, comprising members of staff, parents and sometimes pupils, which schools are legally obliged to set up. Selection procedures vary, with some posts being openly advertised and some not. There are no formal requirements, although in-service training is becoming increasingly important in this respect.

Job mobility in education is low; only 4 per cent of teachers change school or position per school year. It is highest in primary education where 3.8 per cent of teachers change school and 2.1 per cent change jobs internally. Younger teachers (below the age of 30), part-timers and teachers older than 55 are the most mobile. Those above 55 often leave teaching due to early retirement (early retirement scheme, pension or disability). Those in the age category between 30 and 55 years are scarcely mobile at all, either internally or externally (Helderman and Spruijt, 1992). Ultimately, this lack of mobility will have two consequences. Firstly, an ageing of the workforce will occur and secondly, teachers will start to feel trapped. In the long term, the lack of opportunities to change jobs can seriously affect motivation and health.

The traditional image of the headteacher as *Primus inter pares* is changing. After their initial training, teachers have traditionally qualified for headship by gaining practical experience. Current government policy places a headteacher in a new, central position. This started in 1985 with the publication of the government memorandum *More about Management*. Headteachers have since increasingly been ascribed an important dynamic role requiring initiative and leadership. Their behaviour is seen as the single, most determining factor in the realization of good quality education at a school. Changes in the headteachers' role and their growing responsibility for the continuity of the organization have made the question of headteachers' competencies, knowledge and training extremely pertinent. The government has therefore set up special training programmes for school heads in primary and secondary education.

Reorganization and mergers in the Dutch education system have seriously affected the position of managerial and teaching staff. Mergers have contributed to a decrease in the number of jobs for headteachers and deputy heads. This frustrates many teachers with management ambitions: one in five teachers would like to be a member of the school management team (Helderman and Spruijt, 1992). The process of mergers which has had a negative influence on the opportunities for vertical transfer will continue in all sectors of education in the near future.

A positive side to mergers is that they create a need for subject-related 'middle management' positions and staff positions in larger organizations, thereby providing more opportunities for horizontal transfer.

WOMEN IN EDUCATIONAL MANAGEMENT

The percentage of Dutch women employed in education is high in comparison with most other sectors of the labour market: 46 per cent women as opposed to 54 per cent men. However, the position of women is very different to that of men. They are not only more strongly represented in the lower levels than the higher levels of education, they are also underrepresented in school management in all sectors. Table 9.2 compares the percentage of women headteachers and deputy heads with the percentage of women teachers in different sectors of education in the Netherlands. This shows that the percentage of women in management positions is extremely low in comparison to the percentage of women teachers in virtually every sector. Although the percentage of women deputy heads is also lower than that of teachers, the difference is less great. The vocational training and adult education sector stands out from the others with nearly a quarter of the headships and 42 per cent of deputy headships held by women.

Table 9.2 Percentages of women heads, deputy heads and teachers in the different sectors of education, 1995–96

Sector	Heads	Deputy heads	Teachers
Primary education	13	47	76
Secondary education	7	12	33
Vocational training and adult education (1994–95)	24	43	42
Higher professional Education*	12	n/a	40
University education**	4	7	18

* In higher professional education, positions with a salary equivalent to scale 13 and higher are classed as heads.
** In university education, senior university lecturers are classed as deputies and professors as heads. Figures given are for 1995.

Source: Flüggen, 1996.

Table 9.3 shows the percentage of women in management positions over the last ten years and shows how little has changed.

Table 9.3   Percentages of women in education management in the different sectors of education, 1986–96

Sector	1986	1989	1991	1993	1994	1996
Primary	13	13	13	14	14	13
Secondary	5	5	5	6	6	7
Vocational Training	NDA	NDA	NDA	NDA	23	24*
Higher professional Training	NDA	NDA	8	7	10	12
University	1	1	2	NDA	4	4*

Notes
NDA: no data available.
* For the vocational training and adult education sector and for university education the most recent data available are for 1995.

Source: Ministry of Education and Science.

We will now discuss the position of women in management teams per sector and how this has developed in recent years.

Primary education

When the Primary Education Act came into effect in 1985, nursery and primary schools were combined to form new-style primary schools. This had a significant effect on the number of women in management posts. Previously, almost all heads of nursery schools had been women in comparison to 4 per cent in the old primary schools, but in the new primary schools only 12.5 per cent of heads were women (Ruijs, 1990). Ten years later in 1996, the percentage had hardly improved at all (Flüggen, 1996).

In many selection procedures it was automatically assumed that the previous head of a primary school would become the new head. This assumption was even stronger when the head was a man. Nine out of 10 male heads in comparison to 2 out of 3 female heads became head of a new school (Vogelaar *et al.*, 1987).

At the very last moment the Ministry of Education and Science made it possible to appoint two full-time heads in a joint headship as it was apparent that many women headteachers of nursery schools favoured this. There was also a lot to be said in favour of this from an educational point of view as an equal input from infant and primary schools would be assured. However, most of the appointment procedures were at an advanced stage when this measure was introduced. Ultimately about 5 per cent of schools in 1987 had a joint headship comprising a man and a woman.

More than 6,500 women lost their headships as a result of the mergers. About half of them were appointed deputy head in the new schools. Women have also lost ground here. In 1986, 75 per cent of deputy heads were women; ten years later this had dropped to 47 per cent. (The full figures are: 1986, 75 per cent; 1987, 70 per cent; 1988, 65 per cent; 1989, 60 per cent; 1993, 50 per cent; 1996, 47 per cent (CBS, 1996a)). Men are increasingly interested in the position of deputy which has apparently become more important in career planning. Studies have shown that the main reason cited by women for giving up a deputy headship is that it is almost impossible to combine this with caring for a family (Ministry of Education and Science, 1990).

Secondary education

Secondary education comprises a wide range of schools which fall into two categories: general education and vocational education. The schools vary in size and composition but are all co-educational. This has not always been the case. Schools providing secondary education for girls constituted a separate type of school until the end of the 1960s. Generally the headteacher was a woman. When this type of school was abolished the number of female secondary heads dropped considerably. Separate schools for boys and girls also existed in Catholic education. The heads of the Catholic girls' schools were women, usually nuns. Most of the staff were also nuns, many of whom disappeared from the staff rooms and headteachers' offices when mixed schools were introduced in Catholic education.

In the school year 1978–1979, 11 per cent of secondary schools had a woman headteacher. More than three-quarters were heads of home economics schools which were small schools with mainly female pupils. This type of school has slowly disappeared, having been incorporated into larger institutes combining several types of secondary education under one roof and no longer exist as independent schools. Their women headteachers usually lost their position when schools were merged. In 1988 the percentage of women headteachers had dropped to 4 per cent, an all-time low. The most recent figure (1996) shows a slight increase to 7.4 per cent (see Table 9.4).

Table 9.4 Developments in the percentage of women headteachers and deputy heads in secondary education from 1978 to 1996 (%)

	1978	1988	1996
Women headteachers	11.0	4.0	7.4
Women deputy heads	NDA*	10.0	12.0

* No data available.
Source: Central Bureau of Statistics; Ministry of Education, Culture and Science.

Owing to the mergers the number of headships and external vacancies has decreased dramatically in recent years. This is frustrating for women who are ambitious. Given the age of headteachers in office at the moment, 350 positions are expected to become vacant during the next ten years. These vacancies will provide new opportunities to increase the number of women headteachers and deputy heads (Flüggen, 1996).

Both in secondary and primary education research has been carried out on the obstacles to promotion which women encounter. The results of this research in fact confirmed the findings of earlier research carried out in other countries (Koolen and Ruijs, 1984). Job requirements constitute the first obstacle, in particular full-time availability and wide-ranging experience in education, including managerial experience. Secondly, women's underrepresentation in educational management was in itself an obstacle. Women in an exceptional, or token position easily become the target of stereotyping. Lastly, the traditional division of labour whereby women are mostly responsible for the home and family is an important factor. Those women who have succeeded in acquiring a management position said they encountered obstacles while applying for their job, as management qualities are associated with men, as well as opposition during the performance of that job. They had mostly been promoted internally whereas men in management positions tend to be appointed externally (Ruijs et al., 1986).

Following this small-scale research, a large-scale study comprising several sub-studies was instigated. One of these was on the career prospects of teachers and deputy heads in primary education and teachers, middle managers and deputy heads in secondary education (Ruijs, 1990). This research showed that the ambitions of women and men working in primary schools are markedly different. Men are more interested in a management position, preferably a single headship. Women see a management position as a long-term goal and favour a joint headship. The difference is less pronounced in secondary education.

Vocational training and adult education

Vocational training and adult education did not escape the general trend towards mergers and expansion. Following an earlier reorganization there were about 500 institutions in 1992. By 1997 this had decreased to 61, most of them large regional training centres, a kind of community college which combines five sorts of sectors. Women traditionally hold a large proportion, varying from a half to three-quarters, of management positions in two of these five sectors (evening adult education and basic adult education) (bve-procescoördinatie, 1997).

The regional training centres are run by management teams of no more than 3 people. Forty-six of these centres had been established by January 1997. Of the 138 members of the executive boards, 16 were women (about 11 per cent). Three of the chairs of the executive boards were women (bve-procescoördinatie, 1997).

Many of the women who had previously held a management position were not appointed to a top management position at the regional training centres but to a middle management position. They are still head of their old sectors but some of their responsibilities and authority have been transferred to the central management team. Owing to the variety of job definitions, it is difficult to draw any conclusions about the numbers involved. We can give an indication though of the proportion of women in the top management positions of regional training centres on the basis of salary scales, assuming that these scales correspond to the level of responsibility and authority. Recent research shows that of those in the highest salary scales, 16 per cent are women in comparison to 84 per cent men.

Higher professional education

During the 1980s higher professional education in the Netherlands underwent radical changes. As a result of economies of scale and subject specialization about 400 schools were replaced by about 25 large institutes and 45 smaller ones. The system of financing was changed from one based on claims to lump-sum financing. New posts, particularly in management, were created as a result of the change from school to institute, making new demands on heads and deputy heads. The government recognized that this could open up opportunities for women and an equal opportunities policy was developed accordingly (Ministry of Education and Science, 1990). Some institutes succeeded in achieving a balance of 50 per cent women and men in their management team. Nationwide, however, the picture looks very different. Institutes for higher professional education are run by a central management team. Only 4 per cent of the members of these teams and 9 per cent of the sector managers are women. Of all teachers in higher professional education at the moment, 34 per cent are women. Looking at the management salary scales, a small increase in the percentage of women can be seen. In 1993 12 per cent of the higher salary scales for management are taken up by women. (The same salary scales are used as in vocational training and adult education.) Two years ago this was still only 9 per cent. In view of the increase in the percentage of women in the higher salary scales, it does seem that there are some grounds for optimism but there is still a long way to go before proportional representation is achieved.

University education

There are 14 universities in the Netherlands, of which five are state universities, one is Protestant, two are Catholic, one is maintained by local authorities, one is agricultural, three are technical and one is an Open University. The first university was founded in 1575, but women had to wait three centuries before they were officially admitted and the first female associate professor was not appointed until 1917 (Noordenbos, 1994). Until recently, universities had a system of 'automatic promotion' from one grade to the next. For financial reasons this system was restructured and a professional structure was created similar to that of American universities. Automatic promotion is no longer in effect. Criteria for promotion became more stringent and it became much more difficult to obtain tenure. The number of tenured posts at universities was reduced for economic reasons, particularly in the arts and social sciences.

These changes were particularly disadvantageous for women who are generally younger, have less years of experience and due to their childcare obligations tend to take longer to fulfil academic requirements (Noordenbos, 1994). Even the equal opportunities measures taken at this time such as affirmative action programmes, the introduction of childcare systems, careers guidance and positive advertising to attract more women could not counteract this negative effect. Between 1970 and 1990 the absolute number of women academics in universities did increase but the number of women in the top two ranks dropped. In 1970, 2.7 per cent of professors were women (n = 65) whereas in 1990 the percentage was 2.6 (n = 63). The proportion of female associate professors dropped from 9.4 per cent (n = 312) in 1970 to 6.1 per cent (n = 144) in 1990 although the proportion of female assistant professors rose from 11.8 to 15.7 per cent in the same time period (Noordenbos, 1994). The most recent statistics (1995) do show a small rise in the relative number of women professors (4.2 per cent) and associate professors (7 per cent). The overall percentage of women academics in 1995 was 32, although it should be noted that this figure includes a large number of untenured research and teaching staff on short-term contracts (Flüggen, 1996).

Reasons put forward for the particular disadvantages which women academics face include their relative overrepresentation in newly-created vulnerable posts; often part-time and short-term. Many women also entered university employment in the 1980s at a time when it was not a prerequisite for promotion to the level of assistant professor (now reorganized as *Docents*) to hold a PhD. This is now not the case, so women are again handicapped by this. Two-thirds of women academics were on temporary contracts, as opposed to one-third of their male colleagues in 1987 and were employed for a shorter time period. This tendency is now on the increase for both sexes, although after five years on a temporary contract universities are obliged to either grant tenure to or 'let go' of a temporary lecturer. In addition, the option of part-time work and of job-sharing taken up by many women in higher education, results in little time in which to undertake research, limited access to 'old boy networks' and reduced promotion possibilities.

A study by Hawkins in 1990 suggested that women receive less encouragement to attend conferences, obtain research funds and to put themselves forward for promotion than their male colleagues, partly as a result of their dual roles in life. There is also evidence that selection boards give preference to people with 'male' characteristics such as competitiveness and leadership qualities. Women often do not apply for such posts, because they feel that the social and emotional costs of high-level competition are too high, both at work and at home (Noordenbos, 1994).

Although the greater participation of women in educational management has been a priority of equal opportunities policy in the Netherlands in recent years – we will discuss this more fully later – the percentage of women managers in education has not increased dramatically. In primary education there has even been a decrease.

PRESSURE FOR CHANGE

A great deal has already been done and still is being done by the central government to increase the number of women in educational management. Why does the government give such strong support to this goal? Besides the more fundamental emancipatory objectives such as equal opportunities for women and men to develop their talents and abilities, there are two reasons that are of particular importance in education.

Firstly, there is the issue of socialization. Children become acquainted with society through school. Constant exposure to traditional role patterns from a very early age will frustrate every endeavour in the future to instil a more emancipatory attitude. Secondly, there is the issue of quality of management. The character of school management is changing. The increasing autonomy of schools and social developments, such as the introduction of information technology, place other demands on managers in education. As a result certain aspects of school management are becoming increasingly important, namely, working with others, information feedback, process control, remaining focused on the quality of education (and not on the process of managing) and flexibility. Research has shown that these are precisely the qualities in which women school managers tend to be strong. They see themselves first and foremost as educational leaders, with pupils and teaching as high priorities, whereas men compete more with each other. Women also place great importance on an effective group process and on cooperation. They tend to stimulate team spirit and run their schools democratically (Ruijs, 1990; Warringa, 1995). Krüger (1994) placed the differences between women and men as headteachers in the context of research on effective schools. She compared the characteristics of women as headteachers with those of 'effective headteachers'. Her conclusion based on empirical research and a study of the literature, was that women have a number of characteristics that intrinsically make them good headteachers and that therefore a gender balance in educational management was desirable, a view endorsed by the government.

In the Dutch educational system central government has only limited powers with regard to staff appointments. Schools are run by either private school boards or local authorities and it is at this level that promoted posts are appointed. This naturally affects how policy is implemented and at the national level it takes the form of establishing the framework, stimulating and activating. A shift in emphasis is noticeable in the measures taken during the last ten years to increase the number of women headteachers. At first the emphasis was mainly on potential women candidates for headships (management courses, improving conditions of employment, networks, job application training). The accent then shifted to those responsible for the selection of school managers and to school boards (courses on recruitment and selection, information campaigns, subsidies, covenants). Recent developments are targets and monitoring, a statutory measure, a financial bonus and an educational prize. The rest of this section will give a brief description of the measures and their effects in chronological order. In the next section statutory measures and financial bonuses will be dealt with in more depth.

Management courses for women

Motivating and qualifying women for positions in educational management by means of management courses for women was the first aim of governmental policy. These courses were run in conjunction with information campaigns which were aimed at women and school boards, to publicize the courses. An extensive project, carried out between 1988 and 1991, provided courses for women in primary, secondary and higher professional education whose ambition was a management function. An estimated three thousand women attended these courses which were paid for by the government (Ministerie van Onderwijs en Wetenschappen, 1992a).

Research on the effects of the 'Women and Management' courses revealed that the participants became more involved in the management of their schools thereby acquiring a higher profile within the organization. An important learning effect mentioned by the participants was an increase in self-confidence. Their willingness to apply for jobs increased, they became more ambitious and more confident that they would actually be promoted to a management position (Krüger, 1989; van Eck and Vermeulen, 1990; van Eck, 1991).

A small survey of 70 women in higher education who had taken the course one or two years earlier, showed that 24 had secured a management position, while 5 had taken a job outside education (Ministry of Education and Science, 1990). Although the results of this policy were positive in the sense of motivating and qualifying women for management positions, the actual number of women appointed was on the whole disappointing (Emancipatieraad, 1991).

Improving conditions of employment

A second type of measure was aimed at improving the conditions of employment for women in management positions. As women are often responsible for a home and family as well as having a paid job, measures were taken that would make it easier to combine such responsibilities with a career in educational management. Part-time head teaching posts were introduced in 1987 in primary education and in 1988 in secondary education.

In primary education, joint headships have also been introduced; it is now possible to replace the positions of head and deputy head with two headteachers. Unfortunately, this measure came too late to secure the participation of former heads of nursery schools in the management of the new primary schools.

Several general measures were also introduced that were particularly favourable for women teachers. Increased provision for temporarily filling posts during maternity leave and agreements on reducing the teaching load of headteachers and on childcare are examples of these measures. Staffing regulations were made more flexible in higher professional education in 1988 and in vocational training and adult education in 1992. This enabled middle management positions to be created by means of job differentiation, thereby facilitating career planning for women and men. Evaluation has shown that school boards in fact made little use of the opportunity to improve conditions of employment (Emancipatieraad, 1991).

Candidate banks

The fact that an increase in the number of appointments of women to management positions did not materialize brought about a change of policy on recruitment and selection. This policy had two objectives. It aimed, on the one hand, to improve women's chances of success by preparing them for job applications. On the other hand, it aimed to motivate and support school boards and management teams in the selection and recruitment of women headteachers and deputy heads.

Hence, recruitment agencies known as 'candidate banks' were introduced for teachers in primary, secondary and higher professional education with the support of the government. These act as intermediaries between women seeking a management position and school boards looking for women candidates.

Networks

The government provided financial assistance to develop networks as a follow-up to the management training courses. Ex-participants can support each other in their search for a management position and in their performance in that position. Networks, operating on both a national and regional level, provide opportunities for women to gain further qualifications. Informal information circuits can develop as a result of the networks and experienced managers can act as sponsors to others. The aim is that school board members, governors and those involved in school advisory services and similar organizations will also participate in the networks.

An organization representing the interests of women in this field, the Foundation for Women in Educational Management (VrIOM), also receives financial assistance from the government. This foundation organizes national and regional conferences (including the national conference held in Amsterdam in November 1995), publishes a periodical, lobbies, and instigates research in this field.

Recruitment and selection

The experience gained from the candidate banks clearly indicates that a more professional approach to vacancies is an essential condition for the appointment of more women. This involves, for example, drawing up a profile and defining selection criteria in advance. Research shows that this is certainly not the norm in all schools (Ruijs en Mientjes, 1989). The research of de Kool (1994) and of van Eck, Wilbrink and Vermeulen (1994) also confirms that stereotyped decision-making on the choice of candidates is more likely to occur when job requirements are less specific and less explicit. The latter of these two studies also shows with the help of a simulation model that the order in which the different instruments of selection occur, in particular the interview and the psychological test, influences the outcome of the selection procedure, as does the number of women candidates generated by the job advertisement. The very wording of advertisement texts can be a significant factor in increasing the application rate of women, as identified in a survey carried out by Veldhuis, Hubens and Oudejans (1996).

The emphasis on recruitment and selection in policy is a trend that has continued in recent years, particularly in the form of support and encouragement to school boards. In primary education, subsidies have been granted for courses on recruitment and selection for school governors and for the preparation of a recruitment and selection handbook. Subsidies are also available to school boards for expert advice on implementing an equal opportunities selection procedure. In addition, information has been distributed by the central government, professional associations and school board organizations, including the circulation of a leaflet on the subject of women and management to all primary and secondary schools. The subject is also regularly discussed in the professional journals.

Covenants

So-called 'covenants' to increase the number of women in management positions were drawn up by school board organizations, the government and professional associations in vocational and secondary education in 1992 and primary education in 1994. These comprised a number of recommendations to the members of the school board organizations and professional associations who committed themselves to abide by the covenants. They were to formulate targets and develop a policy with the objective of proportional representation of women in management positions; to implement a preferential policy in which women are appointed if they are equally suitable; to endeavour to have at least one woman in the management team; and to pay explicit attention to the position of women in careers policy. Within the framework of these recommendations, additional money was made available to three vocational education institutions to develop a policy for affirmative action and recommendations that are transferable to other organizations. These covenants have contributed to the school boards' awareness of the problem.

Targets and Monitoring

In 1993 the ministry began setting target figures. These figures are checked every year with the help of the 'education thermometer' in the government's magazine on education (*Uitleg*). The education thermometer shows the actual percentage of women in education management per year and what this should be according to the target figures. This means that educational institutions can compare their efforts with the target percentages. The figures also serve as a gauge for policy makers of the desired changes in policy. The target figures are to be attained by the school year 2000/2001. Table 9.5. compares the figures for 1993 and 1996 with the target.

Table 9.5 Target figures for women headteachers and deputy heads compared with the situation in 1993 and in 1996

	1993	1996	2000
Primary education			
women headteachers	13.5%	13.1%	28.5%
women deputy heads	50.0	47.7	52.0
Secondary education			
women headteachers	5.8	7.4	20.0
women deputy heads	11.4	11.6	28.0
Vocational training and adult education			
women headteachers	20.9	24.2*	33.0
women deputy heads	38.6	42.8*	50.0
Higher professional education**	8.8	11.8	23.0
University education			
professor	3.6***	4.2	18.5
associate professor	6.4***	7.0	21.0

*   data from 1995
**   percentage of women in the higher salary scales
*** data from 1992

Source: Flüggen, 1996.

At the present rate the target figures will clearly not be achieved until long after the school year 2000–2001. In most cases the participation of women must be doubled at the very least, which has resulted in the need for the government to step up this policy, taking the form of the following three measures.

Legislation

An important instrument in the process of equal representation is legislation. The law on proportional representation stipulates that all school boards (from primary to university education) must produce a document every two years setting out target figures for the proportional representation of women in management positions in education, the measures that have been taken and the period in which these figures are to be achieved. It was passed by the lower house at the beginning of 1996 and by the upper house in February 1997.

Financial incentives

Another instrument is extra subsidy to cover the cost of pursuing a broad policy of affirmative action. It is only applicable to the vocational training and adult education sector. Concern exists in this sector that the creation of community colleges by merging smaller institutions will result in the same exodus of women from management positions as occurred during the mergers in infant and primary education. A comparable imbalance exists between vocational training and adult education institutions as that between infant and primary schools. Infant schools and evening institutes, the lesser partners in these mergers, have a relatively high number of women managers. These could fall by the wayside in the appointment of new small-scale management teams (Warringa, 1995).

The Sapientia Prize

The Sapientia Prize is a joint initiative of the school board organizations, the Association of Netherlands Municipalities and the Ministry of Education, Culture and Science. A statue representing wisdom, knowledge and understanding, the Sapientia is awarded annually to institutions that pursue an active policy on women and management. The first three Sapientias were presented in March 1996 to three schools and their school boards in primary education, secondary education and vocational training and adult education.

In the next section we will discuss legislation and financial incentives in more detail, both of which were the cause of considerable controversy.

RECENT DEVELOPMENTS

As already mentioned, the role of the government in appointing headteachers is fairly limited. It has been curbed further since schools have increasing freedom to pursue their own policies on educational, material, financial and personnel matters. However, the government wants to retain a special responsibility for women and educational management for as long as women lag behind in obtaining promotions. The government pursues its own policy on the one hand while drawing the attention of the institutions to their responsibilities on the other.

Recent measures must be placed in this context. Two examples of government measures to make the policy on women in educational management effective, taking into account the developments mentioned above, are the so-called 'three hundred thousand guilder measure' and the law on proportional representation of women in management positions in education.

Further financial incentives for affirmative action

The 'three hundred thousand guilder measure' is an incentive measure introduced by the central government in the vocational training and adult education sector to cover the cost of pursuing a broad policy of affirmative action. From the moment that a regional training centre has an approved policy plan for affirmative action and there is at least one woman in the central management team, it is entitled to an additional subsidy. This subsidy of 100,000 guilders (more than £30,000 sterling) is allocated annually for a maximum of 3 years for as long as there is a woman in the central management team.

How this money is used is a decision for the regional training centre and is specified in the annual accounts. It could be used, for example, for an extra post in the central management team or for activities within the framework of the project plan 'affirmative action on equal opportunities for women'. The policy plan must include the following points:

• a description of the 'zero situation' including the current composition of the management of the centre,
• a description of the target situation to be attained by the regional training centre within 3 years,
• a description of the resources and activities required to realize the target situation.

The appointment of a woman to the central management team (for an indefinite period of time) must be realized within 6 months of the plan being approved. It is hoped that in this way regional training centres will develop a human resource policy that will work towards a situation in which the appointment and further promotion of women to senior management positions is the norm in personnel policy.

By linking subsidies to a combination of the appointment of a woman to the central management team and the active development of an affirmative action policy, it is hoped that both short and medium term effects will be realized. In the short term, the objective is to increase the number of women in central management teams. Assuming that all 45 regional training centres take advantage of this measure, at least 1 of the 2 to 4 members of the central management teams will be a woman (bve, 1997). The target figure for the year 2000 stipulated in the memorandum *Equal Opportunities in Education 1993–1996* of the Ministerie van Onderwijs en Wetenschappen (1992b) will then be achieved in one go. In the medium term the project activities, which will form an essential part of the personnel policy of the regional training centres, will make a useful contribution to the policy to be developed on target groups.

At first the measure caused quite a commotion. Press reports talked disparagingly about 'the woman with three hundred thousand'. There was concern that women would only be appointed for the money and not because of their qualities. Just one community college applied for the subsidy in the first year (1995–96). The number of applications has increased considerably during the current school year (1996–97). By September 1997 it will be clear exactly how many community colleges fulfil the conditions for the subsidy. What is already evident is that an increased number of women have been appointed to the executive boards. In February 1997 the chair of the executive board of 3 of the 46 regional training centres, almost 7 per cent, was a woman. There were women on the executive boards of 15 regional training centres (including the chairpersons), one of which had two women members. The total number of members of all executive boards is 138 of which more than 11 per cent are women.

Research by Laemers (1996) provides evidence of a slight increase in 1996 in the number of women in middle management positions. It is essential that these women receive the necessary help and support to enable them to be promoted further when vacancies occur.

The law on proportional representation of women in management positions in education

In view of the disappointing effect of a wide range of non-compulsory measures, there were doubts about the so-called 'self-regulatory capacity' of schools, i.e. the extent to which schools are capable of developing and implementing an affirmative action policy without being compelled to. The government therefore endeavoured to find a measure which would strengthen that self-regulatory capacity. This resulted in the introduction of a law in March 1997. Five years of political pressure, in particular by the pressure group 'Women Headteachers Now', played an important role in the realization of this measure. Members of this platform included representatives of educational and women's organizations, political parties and teachers' unions.

Under the provisions of the law, the boards of schools and institutions in which women are underrepresented in management positions must submit a report to the Ministry of Education, Science and Culture at least once every two years. The report must describe the activities that are part of the affirmative action policy of the institute concerned, explain how the policy is being implemented, including a time plan for the attainment of target figures, and must also discuss the development of activities to increase the number of women in management positions.

The aim of this statutory measure is firstly to encourage the school boards;

it is an appeal to their sense of responsibility, without restricting their freedom of appointment. Schools set the targets themselves and must later account for the results achieved. The law enables representative advisory councils, for example, to draw the attention of the school boards to their responsibilities. Compliance with the measure is monitored by the education inspectorate which then reports to the Ministry.

Implementation will be supported by an information campaign called *Women and Management* aimed at school board organizations in the different educational sectors. *Uitleg*, the official magazine of the Ministry of Education, Science and Culture, will also publicize this statutory measure (Ministerie van Onderwijs, Cultuur en Wetenschappen, 1995). The measure will be implemented for 5 years in the first instance, after which an evaluation will be made and the measure will possibly be extended.

A Broad Range of Measures

Both the three hundred thousand guilder measure and recent legislation encourage schools to formulate a package of measures that together form a coherent whole, stimulating the appointment and promotion of women to management positions in education and enabling them to stay in those positions.

Employing a wide range of measures has proved successful in the past. The ministerial publication produced for the *Women and Management* conference held in Vienna in 1990 cited the example of the Amsterdam Institute of Higher Education (see Ruijs, 1993). This institute is the result of a merger of 12 schools in 1987. Before the merger women held 32 per cent of the management posts. Shortly after August 1987, this figure had dropped to 21 per cent. By means of an active equal opportunities policy the institute has managed to achieve a 50 per cent representation of women in management. The measures included:

- courses on management in higher education for women,
- preferential treatment for women when a vacancy occurs in a field where women are underrepresented (i.e. where they make up less then 50 per cent of the staff),
- career counselling for women teachers and secretarial staff,
- active efforts to recruit women when appointments are to be made,
- equal numbers of men and women on committees,
- the opportunity to work part time in all jobs, including management positions with the minimum requirement of a 60 per cent post,
- childcare leave with the right to unpaid leave or a part-time job while caring for a child under 4 years of age, including the right to return to the applicant's old job with the same number of hours.

A woman head of department at the Amsterdam Institute of Higher Education explains:

In our experience, there are suitable women for all jobs; it's simply a matter of finding them. The organization must be willing to look hard and understand why it is important to do so. Institutions undergoing a process of change, such as ours, are in particular need of management with an eye for the qualities of the staff. Women have traditionally been good at this. At our institute we have seen that a balance between men and women in management creates a better working atmosphere.   (Ministry of Education and Science, 1990)

For the sake of future generations it is to be hoped that the recent developments will ultimately have the desired effect: an equal representation of men and women in educational management. The masculine image that management is similar to man, will hopefully be consigned to the past before long. It is also in the interest of schools to attain a balanced gender ratio in management in order to promote a better quality of management more able to deal with the demands of these changing times.

REFERENCES

BIZA (Ministry of Home Affairs) (1996) *Mensen en Machten in de Rijksdienst* (People and powers in the state administration). Den Haag.

bve-procescoördinatie (1997) Door het glazen plafond. Eindrapportage emancipatie 1992–1996 (Through the glass ceiling. Final report on equal opportunities 1992–1996), *bve-informatief*, no. 43.

CBS (Central Bureau of Statistics) (1995) *Enquete beroepsbevolking 1995* (Survey of the working population 1995). Heerlen, CBS.

CBS (Central Bureau of Statistics) (1996a) *Zakboek onderwijstatistieken* (Education statistics notebook). Heerlen, CBS.

Commissie Toekomst Leraarschap (1993) *Een beroep met perspectief: de toekomst van het leraarschap* (The future of teaching, a profession with prospects). Leiden, DOP.

Commissie Toekomstscenarios Herverdeling Onbetaalde Arbeid (1995) *Onbetaalde zorg gelijk verdeeld: toekomstscenarios voor herverdeling van onbetaalde zorgarbeid* (Unpaid work divided equally: future scenarios for the redistribution of unpaid care work). Den Haag, Ministerie van Sociale Zaken en Werkgelegenheid.

Dekkers, H. (1993) *Onderwijsemancipatiebeleid en economische zelfstandigheid van vrouwen in Noordwest Europa* (Equal opportunities policy in education and the economic independence of women in North-West Europe). Nijmegen, ITS.

Eck, E. van (1991) *Marie maakt het; een evaluatie van de cursus vrouw en management in het hoger beroepsonderwijs* (Mary's making it; an evaluation of the women and management course in higher professional education). Amsterdam, SCO.

Eck, E. van and Vermeulen, A. C. A. M. (1990). *Kwaliteit geboden, kwaliteit gevraagd. Een onderzoek naar de effecten van de managementcursus voor vrouwen in het primair onderwijs* (Quality on offer, quality on demand. A study of the effects of the management course for women in primary education). SCO-rapport 237. Amsterdam, SCO.

Eck, E. van, Wilbrink, B. and Vermeulen, A. C. A. M. (1994) *Doelmatigheid en partijdigheid van psychologisch onderzoek bij de selectie van schoolleiders in het primair onderwijs* (The suitability and partiality of psychological testing in the selection of headteachers in primary schools). SCO-rapport 359. Amsterdam, SCO.

Emancipatieraad (1991). *Advies vrouwen in onderwijsmanagement* (Advice to women in educational management). Den Haag.

Flüggen, M. (1996) Evenwicht m/v is nog zoek. Thermometer Vrouw en management 1996. (M/f balance is still missing. Women and management thermometer 1996). *Uitleg*, no. 30, 4 December 1996.

Gordijn, C. M. N. and Janssen, G. F. M. (1996) in het HBO presteren vrouwen beter, in *Kwartaalbericht Onderwijsstatistieken* 1996–4, Heerlen, CBS.

Hawkins, A. C. (1990) The perception of the work situation of male and female scholars working in universities in the Netherlands, in E. K. Hicks, and G. Noordenbos (eds.) *Is the alma mater friendly to women?* Maastricht, van Gorcum Assen.

Helderman, J. A. M. and Spruijt L. G. M. (1992) *Arbeidsmobiliteit in het onderwijs* (Labour mobility in education). Gravenhage, KASKI.

Kool, N. E. de (1994) *Werving en selectie van schoolleiders in het basisonderwijs* (Recruitment and selection of primary headteachers). Amsterdam, Vrije Universiteit.

Koolen, R. and Ruijs, A. (1984) *Karrièrebelemmeringen voor vrouwen in het onderwijs* (Career obstacles for women in education). Nijmegen, Katholieke Universiteit Nijmegen.

Krüger, M. L. (1989) Female and male school leadership and school effectiveness in secondary education, in J. T. Voorbach and L. G. M. Prick (eds.) *Teacher Education 5; Research and developments on teacher education in the Netherlands* (pp. 125–41). Den Haag, SVO.

Krüger, M. (1994) *Sekseverschillen in schoolleiderschap* (Gender differences in educational management). Alphen a/d Rijn, Samson H. D. Tjeenk Willink.

Laemers, M. (1996) *Vrouwen in bve-management*, Nijmegen: ITS.

Ministerie van Onderwijs, Cultuur en Wetenschappen (1995) *Memorie van toelichting bij: Wijziging van enkele onderwijswetten in verband met het opnemen van een document inzake evenredige vertegenwoordiging van vrouwen in leidinggevende functies in het onderwijs.* Den Haag, Sdu.

Ministerie van Onderwijs en Wetenschappen (1992a) *Beleidsreactie vrouwen in onderwijsmanagement.* (Policy reaction to women in educational management). Zoetermeer, Ministerie van Onderwijs en Wetenschappen.

Ministerie van Onderwijs en Wetenschappen (1992b) *Onderwijsemancipatienota; onderwijsemancipatie 1993–1996* (Memorandum on equal educational opportunities; equal opportunities 1993–96). Zoetermeer, Ministerie van Onderwijs en Wetenschappen.

Ministry of Education and Science (1990) *Women and school management in the Netherlands.* Alberts/Druko, Gulpen.

Noordenbos, G. (1994) Women academics in the Netherlands: between exclusion and positive action, in S. Stiver Lie, L. Malik and D. Harris (eds.) *1994 World Yearbook on Education: the Gender Gap in Higher Education.* Kogan Page, London.

OECD (1996) *Education at a glance*, Paris.

Ruijs, A. (1990) *Vrouwen en schoolmanagement* (Women in School Management). Amsterdam, Swets and Zeitlinger.

Ruijs, A. (1993) *Women Managers in education – a world-wide progress report.* Coombe Lodge Report, Vol. 23, nos. 7, 8, Staff College, Bristol.

Ruijs A., Mens, A., Baggen, C., and Janssen, B. (1986) *Schoolmanagement: een mannenzaak? Verkennend onderzoek naar de positie en de toenemende ondervertegenwoordiging van vrouwen in de schoolleiding van het voortgezet onderwijs* (School management: a man's world? Exploratory research on the position and increasing underrepresenation of women in management positions in secondary schools). Nijmegen, ITS.

Ruijs, A. and Mientjes, A. (1989) *Werving en selectie van schoolmanagers. Een onderzoek naar de sollicitatieprocedures voor schoolmanager in het basis- en voortgezet onderwijs.* (Recruitement and selection of school managers. A study of application procedures for school managers in primary and secondary education). Nijmegen, ITS.

SCP (1996) *Sociaal Cultureel Rapport* (Social-Cultural Report). Rijswijk, Sociaal en Cultureel Planbureau.

Spaans, J. and Veldhoen, M. E. (1995) *Kinderopvang en Arbeidsparticipatie van vrouwen met kinderen* (Childcare and the participation of women with children in the labour market). Eindrapportage per 31-1-1993. Leiden, Research voor Beleid.

Tiedemann, E. (1993) We hadden er een, maar ze ging weg. Vrouw zeldzame verschijning in de top van het bedrijfsleven. (We had one, but she left. The scarcity of women at the top of industry). *Elsevier*, Vol. 49, no. 11, 20 maart 1993.

UNDP (1995) *Human Development Report of the United Nations Development Programme.* Oxford University Press.

Veldhuis, C., Hubens, A. and Oudejans, A. (1996) *Vrouwen in de schoolleiding* (Women in school management). Amsterdam, Regioplan.

Vogelaar *et al.* (1987) *Schoolmanager gezocht (V), (School mananger [female] required).* Aramith Uitgevers, Amsterdam.

Warringa, A. (1995) Meer vrouwen in de schoolleiding (2) (More women in school management). *Uitleg*, no. 30, 6 December 1995.

10

Norway

Jorunn Oftedal

WOMEN AT WORK

In 1960 just 22 per cent of Norwegian women between 25 and 66 years of age were in employment – fewer than anywhere else in Europe. However, because of the Norwegian government's commitment to a policy of full employment and gender equality, by 1993 the situation had changed dramatically, with 72 per cent of women in the labour force. The effect of this 'revolution' has been to lead women of all ages and social backgrounds, and from all parts of the country, to go out to work, so that now there is hardly any difference in the *rate* of employment between young men and young women (Rasmussen, 1994 and Official Statistics of Norway, 1993). However, the division between the sexes in the *type* of work they engage in has led the Ministry of Children and Family Affairs to say that women and men are to a large extent employed in different sectors.

Nowadays young women expect to have paid employment. Of women aged from 16–24 years in 1994, 46.6 per cent had jobs, and a further 6 per cent were looking for work, while the remainder were in education. At the same time, 50.4 per cent of men were in employment. Most young women complete their education and have a job before they start a family. They return to their paid employment after they have children, but often choose to work part time. The rules for parental leave, and changing social attitudes, have made it much easier for mothers to return to work after taking maternity leave.

A high proportion (47.4 per cent) of women in the labour force are classified as part-time workers, i.e. they work less than 30 hours per week, as compared with one in ten men. This sort of work is particularly common in the female-dominated caring professions. Forty-three per cent of women kindergarten teachers and 40 per cent of all other women teachers work part-time after 10 years in the profession, usually for family reasons. Nonetheless, an enquiry carried out in 1993 found that 14 per cent of women part-time workers (aged 16–74 years) wanted more work. Satisfying this demand is to some extent a public responsibility, since women account for 64 per cent of all public sector employees (Norsk Lærarlag, 1994a). Women carry the main responsibility for everyday housework and childcare. Research shows that, on average, mothers of small children spend 6 hours 37 minutes on housework and the care of small children per day. Fathers spend 3 hours 30 minutes on the same tasks. Women spend less time on housework than in the past, and men rather more; young men also tend to give more help with childcare than their fathers did (Likestillingsrådet, 1995).

However, childcare can be a problem for families where both parents work, especially as compulsory school does not begin before the age of 6 in Norway. Although all childcare institutions are subsidised by central government, places in most local authority nurseries are very limited. In 1992, for example, only 43 per cent of children under 6 years of age were offered nursery places, with priority being given to the oldest children. Most families arrange childcare with a grandmother or neighbour – very few employ a nanny to look after their children at home.

Opening hours in nurseries are 7.30 a.m–4.30 p.m., which means that parents with full-time jobs have to live (and work) nearby in order to collect their child at the end of the day. Grandmothers and neighbours are usually more flexible about 'opening' hours. The school day lasts from 8.30 a.m. to 2.00 p.m. Some local authorities provide after-school care for children whose parents cannot pick them up straight after school. Milk, but no meals are provided at school and children bring their own packed lunches. Shopping is less of a problem for families where both parents work full time because shops open late at least once a week.

The cost of having a child in a nursery depends on parental income: the more you earn, the more you pay. However, fees are fixed by law, and unlike informal financial arrangements with neighbours and grandmothers, they can be set against taxable income.

Parental leave is comparatively generous in relation to other European countries. Since 1993 parents have been entitled to a total of 1 year's leave shared between both partners on 80 per cent of salary, or 42 weeks on full salary, and up to 3 years of unpaid leave. The employer's costs are refunded from the social security system. Mothers have to take a minimum of 3 weeks before and 6 weeks after delivery; the father is entitled to a minimum of 4 weeks' leave on full pay, which are lost if not taken. Most fathers take 2 weeks when the mother comes out of hospital and another 4 when she returns to work. Parents are free to divide the remainder of their statutory leave as they wish, although in practice few fathers exercise this right.

Unless they are especially well off, or on a high income, most mothers with three or four children are likely to stay at home with them, since the costs of day care for several children are so expensive. However, in 1990 the average number of children per woman was 1.9. Since 1994, parental leave may be used flexibly. Parents can save a certain number of months, to be used later in the form of reduced working hours without loss of income for a period of up to 2 years. Working parents are also entitled to a certain amount of time off work to care for sick children, on full pay, ranging from 10 to 21 days (RMFA and RMCFA, 1994).

Raising the educational level of women in the labour force is essential if there are to be more women leaders in society. In 1993 45.6 per cent of women in work had received university education compared to 35 per cent 10 years before. However, there are few women in top jobs. The number of women in senior positions in business has remained at approximately 10 per cent for the past 15 years. None of the companies quoted on the stock exchange has a woman director. Of the 10,000 largest companies in Norway, just 67 are run by a woman. However, the proportion of women senior executives between 20 and 29 years of age has risen to 21 per cent in 1993. This may indicate a new trend in the younger generation of businesswomen. Women are now in the majority in the public and private service sectors, but not yet in the more senior posts, as Table 10.1 shows, or at executive level.

Table 10.1   Percentage of women employees in Norway in 1994

	Female employees	Female managers
Private sector	47%	29%
Public sector	64%	43%

Source: Norsk Lærerlag 1994a.

Women now account for 73 per cent of all office staff. However, records show that, in 1994, 15 per cent of male office-workers in the 20–34 year age-group held senior positions, compared to 2 per cent of women (Likestillingsrådet, 1995).

THE NORWEGIAN EDUCATION SYSTEM

Geography and population patterns have had a great influence on the organisation of regional and local schools. Many schools are very small, on remote islands, or in remote valleys.

School attendance in Norway is now compulsory from the age of 6. The 10-year 'basic' school is fully comprehensive, with no streaming, and only minor curricular choice. It provides 7 years of primary and 3 years of lower-secondary education. Although upper-secondary education is non-compulsory, 98 per cent of students currently continue to this level.

Upper-secondary studies are divided into 13 main courses, of which 10 are vocational and 3 academic. Those who opt for academic studies can apply for university after 3 years. Approximately half of all students choose vocational studies, which consist of 2 years of theory at school followed by 2 years of work as an apprentice and a final exam. At this stage, those vocational students who want to can also apply for university, in which case they will be required to complete a final year of academic study at school. Boys and girls have in the past made very different (and traditional) choices in vocational studies. How far this pattern may change is not clear: this structure was only introduced in 1994, so it has not yet been fully evaluated.

Norway has four universities. They are located in Oslo, Bergen, Trondheim (including the Norwegian Institute of Technology) and Tromsoe. It also has six specialised colleges at university level; the Agricultural College of Norway, the Norwegian School of Economics and Business Administration, the Norwegian College of Veterinary Medicine, the Norwegian College of Physical Education and Sport, the Norwegian State Academy of Music and the Oslo School of Architecture. These institutions have a two-fold function: research and teaching. They offer degrees at several levels, requiring courses of study lasting four to seven years.

Norway has 26 regional colleges with divisions spread over almost a hundred different cities. The decentralisation of higher education was a move to make education more accessible and to raise the level of qualified expertise in outlying parts of the country. The programmes offered at these colleges are usually shorter and more occupationally orientated than those at the universities. Courses of study usually last two or three years, but may also be combined with university studies.

There are about 160,000 students at universities and colleges (1993). This figure increased by 60 per cent from 1988 to 1993. There are also more than 8,000 Norwegian students abroad. In 1992 60 per cent of the population had completed upper secondary or higher education.

All state education is free. The State Educational Loan Fund provides financial support for students in the form of loans and grants. The Fund enables pupils and students to acquire an education irrespective of gender, social and financial background (Ministry of Education, Research and Church Affairs, 1994).

There are very few private schools in Norway; single-sex classes and schools were abolished by the 1969 Education Act. Primary and lower secondary schools are managed by the local authorities, while colleges and universities are governed centrally.

Although appointments to senior positions in the school system are generally advertised openly, in most cases they are made from within the existing staff. The formal requirements for such posts are professional teaching qualifications and practical experience of working in schools. In primary schools, being a team leader may be a first step to promotion. In secondary schools, becoming a head of a curriculum area or a director of studies may constitute an intermediate step on the promotional ladder.

The promotion process may differ slightly between local authorities, but the first step is usually for the authority to draw up a job specification. Shortlisted candidates are interviewed by a panel comprising elected representatives from the local county or town council, and representatives of the teachers' association and of the Department of Education. The final decision is taken by a board made up of local councillors and teachers association representatives. If any member of this board wishes, the applications can be sent for consideration by the Council for Equal Rights (if there is one) of the local authority concerned.

WOMEN IN TEACHING

Teaching has traditionally been a high status job in Norway. From 1869 women and men with the relevant educational qualifications have had an equal right to work as teachers, though women teachers were expected to give lessons only to the youngest children. Until 1918 women teachers were paid less than men – and were often preferred by local authorities for that reason.

It is very difficult to get a place in a teacher training college, probably because teaching is thought of as being a 'secure' job, although not very well-paid in comparison with other graduate jobs. A student needs to have completed 12 years of academic education with very good marks to be accepted onto a training course, which now lasts 4 years. The colleges train students who will go on to teach in the 10 compulsory years of education (primary and lower secondary). It is also possible to qualify as a teacher of children in lower and upper secondary schools by studying at least three subjects at university level, followed by 1 year of teacher training.

In the university sector, all assistant professors are now automatically promoted to the rank of associate professors on completion of a doctorate. Full professorships are bestowed by selection committees, whose guidelines stipulate that at least 1 woman should be represented, where there are female applicants. In practice, these committees remain essentially male-dominated (Stiver Lie and Teigen, 1994). Many associate professors are on fixed-term contracts and it is quite difficult to obtain a permanent contract. Whether female candidates lose out in this process is a matter of some debate.

Most teacher training students (72 per cent in 1993) are women. Men and women teachers receive the same basic pay, but on average men earn more than women (Norsk Lærarlag, 1994a). This is partly because wages are calculated according to the number of years spent in training and the number of years worked – and male teachers have generally studied for longer than their female colleagues (e.g. by taking BA or MA degrees after teacher training college). Men also hold more senior, better-paid positions than women, a pattern which will be explored in a later section.

WOMEN IN EDUCATIONAL MANAGEMENT

In 1993 6.9 per cent of all employees in Norway worked in education and research (Official Statistics of Norway, 1993). Women working in this sector generally have jobs with lower status and lower pay than men. A striking example of this imbalance is seen in the high percentage of women working in state-run nurseries, in contrast to the low percentage of women on the academic staff of universities.

Most nurseries are staffed by women, who also hold most of the senior management positions in this sector, as Table 10.2 shows. Women working in nurseries enjoy lower status and salary than their counterparts in other parts of the school system – even though they are required to have the same length of education as teachers and senior staff in schools. Although under 3 per cent of nursery staff are men, 49 per cent of them hold senior positions, compared to just 34 per cent of women. These figures would seem to indicate that men have easier access to higher office than women, and may also be more ambitious.

Table 10.2   Distribution of women teachers in state-run nurseries, 1986 and 1992

	1986	1992
Women headteachers	94.7%	95.5%
Women teachers	96.3%	97.5%

Source: Norsk Lærerlag, 1994a.

Women teachers of younger pupils are in a clear majority in the compulsory school sector, but men still occupy most management posts at all levels. Since 1973 the percentage of women teaching in the years of compulsory school attendance has increased from 52 per cent to 65 per cent. The percentage of women taking up management positions in that period has increased at a faster rate, from 8 per cent to 34 per cent (Norsk Lærarlag, 1994b). This increase might be the result of extra motivation, of management courses arranged by the employer (the local authority), coupled with a general change in attitude among female teachers, that leads them to be more attracted to senior posts. We expect this trend to continue. Table 10.3 reveals how opportunities for women differ between schools for students of different ages.

Teachers and managers in upper secondary schools are predominantly male, although the overall proportion of women teachers has risen from 25 to 39 per cent between 1980 and 1994. The predominance of men in upper secondary education can be attributed to two reasons. Until the late 1980s,

Table 10.3   Distribution of women teachers in state schools in 1994

Type of school	Women teachers	Women headteacher/deputy head
Primary	74%	40%
Lower secondary	51%	24%
Primary and lower secondary under one headteacher	61%	29%
Upper secondary	39%	22%[1]

Note
1. Headteachers only. In that year 31% of deputy heads were women.
Source: Sentralt tjenestemannsregister for skoleverket, 1994.

more men than women studied at university, and so were more likely to have the higher qualifications needed to teach in upper secondary schools. In vocational schools, where experience of working in business and industry is also a requirement, men still outnumber women in courses leading to a teaching degree, except for health-care and social studies, and art. Although 58 per cent of women upper secondary teachers work part-time, the division between full-time and part-time work is not as sex-differentiated as in other countries: 41 per cent of male upper secondary teachers also work part time, as do 7 per cent of male and 9 per cent of female school managers. Table 10.3 shows how women are unequally represented at senior levels in this type of school. However, women now account for 31 per cent of all deputy headships, and many of them may be expected to become headteachers in due course.

In 1993 24 per cent of pupils completing upper secondary education went on to higher education (Official Statistics of Norway, 1993). Women university students are now in a majority, as Table 10.4 indicates. However, women and men students choose very different courses of study. Science and agriculture are still male dominated, although the number of women students in these subjects has increased. Women now predominate in the former male bastions of law and medicine. Since the early 1980s most technical colleges have pursued admissions policies designed to favour women applicants, and this has had the effect of doubling the proportion of women students to just over 20 per cent.

The development of regional colleges has made it easier for women whose mobility is restricted by care responsibilities to continue their education. Other education policy instruments include the awarding of grants instead of loans to mothers, and the provision of better day-care facilities. Universities also receive larger payments for each woman student who completes a Master's degree (RMFA and RMCFA, 1994). Despite the high proportion of women students in universities, female academics remain in a minority.

In the late 1980s, affirmative action resulted in a rise in the proportion of women full professors from 5 per cent in 1985 to 8.5 per cent in 1991. At that time women represented 36 per cent of the academic staff in colleges and 20 per cent in universities. The Norwegian Parliament decided to allow promotion to full professorships on the basis of merit in addition to vacancy of posts, in order to increase the number of women in top university positions. Extra funds were also made available for the creation of full professorships. As Table 10.4 shows, this has had a limited success.

In 1992, the first woman university rector was appointed at Oslo. However, the power structures of Norwegian universities remain dominated by men. In 1993 only 2 deans, and 18 per cent of heads of department were women. At the level of representation on faculty councils and in the ranks of administrative managers, women have greatly improved their representation, to around 33 per cent and 58 per cent respectively in the same year (Stiver Lie and Teigen, 1994).

Table 10.4   Distribution of women students and academic staff in universities and colleges in 1971 and 1993 (%)

	1971	1993
Universities		
Students	30	57
Research students	15	42
Junior lecturers (assistant professors)	8	29
Senior lecturers (associate professors)	11	16
Full professors	3	9
Regional colleges[1]		
Research students	n/a	40
Senior staff	n/a	16
Directors	n/a	2

Note:
1. Regional colleges were not established in 1971.
Source: Pedersen, 1994.

PRESSURES FOR CHANGE

The overriding and common objective of all education in Norway is to provide equal access to knowledge and qualifications regardless of sex, age, health, socio-economic background or regional origin. The principle of equality is emphasised in all official documents. For many years, the Norwegian government has financed campaigns to increase the number of women in political posts. The 1977 Gender Equality Act stipulated that women should represent 40 per cent of members of publicly appointed boards, councils, and committees. Although contentious at the time, quotas are not now an issue. Political representation is not subject to quotas. In 1994, the Prime Minister, 45 per cent of cabinet ministers, and 34 per cent of MPs, state secretaries, and county councillors, were women. In the 1993 elections all 3 candidates (i.e. the leaders of the 3 main political parties) were women. This marked improvement in the political representation of women has partly been the result of the efforts of a flourishing group of women's non-governmental organisations, who have ensured that gender policy has been part of the mainstream for some time (RMFA and RMFCA, 1994).

During the 1960s and up to the end of the 1970s a number of reform Acts were passed to guarantee students equal rights in education. Since 1972 the Ministry of Children and Family Affairs has had responsibility for co-ordinating and promoting gender equality. The basis for a public policy on equal rights was laid in 1979 by the adoption of the Act relating to equal status between the sexes. This provides legal protection against sex discrimination, and ensures the use of special measures to improve the situation of women. Preferential treatment according to gender on approximately equal conditions is recommended where it affects admission to education and entry to recruitment positions.

Following the UN Conference on Women in Copenhagen in 1980, Norway worked out a National Plan of Action for Equal Rights for the period 1981–5. This was approved by the *Stortinget* (parliament) in 1981, and has been renewed every 5 years since then.

Since 1981 the Ministry of Education, Research, and Church Affairs has had a small Gender Equality Secretariat (GES). Its extensive information activities include the publication of handbooks, brochures, and a magazine, lectures, conferences, and joint measures in co-operation with other education agencies. An important aim is to decentralise responsibility to the individual educational institutions and local authorities. Thus, while the Gender Equality Secretariat is responsible for implementing the National Plan of Action, local authorities are supposed to work out their own plans, prepare policy documents, and set up a local Gender Equality Council. Not all local authorities have fulfilled these requirements.

It is now generally accepted that the work of promoting equal status in schools will be helped by having a more balanced proportion of men and women in school management. The Ministry of Education encourages faster recruitment of women to management positions through new rules, training programmes, and other measures.

For a long time successive Norwegian governments have emphasised the importance of giving school managers more management training. Several 'management in education' courses have been arranged for primary and secondary school managers. Though in theory all these have to include 'Women in Educational Management' elements, the emphasis on women has not always been followed up.

Regional colleges, which were established in several cities from the 1970s, have given women who cannot travel far from home access to higher education. This has improved women's competence as teachers and as managers, since a number of local authorities give special grants to women who want to take management studies courses offered at such regional colleges. Women completing these courses obviously have a better chance to compete for senior posts.

In addition to in-service provision for existing school managers, the Ministry of Education also sponsors motivational courses for women who are considered to be potential school managers. These courses place special emphasis on the female perspective in educational management. The courses are arranged at local level, use some nationally-produced materials, and involve local school managers. Apart from their actual content, they have helped to create a highly effective network of women among potential school managers.

The GES also arranges conferences twice a year for people responsible for work on equal rights in primary and secondary schools. These conferences provide information about courses, research material for use in everyday school work, contact with resource staff throughout the country, and information on specific subjects which the GES wants to focus on. They are also important as network-builders.

Only 12 per cent of managers in local authority departments of education are women. However, they tend to be aware of the need for more women in educational management, and to put effort into formulating and monitoring plans of action for achieving this objective. For example, the female leader of the Education Department in Stavanger has doubled the number of women heads (from 6 to 13) during the 5 years she has been in post.

If a short-term management vacancy arises in a school the headteacher often asks a member of staff to help. When this person achieves a certain level of competence he or she is given priority when a permanent management position falls vacant. As more women become headteachers, more women are asked to help in this sort of situation.

Teachers associations play an active part in deciding appointments to educational management positions, and are sympathetic to the promotion of women candidates. Some have produced literature to encourage discussion among their members as to which strategy the association should follow to ensure the appointment of more women managers. Teachers associations arrange special courses to encourage women members to apply for management positions both in the association and in schools. They also hold courses for women members on strategies for managing in a male-dominated society. Several women teachers have taken up leading positions in these associations thanks to the policy of giving preference to women when appointing delegates. A career in a teachers association is often a useful way of obtaining management skills.

In the Norwegian political system, representatives of different parties are appointed to boards where they take decisions on further education matters in their local area. The quota system has had the effect, if not in every case, of encouraging the view that it is quite normal for women to take part in political decisions, and has given more women the opportunity to learn about the political system and to be visible in the public life of the local community. As managers of local education departments, and school headteachers, are in part appointed by politicians in the local authority, people who want to hold such positions need to be visible within the local authority and local politics. There is a well-established tradition in Norway of teachers and education managers being active in politics.

Since 1981 the Norwegian Research Council has set quotas for the number of female postgraduate scholarship holders in the university sector, where they have been underrepresented in certain subject areas. Female scholarship holders have also been given preference for travel grants, sabbaticals, and other forms of assistance. This form of preferential treatment aroused strong opposition in the scientific community. Nonetheless, as a result of this policy, the number of female doctorate holders has increased from around 10 per cent in 1980 to 21 per cent in 1991. This may have the effect of increasing the available pool of talent for more senior posts in the future (Stiver Lie and Teigen, 1994).

RESISTANCE TO CHANGE

Although the Ministry of Education considers work on equal rights to be important, it often gives higher priority to other objectives, such as educational management programmes, school inspections, and provision for children with special needs. In recent years this has meant that less attention has been focused on women in educational management and on discussions about equal rights.

Being a headteacher or deputy head is more time-consuming than being a teacher (Alvestad, 1994). Having overall responsibility for running the school means longer working days and shorter holidays. Women often have housework to do when they finish their paid jobs, and like to spend school holidays with their children. For this reason, although they may be interested in being better paid, they have tended to avoid time-consuming jobs.

In the past, most teachers have had very flexible working hours, whereas management staff have had to work a fixed timetable. Teachers could give their lessons and then go home, fitting in preparatory work whenever it suited them. For this reason, teaching has been an excellent way of combining work and childcare. Central government now expects teachers to spend more time at school in order to co-operate with colleagues and plan their work together. Working hours have also become more fixed in recent years, and teachers' holidays shorter, bringing them closer to those of management staff. In addition to teaching, each full-time teacher must now devote 190 hours per year or 5 hours per week to teamwork with colleagues. However, it is not yet possible to say what effects these changes will have on women teachers' attitudes toward jobs in education management.

There is no obvious career route in classroom-based competencies, rather than school management skills, which deters women from considering management positions. Women tend to be more motivated by the important and interesting work to be done in the classroom and to believe that educational management requires administrative rather than teaching skills (Alvestad, 1994). In addition, the public image of a headteacher is often male, and there are few successful female role models to follow.

A major study of the working conditions of Norwegian headteachers was published by Alvestad in 1994. This research was centred on two key questions – what is the role of the headteacher in 1990, and what importance does gender have in determining this role? It was based on a questionnaire sent to the headteachers of 200 of the 3,700 compulsory schools in Norway. Twenty-three per cent of the heads in this research were women. The resources available to school management are related to the number of pupils. Forty-nine per cent of the schools in the survey had fewer than 100 pupils, and 11 per cent had more than 300 pupils. Headteachers of small schools had to spend a greater proportion of their time teaching than those in larger schools. On average, 55 per cent of each full-time job was spent on management tasks. The headteacher represents the employer when doing management tasks, and works as an employee – and as a colleague of other teachers – when giving lessons. This is a difficult combination. Since 1991, headteachers have been given a more open mandate to work towards achieving the nationally-determined aims in whatever way he or she thinks best. This has made it possible for them to take on a role beyond the previous organisation of schools, which was highly rule-based. Alvestad discerned two different headteacher management styles: the first continued the tradition of the rule-bound administrator, the second took on a more pedagogically-oriented approach to management, based on different ways of action towards the national aims.

The results of the research were as follows:

- although interviews were not yet universal for headship appointments, 15 per cent more women than men had to go through an interview before obtaining such posts,
- more women than men acted as an acting headteacher before being appointed headteacher,
- 30 per cent more women than men had less than 20 years' work experience in schools,
- women headteachers are generally younger than male headteachers; 40 per cent more women headteachers than their male counterparts had less than 5 years' experience in that position,
- far more men (53 per cent) than women (4 per cent) had been headteachers for more than 10 years,
- most headteachers – but more men than women – undertake further education after their appointment (e.g. part-time attendance at regional colleges or universities),
- male headteachers are more politically active than women headteachers.

It was found that women and men have responsibility for different types of schools: 66 per cent of women headteachers run schools with fewer than 100 pupils; 39 per cent of women headteachers run schools for the youngest children (7–12 year olds), while a further 32 per cent manage schools with so few pupils that they have to teach several age groups in the same class.

The study also showed that more women headteachers (26 per cent) were single than male headteachers (4 per cent), and that 48 per cent of women headteachers had children compared to 61 per cent for male headteachers. These numbers indicate different family situations for male and women headteachers. The study also shows that 70 per cent of women headteachers with families also do most of the housework and caring work, compared to just 1 per cent of male headteachers; 17 per cent of women headteachers thought that they shared this work with their spouses more or less equally. Twenty-eight per cent of male headteachers took no part in the daily cleaning and caring work. This also reflects the traditional division of labour for school managers.

Most of the headteachers worked more hours (on average 41–50 hours per week) than would be expected in a normal full-time job. Taken together with housework, this represents a particularly heavy burden for women headteachers.

When the sample was statistically-controlled for school type and size it was found that women heads spent more time on teaching, and were more committed to it, than their male counterparts, who conformed to the traditional stereotype by doing more administrative work. When men expressed concern about 'teaching work' they were usually referring to the priorities they had set for the school as a whole rather than to the time they spent in the classroom.

Further insight into the situation of prospective women headteachers is provided by Waage (1989), who found that courses for educational managers tended to avoid the issue of how women might come to terms with working in jobs traditionally occupied by men. Waage argues that:

- writers on management seldom focus on the role of women managers, but are based on the philosophy that what works for men must work for women,
- women have been obliged to operate within several different realities. Waage also asserted that one result of this is that they have been unsure as to how to develop their own distinct style of management within a traditionally male context.

Similar barriers have been found to exist for women in the academic world. An analysis of three generations of academic women (Kyvik, 1990) showed that women's reproductive and nurturing tasks affect every stage and choice in their lives, resulting in a cumulative deficit across their careers. Although strategies had changed with the growth of the welfare state and new ideologies of equality, all three generations of the women in tertiary education were held back by having to shoulder the main responsibility for care.

The situation is changing. The younger generation start their academic career earlier, and their careers are less interrupted. When they take childcare breaks, they are shorter than those taken by earlier generations. A more equal division of labour can be observed within young academic families, yet even here women continue to have the major responsibility for work in the home. Research into the publication output of male and female academics also shows that these are strongly related to marital status, and number and age of children (Stiver Lie and Teigen, 1994).

Women in the academic world still seem to meet resistance from the system when they apply for permanent, senior posts, for which there is always strong competition. Some women applying for vacancies also seem to lack support from their male mentors, because of the research they wish to pursue, or the methodology they propose to use (Pedersen, 1994). In the 1990s, economic pressures on higher education have resulted in changed conditions of work and salaries. The latter are now to be determined on an individual basis (within categories), and management by objectives and accountability will be the hallmarks of the university system. To what extent this will affect women is not yet clear.

The Research Council of Norway promotes general and applied research in all fields. One of its goals is to integrate gender perspective in all areas of research. The Secretariat for Women's Studies was established in 1982. The SWS seeks to attract more women to research, promote, and co-ordinate research on women, and to disseminate the results of such research. Up to now, women's studies and research have played little or no part in higher education in Norway. Existing expertise has largely been built up through research activities. The Secretariat for Women's Studies at the Research Council of Norway at the universities of Oslo, Bergen, and Trondheim, together with the Network for Women's Research in Tromsø co-operate with educational and research institutions in order to promote and provide information on women's issues. The Feminist University, established in 1993, offers seminars at all levels. Its first-year course, 'Management from a woman's perspective', is particularly worthy of note.

ROGALAND COUNTY: A CASE STUDY OF CHANGE

The potential effects of governmental legislation and pressure for change can be illustrated by a project at a regional level, initiated in 1987 as a pilot supported by the national government. Rogaland County employed over 8,000 permanent staff, working in schools, hospitals, administration and public transport. Statistics showed that most of the approximately 5,600 women employees held jobs with low rates of pay, and only 3 per cent of them had annual salaries of more than NOK 250,000, compared to 28 per cent of men in this higher wage band (Oftedal, 1996).

A four-year plan was formulated at county level, and its main objectives were:

• to create equal conditions for professional and personal growth for men and women,
• to make an effort to promote equal distribution of both sexes in management positions at all levels,
• to aim at a more equal distribution of both sexes in all positions at all levels.

The secondary objectives of the plan were:

• to recruit qualified personnel of both sexes in all positions and at all levels,
• to provide opportunities for personal and professional development so that every co-worker could achieve the knowledge and skills she needed in order to attend to her tasks, even when the character of her post changed,
• to ensure the appointment of more female managers by 1995,
• to contribute to the development of a pay and incomes policy which would provide for professional career opportunities,

• to be instrumental in expanding the number of day-care places for the children of employees.

This plan was to be the prime responsibility of the County's Council for Equal Rights (CER), one of several county initiatives for promoting equal rights for women. The Council is responsible for monitoring all new appointments, and for motivating and training women for new tasks and responsibilities in the County. The specific measures undertaken were organised on a cascade model and comprised three stages of activity.

The pilot project formed the nucleus of the programme. The target group for this project was women with university degrees and/or special experience or interest in management. The aim was to provide opportunities for professional and personal development, and improved career prospects. Thirty women applied and twelve were selected from the health-care, education and administrative sections.

The County wanted, and obtained, concrete results from this project, which attracted considerable interest, and required a great personal contribution from each of the participants. The project lasted for a period of one and a half years, during which time participants formed network groups which determined, reviewed and discussed personal goals for each participant.

One of the project's objectives was to gain experience by trying out previously untried ideas. Another was to make better use of the participants' existing skills. In response, the participants had to commit themselves to working in any future development programmes introduced by the County as resource personnel – as mentors, giving papers at conferences, or by organising development programmes. Seven of the twelve participants now have leading management positions.

The 'Pilot Group' was responsible for starting the second stage of the project, entitled *Management and Growth*, in which the target group was made up of women earning lower levels of pay. The aims were to raise their level of consciousness and to motivate them to seek new challenges within the County. There were many applicants for the course, which was planned to last for one year, and took the form of plenary meetings with speakers, and group work in students' homes between sessions – a popular way of organising courses in Norway. Subjects covered on the course included communication, group processes, and presentation techniques.

By 1995 the course had been run three times, and about 100 women had participated. Those women who took part in the first of the motivation and growth courses are now responsible for running the next one, and are also encouraged to apply for new positions.

The third stage of the project, referred to as QMOR (Quality, Management, Organisation, Results) ran in 1991–92. All of the 41 participants in this project already held management positions; they came from all administrative sectors in the country, and included a number of women active in local politics. The aim was to further qualify women within the designated fields, and to establish a female network which would work in close co-operation with the County's Council for Equal Rights. By 1996, 17 of the participants had obtained further career advancement (Rogaland Fylkeskommune, 1996).

All these courses have been for women only. Reactions have been very positive. The courses have included discussions about the separateness of women in the workplace, and the impact this has had on their professional skills. Seeing so many able and active women in one place has also strengthened the confidence of women employees. The opportunity to discuss professional experiences in a 'female language', and one which is based on the same kinds of experience, has also brought valuable insights (Oftedal, 1996)

CONCLUSION

Despite the Norwegian government's stated commitment to equal rights for men and women, substantial differences remain in terms of the division of labour and leadership positions in the public and private sectors, which give rise to economic disparities. As in many European countries, the Norwegian education system is characterised by the predominant pattern that the smaller the schools and the younger the pupils, the more women teachers and leaders are to be found, while men continue to dominate the best paid positions and university sector.

Concerted action by the government and by the trade unions has had some effect, backed up by a financial commitment to equality measures. In the education system, the following strategies have been deployed with the aim of increasing the percentage of women in educational management:

• positive encouragement by headteachers, employers and in job advertisments for women to apply for vacant posts;
• the provision of free motivational courses and subsidised educational management courses;
• the involvement of teachers' associations in promotion decisions;
• the existence of a formal complaints procedure through the Council for Equal Rights;
• network building among women educational managers;
• sponsorship of research into male and female leadership styles;
• the preferential provision of travel grants, sabbaticals and other forms of assistance to female scholarship holders by the Norwegian Research Council.

Nevertheless, despite these strategies, research cited in this chapter by Kyvik (1990), Alvestad (1994) and Stiver Lie and Teigen (1994) shows that women in educational management and in university posts still bear the brunt of the domestic division of labour in addition to their professional careers. This suggests that many women may consciously 'settle for less' in order to meet potentially conflicting demands. In addition, there is also evidence (Pedersen, 1994) of continued resistance by the system, when women struggle to better their work status in the educational and academic worlds.

REFERENCES

Alvestad, R. (1994) *Rektor i grunnskolen. En kvantitativ analyse av kvinner og menn i rektorstillingen.* Sosiologisk Institutt, Univ.i Bergen.

Kyvik, S. (1990) 'Motherhood and scientific productivity' *Social Studies of Science* 20/1, pp. 149–60.

Likestillingsrådet (Gender Equality Council) (1995) *Minifakta om ungdom og likestilling.* Likestillingsrådet QG-2069, Oslo.

Ministry of Education, Research and Church Affairs (1994) *Education in Norway,* F2600E, Oslo.

Norsk Lærarlag (1994a) *Kvinnelønn – et spørsmål om kjønnsdiskriminering.* Norsk Lærarlag.

Norsk Lærarlag (1994b) *Kvinner og ledelse i barnehage og skole.* Norsk Lærarlag.

Official Statistics of Norway (1993) *Labour Market Statistics. Vol.1.* Statistisk Sentralbryå.

Oftedal, J. (1996) Examples of Good Practice by board and managers in Rogaland County, Norway. *Context,* Vol. 12.

Pedersen, T.B. (1994) Vil Akademika ha flere kvinner? *Nytt om kvinneforsking* 3/94, pp. 5–20. Oslo, Norges Forskningsråd.

Rasmussen, B. (1994) *Kjønn og ledelse: Menn, makt og kvinnelige inntrengere.* Rapport fra en konferanse om kvinner i 90-åra. Arbeidsnotat 1/94, pp. 195–203. Norges Forskningsråd.

RMFA and RMCFA (The Royal Ministry of Foreign Affairs and the Royal Ministry of Children and Family Affairs) (1994) *Gender Equality in Norway. The National Report to the 4th UN Conference on Women* (Beijing 1995), Oslo.

Rogaland Fylkeskommune (1996) *Rapport fra Pilotsprosjektet og KLOR-prosjektet.* Stavanger, Likestillingsutralget.

Stiver Lie, S. and Teigen, M. (1994) 'Higher Education in Norway: a Nirvana of Equality for Women', in S. Stiver Lie, L. Malik, and D. Harris (eds.) *World Yearbook of Education: The Gender Gap in Higher Education.* London, Kogan Page.

Waage, K. (1989) *Kvinners vilkår i menns jobber.* RVO-publication Vol. 103.

11

Spain

Montserrat Santos

WOMEN IN THE WORKPLACE

Over the past twenty years Spain has been held up as an example in the developed world for the speed with which Spanish women have been assimilated into the workplace. In a 1995 OECD report Spain showed the largest growth in female employment of all member countries, after Australia. Between 1981 and 1990 over one million women joined the employed sector, increasing their representation in this area by 27 per cent; in the same period, the number of gainfully-employed men increased by just 5 per cent. This spectacular rise in female employment was due to the incorporation of middle-aged married women, as they broke with the Spanish tradition that required them to stay at home to look after their husbands and children. This tendency gradually stabilized between 1990 and 1996, but by the end of this period women's share of the job market had risen to 34.9 per cent, as Table 11.1 illustrates. Although a comparatively small proportion of the workforce is employed part time, women comprise over three-quarters of this total (Eurostat, 1995).

Table 11.1 Employment activity rates 1976–1996 (%)

Year	Men	Women
1976	78.6	19.5
1981	73.9	27.4
1988	66.5	32.3
1990	66.8	33.4
1996	65.1	34.9

Source: INE (Instituto Nacional de Estadística) 1996, 3rd quarter, Labour Survey, Madrid.

In recent years, a new element has been added to the two variables in family life that were so characteristic of the 1980s: the improvement in the level of education reached by women in Spain, and the relationship between changes in work patterns and education. The published data on these two variables show that women are still relatively disadvantaged, though, of course, much less so than was the case before. Thus, 83.4 per cent of men who have completed higher education are in work, compared to 72.1 per cent of those who have only completed basic education; the corresponding figures for women are 80 per cent and 26 per cent (Instituto de la Mujer, 1996).

While we can observe the progress made by women in relation to job opportunities over recent years, on close examination the situation is not so satisfactory. Although women now constitute more than one-third of the workforce, only 5 per cent of them reach management levels in the private sector, compared to 14 per cent in the state system, where objective employment criteria apply. This distortion of the labour market flies in the face of the objective reality – which is that 50 per cent of new graduates, and 40 per cent of those qualified at Masters level, are women. What happens, then, to these better qualified women, those who have completed degree courses? Most of them tend to fall victim to the imbalances of the structure of the labour market in Spain, where taboos continue to deny them an equal chance of securing employment, despite warnings by analysts that employers will suffer increasingly from the effects of a sudden demographic decline, to which female employment will be the only answer. The same sources urge women to work at improving their skills. However, few of them will admit that the real problem for women in securing management-level jobs, including those within education, is the social structure itself, which simply has to change. If this does not happen, women may well be absorbed into the workforce in larger numbers, but only at the lower levels – which is precisely where they are at the moment. While we wait for more rational and equitable practices to be adopted, we can identify significant differences between the two basic sources of employment. There are such clear advantages for women working in the public sector that their skills are often lost to the private sector, which for all practical purposes is run entirely by men.

The private sector

Male domination in top private sector jobs is a matter of record. Estimates suggest that women hold only 5 per cent of senior jobs in business, and that even those fall within a limited range, including services, new companies, or small, usually family-run businesses. Table 11.2 illustrates how poorly women are represented in senior management. The figures speak for themselves: the higher up the promotion ladder, the fewer women one finds.

The type of work carried out by women is a good indication of the quality of the jobs open to them. An analysis by sector indicates that women have a 45 per cent share of jobs in the textile industry, 64 per cent in the shoe and leather industry, 42 per cent in commerce, 38 per cent in restaurants and related trades, 60 per cent in education and research, 63 per cent in health services, 62 per cent in social care and community services, and 83 per cent in domestic service. It is interesting to note, however, that from 1990 to 1996

Table 11.2   Employment of women in the private sector by professional grade, 1994

	%
Managing Director	0.79
Director 1	4.19
Director 2	5.44
Senior Manager	8.99
Middle Manager	10.44
Line Manager	11.42
White-collar Employee	23.96

Source: CEINSA (Centro de Investigacion Salarial) Barcelona, 1994.

the number of women working in textiles and public services remained stable. Over the same period there was a very sharp rise in the number of women working in estate agency (Instituto de la Mujer, 1996).

Another point worth noting is that the average age of women holding executive positions is only 36 years, compared to 43 years for their male counterparts. Women's academic qualifications are also slightly higher, which is largely explained by the age difference. Younger executives, whether male or female, tend to be better qualified than their older colleagues (Instituto de la Mujer, 1996).

The public sector

The number of women employed in the public sector has increased by more than 52 per cent since 1984. At the time of writing (1996) women occupy 10.57 per cent of the most senior jobs, though as Table 11.3 shows, they have achieved a higher share in previous years.

Table 11.3   Women in the most senior civil service posts, 1994–1996

	1994			1995			1996		
	Women	Men	% Women	Women	Men	% Women	Women	Men	% Women
Ministers	3	12	20.00	3	12	20.00	4	10	28.57
Secretaries of State	5	15	25.00	5	15	25.00	0	25	0.00
Under-secretaries	2	20	9.09	2	20	9.09	4	53	7.02
Director Generals	37	232	13.75	37	232	13.75	27	208	11.49
Other senior posts	1	10	9.09	1	10	9.09	–	–	–
Total	48	289	14.24	48	289	14.24	35	296	10.57

Source: *Ministerio de Administración Pública* (MAP) Madrid, 1996.

The fact that the Spanish civil service offers women an environment for professional fulfilment, is largely as a result of the competitive entry system, whereby personnel evaluation is based on objective, standardized tests, designed to highlight individual ability. Businesses, by contrast, tend to use a different selection process, based on attitudinal and motivational tests, and on enquiries into the individual's circumstances, their potential, and their personal commitments. In the last of these areas, a woman applicant's family responsibilities can represent a serious obstacle to her being offered a position.

Profile of the woman executive in Spain

All of the determining factors we have indicated add up to a profile of a woman executive quite different from her counterparts in other European countries. According to the *Instituto de la Mujer* (Institute of Women's Affairs, a research and campaigning unit under the aegis of the Ministry of Culture) the woman executive in Spain, especially in the private sector, is young, between 25 and 45 years of age, with a university degree and further specialized training, and married with one or more children. In most cases she will have chosen her first job objectively, and become a manager as a result of internal promotion; her principal encouragement tends to come from her husband, immediate manager, and parents. Her working week is never less than 40 hours, which leaves her with only 10 hours of leisure time per week. Her monthly salary never, or hardly ever, exceeds 500.000 pts (£2,220) (Nueva Empresa, 1993).

Professional development: opportunities for women

According to a study undertaken for the *Instituto de la Mujer* in 1992, the professional careers of women executives are marked by a series of windows of opportunity, and by a series of obstacles which they have to overcome in order to achieve senior professional status. The study was carried out with nine discussion groups composed of women executives and middle-ranking managers from the state administration and business sectors, with as many again from private, public, and multinational companies. There was a tenth 'control' group, made up by human resource directors from the same types of organizations (*Instituto de la Mujer*, 1992).

The first group of encouragingly positive factors had to do with the socio-cultural, economic, and political levels which Spain is beginning to achieve. Faced with the traditional male view that women lack the time or energy needed to occupy the highest levels of employment, because of their other responsibilities – caring for children, running the home, etc. – society itself is undergoing a series of changes which tend to help women, and make it possible for them to have a professional career. These changes include the fact that Spain now has one of the lowest birth rates in Europe at 1.4 births per woman in 1993 (Eurostat, 1995). The trend towards later marriages and later, planned, parenthood, gives women more time to dedicate to their careers, and a degree of very positive economic independence within the relationship. Finally, improvements in domestic appliances, convenience foods, one-stop shopping, etc. have also helped to give women time for other activities.

Conditions for statutory maternity leave arrangements are average, in comparison with other European countries. Mothers may take 16 weeks of leave, paid at 75 per cent of earnings. Either parent may take up to one year of unpaid leave. Provision of state-funded preschool education is available comparatively widely, encompassing 40 per cent of 3-year-old children, and over 90 per cent of 4–5-year-olds. The comparatively lengthy school day of 8 hours is more compatible with the needs of working parents than in many other European countries (Eurostat, 1995).

These changes are determining factors, as are a second group related to women's qualification for employment, in particular the fact that 50 per cent of them now have access to higher education. Women have also increased their professional skills thanks to specialization, and the increased experience they have gained from being more widely represented in the workplace.

Other changes have resulted from developments in the employment market as a whole, and the market for specialized and skilled jobs in particular. The demand for a wider range of varied and specialist management skills has led to women being recruited for jobs in senior management on a larger scale than ever before.

The general increase in consumption in Spanish society in recent years, together with the other factors already described, has given rise to a new middle class, in which the woman's earnings are essential to maintaining social status, and for raising the overall family income.

One consequence of all these changes is that it has become more usual for women to plan for a professional career. They also take care to select courses that will improve their career prospects, and to consider working in less traditional areas if they seem to offer better opportunities for professional development. It is also noticeable that there is more competition between 'career women', and that society is more prepared to accept women as professionals rather than as the unskilled workers they were considered to be in the past.

In terms of political representation, women have yet to make substantial headway. In 1993 just under 15 per cent of members of the Spanish parliament were women (Eurostat, 1995).

Spanish women executives and the glass ceiling

Although opportunities for professional women have improved, many obstacles still stand in their way. Of these, the one most often identifed is discrimination, an unfair process operating against women which is mostly observed at the organizational level, and in business rather than in the public sector; in many companies women cannot aspire to a job at management level because, whether explicitly, implicitly, or informally, promotion to a senior position would go against company policy (Instituto de la Mujer, 1992).

The image of the woman manager also has to contend with the chauvinistic, 'men-first' assumptions often accepted without question in the workplace. The pressure this puts on women may lead them to try to out-do men in their behaviour, with the result that they can appear to be over-demanding and inflexible. The framework of masculine values perpetuates the negative tendency for men to communicate exclusively with other men. The strategies of male power in organizations often seem to by-pass the women, effectively excluding them from a part in the company's internal politics. This is important because groups and networks play such an important part in professional advancement: as individuals are promoted within the hierarchy, the prospect of making further progress often depends on informal recommendations and evaluations.

Older women tend to start at a disadvantage because, having traditionally received a narrower and more limited education than men, they may have to go to the expense of further professional training if they want to compete with their male counterparts on equal terms. The fact that this is still the case suggests that, even now, women's education fails to provide them with the necessary skills, or the self-confidence and determination needed to rise to the top. This lack of social orientation towards professional competitiveness is a serious drawback, since it can leave women defenceless in inter-organizational relations.

While these educational failings are important, the two main factors that deny women access to management are their family responsibilities, and the time and energy needed in order to carry them out. Put simply, having children represents a serious obstacle to a woman's professional success. In companies, as in other types of organizations, a manager is expected to be available at all times, and to be fully committed to the work in hand; if the woman manager is also expected to cope unaided with the family unit, the problem becomes very serious, since the two roles may not be compatible. The trend towards marrying later, having fewer children, and being able to plan families, has given women more free time and a new status, but it is still the case that most women marry and have children, and that this has not resulted in a fair division of domestic work: women continue to take an unfair share of responsibility for the home and family (Instituto de la Mujer, 1992).

Having to divide their energies between office and home at all times puts working women under great pressure; they can suffer high levels of stress, not helped by the feeling that they are being watched for signs of weakness. Any difficulties that do arise from their dual role tend to be penalized more heavily in private companies, although, increasingly, the same can happen in the public sector as well. The threat of being singled out because of their 'divided loyalty' forces many women to adopt a cynical or devious attitude – they feel they might be marked down because of their outside commitments, always assuming that they have not been obliged to give up having a family in the first place in order to further their professional career.

All these pressures can lead women to become unduly self-critical, and to experience a lack of self-confidence, to the detriment of their own professional performance. In spite of this, women remain strongly motivated towards making a successful career, and see becoming a manager as an excellent opportunity for personal development. For this ambition to flourish, the workplace, and social life in general, should become 'complementary' in space and time, not a predominantly male domain, but an environment in which both sexes can meet on equal terms (Instituto de la Mujer, 1992).

The place of women in the Spanish education system today

In 1960, education in Spain went through a profound period of transformation. Compulsory attendance was established between the ages of 6 and 14, and co-education was introduced. The reforms involved a deliberate transfer of responsibilities from the centre to the regions and the deployment of thousands of new teachers. Further reforms in 1990 raised the school leaving age to 16, and the system now comprises:

- preschool education for 0–6-year-olds;
- primary or basic education, consisting of two stages, from 6–12 years and 12–16 years;
- upper secondary education, from 16–18 years, which is subdivided into an academic programme, leading to the *Bachillerato* (academic school leaving qualification) or *Formación Profesional* (vocational education). Those who pursue the latter option are enrolled on a specific two-year (extendable) programme out of a wide range of options. The academic programme lasts three years, with a fourth year for university preparation, the COU (*Curso de Orientación Universitaria*);
- higher education, comprising universities, polytechnics and higher technical schools (ETS), offering courses of 1–3 years' duration and university schools, which offer one-year courses of lower status.

About a third of Spanish schools are private, the majority of which are Catholic. These receive substantial state aid, and are required to follow the same curriculum (Alberdi and Alberdi, 1991).

The education system is a basic social institution. As well as knowledge, it transmits social attitudes and values. This is why it is important in analysing the situation of women in Spain. Two key changes in the Spanish education system are having an important effect on the higher education of women.

The first change occurred as women entered the workplace in very large numbers during the 1980s. At the same time there was a large increase in the number of girls staying on in the non-compulsory stages of education, to the point where, in 1996, they accounted for over half of all students completing university education. The second change was the extension of compulsory education to the age of 16, with the approval of the 1990 General Law for the Overall Organization of the Educational System (LOGSE), which finally gave women equal rights within the education system. It has to be remembered that historically, in what is still a mainly rural country, the fact that women played a key role within the family did not entitle them to any professional or work-related status, and little attention was given to their educational needs.

Data from the Instituto de la Mujer (1996) suggest that while women are still receiving a lower level of education than men, the gap is narrowing all the time. The illiteracy rate for women, while still higher than for men, has also fallen sharply, from 10.3 per cent in 1982 to 5.3 per cent in 1996; male illiteracy during the same period fell from 4.19 per cent to 2.3 per cent, with the highest rates of illiteracy found in people aged 60 years and over. However, it should be noted that the numbers of men and women continuing to study beyond primary level are rising steadily. Over 38 per cent of women have completed secondary studies or vocational training, and 13 per cent have completed higher education, compared to 15 per cent of men.

The education/age relationship shows two trends: as explained, the percentage of illiterate women over 60 years of age, while still higher than for men, is falling significantly, while amongst younger people (under 30 years), literacy rates between the sexes are almost identical.

On average, rather more women than men complete their primary education at the expected age. The number of students of both sexes who complete the compulsory primary and secondary levels of education is very similar; such differences as we can observe at these levels are more qualitative in character (types of studies, academic performance, etc.) than quantitative (numbers of children in school).

In the area of post-compulsory education – the *Bachillerato* and the University Orientation Course (COU) – more women (54.11 per cent) than men are taking courses; women COU students achieve better results than their male counterparts, and the percentage of women students successfully completing COU rose from 64 per cent in 1982 to 73 per cent in 1995. The figures for male students are slightly lower, at 69 per cent in 1995 (Instituto de la Mujer, 1996). Where students are offered a free choice of subjects to study for the *Bachillerato*, most women students choose arts courses. They showed relatively little interest in science and technology in 1995 – only 39.79 per cent chose these COU options.

The number of women who choose vocational training has also risen significantly, from 40 per cent of the total in 1982 to 45 per cent in 1996. More women than men now complete vocational training – although the percentage who complete this course of study never rises above 24 per cent. However, they tend to make stereotypical course choices, and are in a majority in areas leading to what have traditionally been considered to be 'women's jobs', such as hairdressing, secretarial and social studies, etc. (MEC, 1994).

The increased presence of women has been most noticeable at university level, where their numbers grew by 157 per cent in the period 1975–93: at the time of writing women account for 50.3 per cent of all university students in the context of a general mass expansion of higher education. In spite of this extraordinary growth, their choices at this level also continue to follow traditional patterns: only 14.9 per cent chose a technical course in the higher technical (ETS) schools. In 1991–92 women accounted for 65 per cent of medical science graduates, 60 per cent of humanities graduates and 15 per cent of engineering graduates (Eurostat, 1995). Women outnumber men on social studies courses, while men are in a majority on technical courses. A study carried out by the Women's General Directorate (DGM) in 1993 reported that although equal numbers of men and women are graduating now, 'market forces' mean that even those courses with a high percentage of women students end by producing a male academic élite (Instituto de la Mujer, 1996).

Postgraduate (doctoral) studies represent a further advance in the specialization and academic training of women. In recent years the number of women completing higher degree courses in the applied and natural sciences, social sciences and the humanities, and medical science has fallen. However, their numbers have increased significantly in agrarian sciences, engineering, and technology.

THE TEACHING PROFESSION

There are over 300,000 women teachers in the Spanish education system, accounting for 7.41 per cent of all women in work. Sixty-five per cent of trainee teachers are educated within the state system; those in private education follow broadly similar courses to the state colleges, so in terms of content and approach they can be considered together. Where differences are found is in the teachers' terms of employment: those in state education are appointed through a system of competition, and become public employees for life; their salaries are higher than those paid in the private system, and they have fewer classroom hours. In Spain teachers' salaries vary according to their teaching level and the number of years they have been working. State trained teachers also receive an automatic rise in salary every six years, based on completion of an agreed number of in-service training hours. In broad terms, a primary school teacher in state education, with around fifteen years' experience, has a net monthly salary of approximately £ 1,000 (200.000 pts), a secondary school teacher of £1,250 (250.000 pts), and a university lecturer of £1,625 (325.000 pts). The number of class contact hours ranges from 20–25 hours in primary education to 15–18 hours in the ESO (Compulsory Secondary Education) and 6th form (*Bachillerato*) years, to 6–9 hours in universities. Rates of pay for teachers in rural and urban schools are the same (MEC, 1994).

The higher education system in Spain is highly centralized, with a curriculum designed by the Ministry of Education and the autonomous governments at regional level. Tenured staff have the status of civil servants. Tenure is obtained through a system of national exams in prescribed areas of knowledge and candidates are examined by a public tribunal of university professors. Despite the increasing percentage of women among university academic staff, only 8 per cent of full professors are women. There is a distinct lack of a female presence among university chancellors, deans or departmental directors, which are all elected posts. Women also tend to be disproportionately underrepresented on elected university governing bodies. In common with school teachers, women face barriers in coping with the dual role of work and home. In addition, women tend to shy away from the micropolitics of universities and to feel inhibited concerning competitiveness. Their lack of representation at the top also creates a cycle of reproduction, where they are not seen to fit the professional role (Nash, 1995).

Teaching in Spain is not a high-status profession, whether at the level of compulsory or higher education. In general, the social standing of teachers is quite similar to that in other European countries. Nor is the public image of teachers particularly positive. For many women, teaching simply represents a second income to help balance the household budget; for men, it may be taken to mean that they have not been able to find a better job.

Numbers of men and women teachers are approximately the same, which is not to say that they are fairly distributed across the full range of schooling. Thus, women are in a majority in preschool education (96.09 per cent), special education (75.05 per cent), and primary education (65.29 per cent), but account for less than 31 per cent of university lecturers, and a mere 12.8 per cent of teachers in higher technical (ETN) schools. Although there are more women than men teachers (see Table 11.4), this is not reflected in the hierarchical distribution, or in the roles carried out by women.

Table 11.4 Teacher training by educational category, level, and gender, 1993–94 (includes public and private centres)

	No. of students	% Women
Infant/preschool	51,654	96.09
Primary/EGB	227,649	65.29
Special Schools	5,852	75.05
Secondary/*Bachillerato*	175,561	48.54
Special Needs Teaching (ERN)	15,419	48.99
Other secondary-level teaching	641	7.33
Distance learning	672	46.88
Adult education	11,787	39.98
University	71,297	30.03
Grand Total	550,532	57.41

Source: Instituto de la Mujer, *Datos de la Enseñanza en España* (1996)

There are no readily available official statistics showing the number of women and men in senior management posts in the Spanish education system. This is an understandable situation, bearing in mind the education model, explained below, and the limited interest shown by teachers in seeking managerial posts. The proportion of heads who change jobs annually is really alarming, and as a result figures for distribution by sex are approximate.

School inspectors employed by the Ministry of Education and Culture (MEC) have suggested that during the academic years 1993–6 only 3.5 per cent of all women in state education were heads of schools. This figure compares unfavourably with the figure for men – 7.4 per cent – for the same period. Having said that, there has been quite spectacular growth compared to 1985 when the percentage of women heads was 1.3 per cent – less than half the present level. European sources indicate that in 1995, 74 per cent of primary and 50 per cent of secondary teachers were women. However, figures on headships are only available for 1985, when 47 per cent of primary and 20 per cent of secondary heads were female (Laemers and Ruijs, 1996).

The educational management model in Spain

The Spanish education system has been undergoing major structural reform since 1985. Under the new system, education is compulsory up to the age of 16 years. There is a comprehensive model, with some options in the final years. The curriculum is designed to be adapted to the reality of the school, defined in terms of values, of shared responsibilities, of consensus in decision-making; the students are seen as the object in the teaching–learning process, the teacher as the instrument to bring it about. Schools are therefore undergoing a process of change. They are expected to be more open to the outside world; the school community as a whole is encouraged to take part in the management and policy-making of the school. This decentralized model was originally introduced, over a period of time, in Scandinavia and other European cultures with democratic traditions. Spain's history has, of course, been quite different: the authoritarian model of the 1970 Education Law was designed for teachers trained to be mere transmitters of a curriculum drawn up by the Ministry of National Education. The new system encourages schools to be open to the surrounding community, and the open curriculum is intended to cater to every special educational need. In this situation, teachers must be helped to adapt to change, which everyone agrees is no easy or short-term task. These circumstances have to be taken into account in order to understand the special character of the Spanish management model, when seen alongside well-established models operating in the rest of Europe.

As previously noted, two major education laws – the 1985 Basic Law of the Right to Education and the 1990 Law for the General Organization of the Educational System – have encouraged school autonomy and participation by members of the school community in the government of the school, by creating a governing body called the school council. This comprises teachers, parents, students, non-teaching staff, and one public representative from the state or local administration. In addition to taking general decisions that help the day-to-day running and development of the school, the governing body is responsible for electing the school head. In this area it is able to act entirely independently of civil service or any other external interference. Candidates have to be members of the school's teaching staff, with at least five years' teaching experience. Up to 1996 the conditions needed to apply for the headship were so broad that they would be met by 99 per cent of all teachers. The only requirement was to appear before the school council, which chose whoever it decided was the best man or woman candidate. Once elected for a period of four years, the head would then either return to his or her previous teaching post within the same school, or reapply for the headship. In spite of these provisions, about 50 per cent of the available headships in any year went unfilled for lack of candidates, so the administration would have to appoint a supply head for one year. This led to curious cases of teachers who held a headship indefinitely, in the absence of other candidates, while in other schools the head would change annually.

In November 1995 a new law concerning school governance was passed, which changed this system to some extent, by introducing the requirement that applicants for headship must be accredited by the state administration, in addition to the existing criteria. Headteachers with more than five years' experience were accredited automatically. Other applicants for accreditation are now to be selected on the basis of teaching excellence or qualifications by the state inspectorate. The consequences of this change of policy are not yet clear, although unofficial sources report a drastic decline in the number of candidates for headship, perhaps limited to those who are really motivated to apply.

How are we to account for the general lack of interest in headships in recent years? In the writer's view this resulted primarily from the teacher training system operating at the beginning of the democratic process. Most teachers recruited at that time rejected the discredited authoritarianism, which tended to be associated with the figure of the school manager. A second reason, particularly for male staff, was the lack of positive incentives, whether economic or of some other kind. It is worth mentioning here that all school managers, including the principal, have to teach for 6–12 hours of classes per week, in addition to their other responsibilities. Thirdly – and this is a personal opinion which is at odds with various studies carried out by the European Forum of Educational Administrators in Madrid (EFEA, 1993) – the management model was based on traditional male role-figures, a bias which the state administration endorsed by appointing men to over 80 per cent of all management posts. This educational model led women to reject the role of school head, since they could not identify with it.

The legacy of this situation still obtains today. However, the Ministry of Education and Culture, the MEC, tries as best it can to overcome some of the model's failings: salaries paid to heads of school have increased substantially in recent years; where a head's performance has been positively appraised this will be recognized in her or his salary as a teacher; training programmes have been introduced to prepare teachers for possible promotion to head of school. However, the regulations still require the head to be a teacher from the same school, who has to return to her or his normal teaching work once their mandate is over. It is too soon to know the outcome of these changes, but everything seems to indicate that interest is increasing amongst both men and women teachers, chiefly in response to the economic incentive (MEC, 1994).

Women teachers' views on school management

According to studies conducted for the Foundation for Co-operation and Education (FUNCOE, 1992), and for EFEA (1993), women teachers view the management function from three different perspectives. The first of these is comparison, i.e. they compare teachers with tenure to teachers without tenure, and consider that the former are in some way ahead of the latter. The following list shows the opinion of women teachers on school managers:

Male/Female teachers with tenure

• Teach fewer pupils, for less hours
• Receive merit points
• Can undergo training in school time
• Have access to relevant information
• Earn more

Male/Female teachers without tenure

• Teach more children for longer hours
• Do not receive merit points
• Have to train in their own time
• Lack relevant information
• Earn less

(*Source*: EFEA, *Estudio sobre la mujer directiva en la escuela*, Madrid, 1993)

Tenure can offer a number of advantages. It normally leads on to internal promotion, which will be useful later when applying for a transfer to another school, or for an internal post decided by competition; opportunities for training in working hours may in due course be recognized in a salary increase.

The second viewpoint reflects the fact that women teachers in Spain place a great deal of importance on the manner in which people are appointed to management jobs. They consider that this is one of the factors that will determine the attitudes of their colleagues, and of the management, towards the rest of the teaching community (see Table 11.5).

In the FUNCOE (1992) study the teachers do not distinguish between the way men and women are appointed. However, they do believe that gender differences have a bearing on whether men or women are appointed to a management position. The following list shows the reasons why men and women are/are not promoted to a headship.

Women teachers whose applications are successful

• Are the youngest
• Come from new schools
• Have no dependent family
• Feel the need for change or innovation

Table 11.5 Jobs with tenure, by manner of appointment

Manner of access	Aims	Feelings generated	Attitudes arising
Voluntary	• Renewal • Prestige • Economic	• Enthusiasm • Frustration	• Bureaucratic

Prescriptive	• Designated by
	  the Inspectorate
		• Apathy
		• Rejection
			• Refusal to
			  accept the
			  situation

Source: FUNCOE, *Las profesoras y los cargos directivos*, Madrid, 1992.

Women teachers whose applications are unsuccessful or who do not apply

• Are too old
• Have a dependent family
• Are expected to work over-long hours
• Are asked to assume too much responsibility
• Do not get on well with colleagues and parents
• Prefer teaching to managing
• Prefer an easy life

Male teachers who make successful applications

• The job is more suitable for a man
• Prefer to be in charge
• Don't experience teaching in the same way as women
• Want prestige and recognition
• For financial reasons

Male teachers who make unsuccessful applications or who do not apply

• Too much responsibility
• Would not be compensated for extra hours
• Do not get on with their colleagues
• The job is not permanent
• Not possible to make real changes

(*Source*: FUNCOE, *Las profesoras y los cargos directivos*, Madrid, 1993)

The opinions given in this list for not accepting a management position tend to confirm the main points raised at the beginning of the profile of the woman executive in Spain, above.

Conclusion

Spanish women heads of school are not very different from women professionals doing the same work in other parts of the Western world. From the studies we have carried out on this topic (EFEA, 1993) we suffer from the same fear of having power, the same sexist prejudices, and the same problems in getting used to role-reversal, as our counterparts in Europe. However, our chief difficulties stem from the family structure in Spain. For many women teachers, the second income allows them to maintain a certain social status, in a job which leaves enough spare time for family requirements. Lack of time is one of the chief problems mentioned by those currently doing the job: 'To have children of school age, a traditional home life that works, and at the same time be looking for a highly responsible job is virtually out of the question so long as the roles imposed by society do not change' (Hernandez, 1993). Added to this lack of time, the Spanish women, juggling the responsibilities of mother, wife, and school head, may also have to overcome fears of conflicts and loneliness. These four variables, which emerge prominently in our surveys and interviews, confirm they have a lot in common with other Spanish women executives.

There is, however, a social pressure for change. Women want to play a part in the world of work, want to hold management jobs, and are getting ready for that day. Social forces, too, are gradually coming to accept that women are the future wealth of the country. To this end, recent Spanish governments have been developing instruments of promotion, through the Ministry of Social Affairs and the Equal Opportunities Ministry, with plans for an Equal Opportunity Ministry of Promotion with Equal Opportunity Plans. The First Equal Opportunities for Women Plan (1988–92) focused on very general points that were based on investigating in detail the social situation of women, and developing positive steps to resist sexual discrimination. Under the watchful eyes of European colleagues more informed in these matters, our politicians have now set more ambitious targets, of which the most important are: promoting the equal division of domestic responsibilities; helping to create a social image of women that reflects their everyday reality; increasing women's social and political participation, and generally opening up women's access to decision-making jobs. If all these objectives are achieved, in the 21st Century Spanish women may achieve the same employment levels as our sisters in the European Union.

NOTES

The data on which I have based my study are taken from a range of published sources, but I have used three in particular: the data provided by the Ministry of Education and Culture from their own research refer to 1994, the latest date for which details are available; data from the Employment Survey for Terms II and III 1996 were provided by the National Statistics Unit (INE/*Instituto Nacional de Estadística*); I am grateful to the *Instituto de la Mujer* for their very useful studies, up-dated in 1996.

REFERENCES

Alberdi, I. and Alberdi, I. (1991) Spain, in M. Wilson (ed.) *Girls and Young Women in Education: a European Perspective*, Oxford, Pergamon Press.

CEINSA (Centre for Research on Salaries) (1994) *La presencia de la mujer en cargos ejecutivos* (Women in executive jobs), Barcelona.

EFEA (European Forum of Educational Administrators) (1993) *Estudio sobre la mujer directiva en la escuela* (A study of women heads of schools), Madrid.

Eurostat (1995) *Women and Men in Europe: a statistical portrait* (1992), Luxembourg, Office for Official Publications of the European Communities.

FUNCOE (Foundation for Co-operation and Education) (1992) *Las profesoras y los cargos directivos* (Teachers and management), Madrid.

Hernandez, C. (1993) *La mujer y su entorno* (Women and their environment), Comunidad de Madrid.

INE (Instituto Nacional de Estadística/National Institute of Statistics) (1996) *Labour Force Survey (3rd quarter)*, Madrid.

Instituto de la Mujer (1992) *Oportunidades y obstáculos en el desarrollo profesional de las mujeres directivas* (Opportunities and obstacles in the professional development of women managers), Madrid.

Instituto de la Mujer (1996) *Datos de la Enseñanza en España 1993/1996* (Data on Education in Spain, 1993/1996), Madrid.

Laemers, M. and Riujs, A. (1996) A Statistical Portrait, *Context*, no. 12, pp. 7–15.

Ministerio de Administracion Publica (MAP) (1996) *Mujeres en los altos cargos de la administración* (Women senior managers in administration), Madrid.

Ministerio de Educacion y Cultura (MEC) (1994) *Data on Education in Spain*, Madrid.

Nash, M. (1995) Equal Opportunities Policies for Women at Spanish Universities: A Strategy for the Future? in C. Farber and A. Henniger (eds.) *Equal Opportunities for Women at European Universities*, Freie Universitat Berlin.

Nueva Empresa (1993) La mujer en la empresa (Women in enterprise), no. 376, May, pp. 68–72.

12

Overview

Maggie Wilson

The preceding chapters illustrate the substantial problems involved in cross-national and cross-cultural comparison, particularly where changing economic forces and policies are currently having an impact on educational systems and processes. In the case of Hungary, the transition from a state socialist to a market economy is having a profound influence on the overall situation of working women and on the social infrastructure, which in turn determines the quality of life in education, whether as a student, teacher or headteacher. The unification of Germany represents another such major transformation, in which the incorporation of the new *Länder* on the terms of the old can be seen to have been disadvantageous for women teachers and lecturers with respect to promotion possibilities. In other countries such as England and Wales and the Netherlands, relatively minor reforms, such as school mergers and closures have had an impact on women's chances of promotion. Nonetheless, while other countries represented in this book have not experienced the same level of change, broad patterns emerge in relation to overall trends in the teaching profession and in the barriers to women's advancement which persist in schools and universities and in the wider world of work.

WOMEN IN TEACHING: OVERALL TRENDS

The detailed data presented in this book confirm the overall picture presented in the introduction of a profession which is in general becoming increasingly feminised but which is also highly differentiated internally according to status and gender. Tables 12.1 and 12.2 give an indication of the distribution of women personnel in the relevant education systems. Differences in the availability of official statistics and in the frequency and level of monitoring are significant in terms of governmental attitudes towards the situation of women in teaching, but also complicate comparison. Thus, for example, the Netherlands and England and Wales are relatively well served in the production of official statistics by the relevant education ministries. At the other end of the spectrum, the decentralisation of monitoring procedures to *Land* level in Germany produces a highly patchy and incomplete picture, reflecting the uneven degree of official concern given to such issues among the *Länder* of differing political compositions.

Table 12.1 Representation of women in educational management in selected European countries (%)

	primary teachers	primary heads	secondary teachers	secondary heads
England & Wales (1992)	81	49	49	26
France (1995)	79	64	56	30
Greece (1995)	50	41	53	36
Hungary (1995)	85	33	97[1]	30
Ireland (1996)	78	46	54	29
Italy (1995)	93	46	63	30
Netherlands (1996)	76	13	33	7
Norway (1994)	74	40	39[2]	22[3]
Spain (1995, 1985)[4]	74	47	50	20

Notes
1. Figure given is for *Gymnasien*; 60% of vocational school teachers are women.
2. This figure is for upper secondary schools; 51% of lower school teachers are women.
3. This figure is for upper secondary schools; 24% of lower school headteachers are women.
4. 1995 figures are given for the precentage of women primary and secondary teachers; 1985 figures are given for the percentage of women headteachers.

Table 12.2 Representation of women in university education and educational management (%)

	undergraduate students	lecturers	professors
England and Wales (1995)	50.0	28.0	8.0
France (1995)	55.0	35.0	13.0
Greece (1996, 1992)[1]	51.0	26.5	7.6
Hungary (1995, 1996)[2]	51.0	37.0	3.0
Ireland (1996)	53.0	21.0	5.0
Italy (1992)	50.0	24.0	9.5
Netherlands (1995)	45.3	32.0	4.2
Norway (1991, 1993)	57.0	20.0	9.0
Spain (1995)	50.0	31.0	8.0
West Germany (1995, 1991)[3]	41.5	22.5	5.7

Notes
1. 1992 figures are given for the percentage of women undergraduate students; 1996 figures for the percentage of women lecturers and professors.
2. 1996 figures are given for the percentage of women undergraduate students; 1995 figures for the percentage of women lecturers and professors.
3. Figures for West Germany are given in C. Färber and A. Henniger (eds.) (1995). *Equal Opportunities for Women in European Universities,* Freie Universitat Berlin.

Nevertheless, data produced for this book whether officially or in some cases by the author's own compilations, do support the overall picture of a pyramidal structure of the job hierarchy. The very high percentage of female primary school teachers in all countries, with the exception of Greece, does not result in an equitable representation at headteacher level. At the level of secondary education, a similar disparity between the percentage of women employed and the proportion who attain headships is to be found at a lower baseline of female employment. Where secondary education is divided into either lower and upper secondary level or into organisational strands of differing degrees of prestige, women are less well represented in the more senior or favoured areas. Thus for example, the proportion of French women *agrégés* or German women *Gymnasien* teachers is lower than that of their less prestigious counterparts in secondary education. Regrettably, detailed statistical monitoring does not reveal whether these patterns are further reinforced by equally disproportionate representation at the level of social leadership. Only in Hungary, where vocational and technical education has enjoyed a different status in relation to academic education, is a far higher proportion of women *Gymnasien* or grammar school teachers to be found. Here it is clear however that this does not result in any superior chance of promotion.

At the level of compulsory education, only two chapters, namely those concerning Greece and England and Wales, feature data on the relative chances of promotion in rural and urban areas. These limited examples suggest that women's chances of promotion are higher in metropolitan rather than rural areas, arguably because of prevailing political forces, a point which deserves further exploration. In those countries which retained single-sex schools, namely the Netherlands, Ireland and England and Wales, better chances of promotion in girls' schools appear to have existed for women teachers. Detailed data are also provided in the case of Ireland on the application rates of women teachers for headships in order to explore the often expressed argument that women do not apply for promoted posts and are thus to blame for their unequal status. The lower application rate of women can be read in many ways: as a sign of lack of motivation or confidence; as a sign of greater self-awareness and judicious selectivity; as a reflection of the onerous nature of school leadership positions in many countries. The limited data presented nonetheless do suggest that women applicants are slightly more successful than their male counterparts, which may reflect a greater determination to succeed. Whatever the case, it is clear that detailed monitoring of such rates across a broader spread of countries would help to elucidate this particular issue.

Table 12.2 confirms again the underrepresentation of women teachers in university education and in particular at the most senior levels, in contrast to the near equalisation of the gender balance at undergraduate level. In only four of the countries reviewed were data available on the representation of women at the apex of the system, namely the level of vice-chancellor or rector. These figures were broadly similar for Greece, France and the UK at 6 per cent or under. An exceptional case was that of Norway, where one out of four universities was headed by a woman.

It could be argued that this kind of tabular representation masks significant differences in the organisation of hierarchies within higher education systems and thus the promotion prospects of women within these. Thus for example, it is far more difficult to obtain promotion or indeed any chance of a secure future in Germany, where the majority of teaching personnel are at the untenured *Assistenten* level, than in countries such as Greece, Ireland and France, with more stratified systems, which should in theory give rise to a greater degree of mobility. Indeed, a further criticism of the kind of snapshot presented in Table 12.2 is that such data present too static a picture of a rapidly changing scene. Just as female students have substantially increased their enrolment levels in upper secondary schools and higher education since the 1970s, it is only a matter of time, so the argument runs, before a similar process of equalisation will work its way up the system. This kind of argument can only be proven or disproven with long-term monitoring. Evidence from England and Wales, the Netherlands, Greece, Ireland and Norway suggests that significant changes in the composition of the lecturing force are occurring, but at a much slower rate than in the composition of the student body. Where data are given on the middle ranks of academic staff, a progressive decrease in the proportion of women teachers is to be observed. With the funding of higher education a matter of increasing concern in many countries, the expansion of opportunity for students has often been facilitated by the employment of a growing number of casual staff on short-term contracts, largely unrepresented in official figures, as reported in the chapters on Ireland, France, the Netherlands and England and Wales. While this issue clearly affects both sexes, evidence suggests that women are overrepresented in this group. Such developments are generally not monitored regularly and in the kind of detail presented in the English case study, a situation which clearly needs to be improved.

In the Greek chapter, interesting data are presented on the promotion prospects of women educational advisers and administrators, with the suggestion that opportunities are better for women who have specialised in subject areas in which they were in a substantial minority, perhaps reflecting a higher degree of determination to 'beat the odds'. While data are provided on the presence of women lecturers in higher education subject areas in the chapter on England and Wales, patterns of relative promotion prospects are not generally available.

Within higher education systems, institutions may bear varying degrees of prestige. Thus in the French system, the *Grandes Ecoles* furnish the senior ranks of French industry, the civil service and political system. However, such institutions are often more closed than those of a mass character and like the English private schools, are not amenable to statistical monitoring, with obvious consequences for discerning overall trends. Likewise, whole sections of post-compulsory provision are not as yet charted, such as the various technical universities and institutes which exist in many countries. Whether this is as a result of their status or more masculine ethos, in most cases is open to question. Where documentation does exist, as in the cases of Dutch vocational training and higher professional education, the Spanish higher technical schools and the English colleges of further education, a predictable pattern of female underrepresentation emerges.

In terms of the administration of education, significant but incomplete information is available. Where figures are given for the representation of women within ministries of education, as in the cases of Italy, Greece and Ireland, there is evidence that women are greatly underrepresented in senior positions (at around 12–14 per cent), even where they constitute the bulk of lower-level administrators. Figures for regional directors of education are likewise very low; 3 per cent of Greek heads of primary education and 8 per cent of secondary education officers; 17 per cent of French regional directors; 15 per cent of English Chief Education Officers and 4 per cent of heads of education offices at *Land* level in Germany. Despite the variety of arrangements which exist for the inspection of schools and for advisory services to teachers, similar patterns of underrepresentation can be discerned. In France, Germany and Ireland women constitute under 16 per cent of chief or senior inspectors. Detailed information about the Greek advisory service at central and regional levels shows a striking disparity in the proportion of women advisers and administrators, despite their substantial level of representation in certain subject areas or at the level of primary education.

THE STATUS OF TEACHING AND THE DEMANDS OF EDUCATIONAL MANAGEMENT

Although school teaching has been something of a stronghold for women in the postwar era, variations can be discerned in relation to the status of the profession and its attractiveness to male and female recruits among countries and over time. In countries such as the Netherlands, France and Germany, civil service status has bestowed on the profession a certain social respectability and perceived stability, although this may be on the wane. In Norway, teaching is still considered to be an attractive option, while in Ireland the status of being a highly educated member of the community has traditionally compensated for modest levels of remuneration. In contrast, in Italy, Spain and Greece, teaching is clearly not considered to be a prestige occupation and the Italian and Greek chapters draw the reader's attention to the social class origin of recruits, combined with geographical origins. Thus in these cases, teaching can be seen to have drawn from a pool of middle-class girls from rural areas and of working-class boys. In the Netherlands and England and Wales, changes in the teacher's role are seen to have been particularly stressful and to have resulted in an exodus from the profession.

In all countries, a slow but steady trend towards the feminisation of the profession is reported as more girls seek an occupational future in the wake of higher enrolment levels in upper secondary and higher education. One exception is the case of Hungary, where women have already been entrenched in teaching for some time. A consistent theme of the book is that of the association of teaching with nurturing, caring and creative qualities and the practicalities of the compatability of the school year and school hours with the job for women with children. This is particularly significant in those cases, such as in Germany, where the school day is very short and after-school care virtually non-existent. A common theme throughout the book is that the process of feminisation has distinct consequences. The first is that the more women who enter the profession, the lower the occupational status and often remuneration of the profession; a classic self-confirming contradiction. This can be seen clearly in the case of Hungary where teachers' salaries are some 40 per cent lower than those of other salaried professionals. The second is that those men who enter teaching tend to exhibit a higher motivation to 'succeed' in obtaining promotion in order to compensate for their relative lack of status. The third consequence is that many female (and some male) teachers draw a sharp distinction between the reasons why they entered teaching and the perceived demands of headship. The role of the headteacher is seen to involve long hours, often for relatively little extra remuneration, increased stress, a more bureaucratic workload and more distance from the warmth of the primary classroom or the creativity of involvement in curriculum development. Indeed in Norway, France, Ireland, the Netherlands and England and Wales, the role of the headteacher is reportedly becoming more bureaucratic with increasing task demands. In the Netherlands and England and Wales this involves complex financial management and a changed definition of the role of the headteacher. The fact that classroom teaching itself is also becoming more demanding in these countries, only serves to act as a further disincentive.

To some extent, these arguments explain the different application rates of men and women for promoted posts where this has been proven to be the case. All too often, this explanation is based on assumptions not supported by empirical analysis. The issue of women's non-application is a more complex phenomenon than is suggested by conventional accounts, as the preceding chapters suggest.

BARRIERS TO WOMEN'S ADVANCEMENT IN TEACHING

An earlier account of these issues, which summarised the findings of the 1990 Vienna Conference on Women in Educational Management, highlighted a distinction between social and organisational barriers (Ruijs, 1992–3). The presence of young children in a family, the uneven distribution of domestic responsibilities between male and female partners, career breaks, the psychological status of combining the dual role of parenthood and teaching (thinking about birthday cakes in the middle of a board meeting, as Ruijs aptly exemplifies) are all factors which are also emphasised in the majority of chapters in this book. The absence of family leave to care for young children, inadequate provision of childcare facilities for preschool children and differing levels of maternity/paternity leave are also significant variables, which can impede women in the workplace in general, let alone those with promotional aspirations. However they also constitute obstacles which are amenable to remedial action at the levels of the workplace or government, as usefully outlined by the Hansard Society in the chapter on England and Wales (see Table 2.11).

The issue of part-time work is also often given as a sufficient explanation for women's lack of career prospects. However, the situation is more complex in detail. In some countries, such as Italy and Hungary, the rate of part-time working is low overall and not very different for men and for women. In others, such as Germany and Norway, a relatively high proportion of both male and female teachers work part time, while in others, such as Ireland and England and Wales, the majority of part-time teachers are women. In the latter case, part-timers are not included in data on the gender distribution of teachers, though they constitute a third of the female teaching force, and the promotion of part-timers is very rare. In contrast, in Norway, the Netherlands and Germany, part-timers have been promoted to school management positions and experiments in job-sharing such roles carried out.

Less amenable to intervention are factors which pertain to an accrued absence of women in management roles. The organisational culture of many school and university staffrooms is not particularly 'friendly' to the female manager, as documented in the chapters on France, England and Wales and Germany. The absence of female role models for aspirants to headship and the visibility and isolation of female headteachers or university professors can act as a deterrent to other women. This is seen to be particularly the case in higher education, where the female lecturer is a rarer breed. Where a lack of guidance prevails, women can all too often 'drift' in career terms, unsure where to place their energies and opting for 'safe bets'. This is documented, for example, in the case of Dutch and French women lecturers and at a lower level, in terms of the subject choices which girls make in upper secondary and university education. As the Greek and Dutch chapters stress, this apparent lack of confidence and self-exclusion may mask other realities. A question also raised in, for example, the chapter on Spain, is whether the motivation of women teachers differs from that of men.

Long-standing organisational practices can also lead to indirect discrimination. Countries where a 'free market' exists for applications for promoted posts may present better opportunities for working couples than those where applicants to a central authority are directed towards posts anywhere in the country, such as in France. Career structures vary among the countries represented in this book at both school and university level. Some are organised more hierarchically than others, with a greater degree of differentiation between grades. Whether this offers more scope for positive appraisal or affirmative action is open to question. The Spanish model of management, based on a 3–4 year rotation of headships, offers an unusual alternative, although one which has yet to deliver a greater degree of gender equality. In higher education in other countries such as Germany, the requirement to move for the purposes of the *Habilitation* and subsequent postings clearly constitutes a disadvantage for couples, particularly those with children, and a review of traditional arrangements is clearly long overdue. A further practice in higher education which could be said to constitute indirect discrimination is the link between research 'productivity' and advancement, documented in the chapters on Norway, Ireland, Hungary and England and Wales. Where research funding is awarded to those with the most time in which to undertake research, usually men, a self-fulfilling cycle of advantage continues.

In terms of the selection process itself, possible direct discrimination is mentioned in the chapters on Germany, England and Wales and Ireland. However, this is notoriously difficult to prove or document, particularly when selection procedures are not open to scrutiny, as is the case in most countries. Although several countries feature a system of ostensible open competition – in Hungary, Spain, Italy, France and Greece, for example – this does not seem to result in any better chances for women. Most systems are also based on interviews, where subjective criteria about the suitability of a candidate along stereotypical lines may creep in. Without published criteria for the job specification, short-listing and appointments, there can be no guarantee that equal opportunities criteria are applied. The composition of selection committees for school and university posts is not well monitored in most cases. Voluntary guidelines on the membership of committees can also be routinely flouted, as in Ireland. Although a quota on the proportion of male to female members of public appointment boards, as in Norway, does not guarantee gender fairness, it could be seen as a first step in improving the appointments systems of many countries.

In higher education, the system of obtaining successive degrees and passing formal tests may offer more objective chances of promotion than a closed system of the 'kingmakers' appointing heirs in their own image. However the demands of the promoted role may require more than a superior knowledge base and understanding of a subject specialism, especially as the character of higher education is changing in so many countries. Again, objective job specification procedures would seem to be a prerequisite for a more gender-fair system of appointments at professorial level.

STRATEGIES FOR CHANGE

In each country-based chapter, the seeds of change are to be found. In many cases, the prime movers of change have been at the grass roots level: women's networks in the Netherlands, Norway, Italy, England and Wales; teachers' associations or unions in Ireland and Norway. In some cases the actions of such groups, coupled with pressure from international sources have led to substantial changes in employment policies, which have benefited the female workforce in general, such as the improvement of parental leave arrangements. The example of Norway illustrates the upward spiral which can develop when more women are enabled to participate in employment and political life, and then begin to constitute a critical mass to effect further change. It is significant that quotas in public and political life are not considered to be 'an issue' in a country which has taken a strong governmental lead on equality issues for some time, in contrast to the controversial nature of such proposals in France, where, in common with many other European countries, women are poorly represented in the political sphere. This strong central impetus given by the Norwegian government is partly facilitated by the small population size of Norway. In the Netherlands, a balance between the central state and the autonomy of municipalities and institutions has been struck, with a resulting policy combination of incentives and legislation to introduce equal opportunities policies. A relatively established programme of affirmative action by the Dutch government has again resulted in a higher degree of acceptance of such measures as targets and preferential treatment.

Other areas amenable to action by central government include the provision of enhanced maternity leave, as in Germany; improved childcare arrangements preschool, as in France, and after school, especially where the school day does not correspond with the working day. At the level of local or regional government (depending on the size of the political unit) a vital public service is the provision of equal opportunities training programmes for the 'power-holders' and the establishment of fair and binding selection and promotion procedures. At both central and local government levels, the provision of public information through monitoring is a necessary starting point for affirmative action programmes – not a destination, as some would represent! At local government level, the provision of women-only management training courses, as in the Norwegian and German case-studies, may serve to improve confidence levels, facilitate working and lead women to apply for promoted posts. It is at the institutional level that mentoring and appraisal schemes are critical in shaping women's career paths and in encouraging them to 'have a go' at applying for posts, like their male peers. It is at this level again, that flexible working arrangements such as annualised hours, supportive and extended career breaks schemes and job-sharing come into play. The case studies from the English and Dutch universities cited and from the German and Norwegian systems give an indication of positive change in this respect.

In terms of selection procedures, it is still apparent that a considerable amount of work needs to be undertaken, as indicated in the preceding section. All too often it appears that a loose definition of the requirements of the promoted post act to the disadvantage of women. This becomes particularly acute in the context of part-time management. Could the post be organised in a different way in order to benefit from the strengths of potential candidates? Are all the tasks assigned to the post appropriately carried out at this level or have they grown in an unsystematic way, based on a set of assumptions about the nature of the job? Apart from the need for external assessment of such issues, and a minimum standard of female representation on selection committees, fair selection procedures would also include an open appeal system and guidance to unsuccessful candidates.

In a broader context, questions must be asked about the direction and rationale of change in this area. It is interesting to note that only four of the chapters, namely those concerning Germany, the Netherlands, Norway and England and Wales, present research on differences in management styles and aims between men and women, in contrast with the ample research bases for such work in the USA and Australia (see Shakeshaft, 1993; Blackmore and Kenway, 1993). Is it simply a matter of gender-fairness, of ensuring that both sexes have equal chances of success in a competitive system? Is it a question of the wastage of the potential talent of able but overlooked women? Should women who opt for a more balanced lifestyle rather than the single-minded pursuit of promotion in an inegalitarian context be portrayed as lesser mortals? Do those who succeed in climbing the slippery slope against the odds make a difference to the lives of pupils, students and colleagues?

It is surely significant that such questioning of the qualitative aspects of managerial work has arisen from practices developed to effect quantitative change, i.e. more equality in numbers. It is now established that pressure for fairness on this basic level is resulting in a re-evaluation not only of women's abilities in the workplace and of their roles in the family, but also of the corresponding roles of men. The growingly stressful experience of management as opposed to its promised attractions, may in the end compel both men and women into changed working relationships with tasks seen as different rather than superior or inferior. That destination, if it be the ultimate one, lies at the end of a long road.

REFERENCES

Blackmore, J. and Kenway, J. (1993) *Gender Matters in Educational Administration*, London: Falmer.

Ruijs, A. (1992–3) Women Managers in Education: a Worldwide Project, in *Coombe Lodge Reports*, Vol. 23, nos. 7–8, pp. 519–676.

Shakeshaft, C. (1993) Women in Educational Management in the United States, in J. Ouston (ed.) *Women in Educational Management*, Harlow: Longman.

Index

OTHER WOMEN IN MANAGEMENT TITLES FROM PAUL CHAPMAN PUBLISHING

DANCING ON THE CEILING

A Study of Women Managers in Education

Valerie Hall

The book is about leadership and gender. It draws on the author's experience as a teacher and management development consultant in education, as well as her research into gender issues over a number of years. It will be of interest to women and men in education, as well as making a theoretical contribution to the debate about educational leadership.

1 85386 287 2   Paperback   1996   244pp

EUROPEAN WOMEN IN BUSINESS AND MANAGEMENT

Edited by Marilyn J. Davidson and Cary L. Cooper

Throughout the European Union the proportion of women in the workforce has increased dramatically. Between 1985 and 1988, 58% of the 4.8 million jobs created in the EU were occupied by women.

With more women working, there has been an increase in the number of women entering business (including entrepreneurs) and management throughout all the EU countries. This book explores the past, present and future position of women managers in each of the respective EU states.

1 85396 138 8   Hardback   1993   208pp

THE BLACK AND ETHNIC WOMAN MANAGER

Cracking the Concrete Ceiling

Marilyn J. Davidson

Based on the author's analysis of in-depth interviews and relevant research literature, this book investigates and explores the experiences, problems and pressures faced by black and ethnic minority women managers in the UK. To date, research addressing the issues of black managers has been almost exclusively American, predominantly about black African–Americans, and the overall amount of published research has been limited. Indeed, studies of black and ethnic minority professional women, especially in corporate settings, have been virtually excluded from the growing body of research on women in management. This book has been written to fill this gap.

1 85396 299 6   Paperback   1997   144pp

WOMEN AND THE EUROPEAN LABOUR MARKETS

Edited by Anneke van Doorne-Huiskes, Jacques van Hoof and Ellie Roelofs

Labour market inequalities are a feature which all European countries share. This book provides a comparative perspective of sexual inequality in the 12 member-states of the European Union. Different aspects of inequality are discussed and presented: participation rates, occupational segregation, income differences, careers and the division of unpaid work.

The book concludes with an exploration of what the future has in store for women in the EU.

1 85396 298 8   Hardback   1995   272pp

COMPLETE CATALOGUE OF WOMEN IN MANAGEMENT TITLES AVAILABLE ON REQUEST